Title	*Life's Pu*[...]	
	FOR THE BELIEVER AND T[...]	
1/A	SUGAR IN THE WATER	2
1/B	THE ARRIVAL OF THE QUESTION	12
1/C	A SINGLE ENTITY OF TRUTH	30
1/D	WHAT TO DO NOW!	42
2	THE WAY AHEAD IS IN HARMONY	65
3	WHO ARE "YOU"?	93
4	WHERE IS HEAVEN OR HELL	98
5	WHAT IS ENLIGHTENMENT?	109
6	HOW THE CREATION PURSUES GODS' HARMONY OR NATURES HARMONY FOR THE NON-BELIEVER	153
7	FALSE BELIEF SYSTEMS	182
8	ALL IS UNDER THE LAW OF HARMONY	200
9	THE TARGET AND PURPOSE OF GOD OR OF NATURE FOR THE NON-BELIEVER	223
10	HOW TO MEDITATE AND THE PURPOSE OF MEDITATION	227
11	A FINAL NOTE: <u>The truth being that everything that exists is "You"!</u>	249

THE AUTHOR

1/A SUGAR IN THE WATER

"Life's Purpose" is a narrative historically emanating from Russia's Far Eastern Siberia. It is dedicated to a Russian Group of university students who lived in Birobidzhan and who asked me the question, *"Do you believe in God, for we in Communist Russia have always been told to believe in nothing?"* This blunt question was being asked to me after my economic "management" presentation to a group of teachers and it was a question which I received after my ten years of working in new Russia in order to support their "Market Economy" development. This arising question was asked of me on my invited September 1999 journey to Russia's Siberian far-east. For certainly, has an English individual I had never been called upon to "officially" speak about religion in Russia and it was certainly not one of the reasons why I was being financed to go to meetings in Russia – in order to support their new "Market Economy" manufacturing needs. So the question took me by surprise, for it seemed to be coming from a new awakening.

However, let me set the scene concerning my previous ten years of "consultancy" work in Russia! These being visits in order to economically support the state and also private manufacturing and development of "Market Economy" goods which actually began in 1988. It all started when the Bradford branch of the UK "Chamber of Commerce and Industry", in which I was member, stated that the "British Chamber of Commerce and Industry" had been invited to send, with all expenses paid, a representative to attend a Russian "joint-venture" business presentation that was to be held in Moscow. This being a "joint-venture" business presentation which was to be given by "Vneshcomonservice", which was a Russian organisation, whose work was similar to the UK "Chamber of Commerce and Industry". I was then personally asked if I would like to go and represent them at a Moscow "Joint-Venture" meeting and of course I immediately said "Yes"! The reason for my saying an immediate "Yes" was that I was actually unemployed at that time! This invitation being after I had just been forced to close my work-wear clothing manufacturing company in Bradford and sadly I also had to dismiss over 80 people who did work for me! This sad event happened after our Government permitted China to sell their manufactured work clothing into the UK at subsidised prices that were less then I could buy the needed cloth for.

Now, these past Russian nine years of venture, which where prior to the time of this current Siberian Birobidzhan meeting, is an interesting story so a little more about me and my past! For it is known that my first invitation to Moscow, with all expenses paid, was to attend the Russian Chamber of Commerce and Industry has a representative of the British Chamber of Commerce and Industry! This being a business invitation to visit Moscow which did actually happened long after my motorcycle accident that had painfully occurred in 1961. This being an accident which happened at my age of 23 when the motorcycle I was riding was hit head-on by a speeding car that was coming round a bend on the wrong side of the main road, this being that fact which did end my merchant navy career and also the visiting of countries which had very different cultures.

An interesting "reality" happened at this accident, for when I was going down the dark tunnel towards a distant white light a voice said to me *"Go back, you have work to do!"* At this point I tried to stand up which startled the policeman who had covered me with his cape because he had checked me and thought I was dead. The next thing that I remember, after the accident, was me being awakened on the hospital operating table by a request to sign my name on a piece of paper, after which I heard them say that they were now going to take my leg off – at which I screamed loudly *"You do not take my leg off"* before fainting. It is good now to mention that they did not take my leg off and I was told later that they no longer take legs off under such conditions.

It actually took a year in hospital and then another year of bodily healing before I could seek employment again! I was also still using a walking stick and was informed that I must also work in an office and not anywhere on a factory floor, which did sadden me. So in this new return to work I first began has a "Work Study" trainee which meant that I would also work on the factory floor – i.e.: amongst the productive workers! This being after I had offered to work for £10 a week, for they had first refused to employ a walking stick me and this was in the year1962!

I was pleased because my office work also included work on the factory floor, for it included my establishing a time in "Standard Minutes". This being the actual payment time that was given to many machinists for completing a repetitive job that eventually led to the completion of the garment being manufactured! I quickly learned how to install new manufacturing system in the clothing trade and then, after three years of going to night school, I passed all exams and so was enabled to become a "Fellow of the Institute of Management Services" and so had professional qualifications that were deemed higher than a bronze degree. This being an institute of management whose main objective was to promote within all industries "Scientific Management", this being the root and the purpose of all Management Services!

In those days' within the 1960's, management and workers had VERY different "separate" opposing cultures and so my past culture has a "worker" allowed me to beneficially install a "Time and Motion" system that was believed by the operators that I motivated. This mainly being in payment systems that were based upon a person's given time to do a job! It was also a time allowed which included the best method that was needed to do an operation, especially for "repetitive" work. I also attached within my issued "times to do a job" the improving, via bonus payments to all supporting "Management Services", which ensured a good "constant" supply of all the work being given to the productive workers. For certainly, this supervisory supporting of work was based upon a management science which did scientifically establish that activity which promoted only "Wage-payment" productivity concepts. This being the "Time-Taken" and methods used to complete a job, a reality which gained the satisfaction of all employees and employers. I then became a free lance "Management Consultant" and developed five clothing manufacturing factories before creating my own company which lasted for eight years - until UK allowed competition from China closed me down.

But now let us go back to the question that was asked by Nastya Nelzina of Birobidzhan, who did say to me "Do you believe in God?" It was also said in such a way that it did take me by surprise, for it seemed to be coming from a new awakening which touched upon the fact that religion had been severally frowned upon for many years by the communist government and my answer to this question was a simple "Yes!" This new business development meeting in "Birobijan" was after my ten years of working in Russia and this trip was also financed by the "British Executive Service Overseas" (BESO) company. This being the British Executive Service Overseas which was conceived in the UK in 1972 when a group of businessmen collectively decided that they wished to put something back (i.e. their experience) into the developing countries. It was founded by the UK Government, the CBI and Institute of Directors as an independent (not for gain) charitable organisation. This being a charitable organisation which was conceived in 1972 when a group of businessmen collectively decided that they wished to put something back (i.e. their experience) into the new worlds developing countries. It is certainly a good organisation which teaches to these newly developing foreign companies that which is known to be good management "Know-How" and on this occasion, they did finance my trip to a town called "Birobidzhan", which is in the Far East of Siberia.

This "Birobidzhan", location was actually known has Stalin's Jewish "Autonomous Region", which was engineered in 1934 as the National Homeland of all Jews who actually made up about twelve per cent of the city's population. Stalin did place it in the Far East of Siberia and from that date it has been economically and socially not been contacted by world Jewry, a reality in which Stalin must accept responsibility. Agreed that this is a great pity, but I do not feel concerned about these Great Russian Europeans. I say Europeans because in 1960, when we first began the European Union, I said to everyone that I disliked this idea of joining Europe. I further stated that *"I am not European; I am British."* I even stood to be elected to parliament when I became a "Prospective Parliamentary Candidate", this realty being twice, first for the "Referendum Party" and then for "UKIP", the "United Kingdom Independence Party" which is a political party in the United Kingdom whose policies are to promote conservatism, national conservatism and Euro scepticism. Indubitably, this was because I was parochial in my thinking.

Now I know how silly this past thinking was, for after my trips to Russia I now understand, that the whole of north of the "Northern Hemisphere" is full of Europeans, this being a tribe in which most people pursue a knowledge which was birthed within the Christian Bible. I also found that the people of Birobidzhan do live a very hard city life and that they also had very little or no knowledge about private enterprise and its tendency to supply good things for its surrounding population.

MY ECONOMIC MANAGEMENT MEETING
MOSCOW CITY COUNCIL

I also understand that these European Russians, who were forced to live in Birobijan, actually reside in climates of twenty-five degrees in summer and minus twenty-five degrees in winter!

I also further and quickly understood that they certainly know how to absorb all these conditions. For instance on many occasions, the workers currently re-installing water pipes within the building in which I was sleeping, kept stopping the water flow to all this buildings rooms. Then, without warning, they would turn on the water flow again, this being after they had repaired that part of the water pipe that they were working on. But at one time, before a repair had taken place, I filled a bottle with dirty water from the tap in my room and took it to that mornings scheduled meeting. I then held it up at the group meeting in which I was talking about a subject called – "No economic Gain without Social Pain". I then asked the question *"What are these bits floating in this tap water"* and immediately after this question, many voices laughingly shouted, *"It is sugar"*. We all roared with laughter as I suddenly understood that these Russians saw these unusual economic side effects as just sweeteners that were occurring has they moved towards a new life without communism. I then thought what an excellent title for a story about Russia's new democratically based development which could be called *"Sugar in the Water."*

Well, now a little about this town of Birobidzhan, in which I was at this time asked to work! It is eleven time zones away from my home city of Leeds. So this travelling from Leeds to Birobidzhan did mean to me a one-hour journey by plane from Leeds to London. Then a three and a half-hour journey by plane from London to Moscow. Then upon arriving in Moscow I took a "taxi", these being private cars that were acting has taxis which took me from Moscow's international airport to Moscow's domestic airport - which was for flights that stayed within the Russian Federation.

It was from this airport that I began the nine-hour flight to my destination's regional capital, this being a city called "Khabarovsk," which is a city on the Amur River in south-eastern Russia. After landing at this airport I then needed to take a final journey of four hours by car to my destination, which was this city of Birobidzhan! It was also interesting that I actually arrived there just as the sun was dropping through the horizon. I remember that this sun settling was a magnificent sight for the car I was in was running directly into the sun, and I can assure you dear reader, that when I came to our place to stop, I felt that I had really arrived.

It was a good arrival feeling which was also supported by the knowledge that my baggage did contain many years of business experience which I would reveal to the people of Birobidzhan. This being about controlled business development experiences which I had personally written for Russian understanding which was "Business-Wise" needed in order to give to all listeners a necessary "NEW" business "Start-up" concept. These being the creative concepts that were needed to be supported by good economic "Know-How" and motivational understandings regarding the much needed application of cost cutting within existing business strategies – this to be for all the newly freed Russian people of Birobidzhan?

For instance, on this trip, I had prepared five business development presentations that I had carefully created when I was lecturing at the Russian "Modern Humanities University" in Moscow! These all being business development presentations that had been targeted by the requests of a British charitable organization that had an official base in Moscow. This was also the organisation which was actually financing all my occurring Russian Rouble expenses. For certainly, I also felt really ready and was therefore primed to deliver these "Business Development Gifts" to the people of "Birobidzhan".

For certainly, these gifts were actually "Know-How" gifts that were created from my degree in "Work Study"! This "Work Study" statement being a generic term for those techniques particularly method study and work measurement, that are scientifically used to systematically compare all methods that affect the efficiency and the economic development of all the potential working methods which can be used to find the lowest cost of a quality based production! Thus, said again, all my Russian development presentations where based upon my thirty-five years experience in "Work Study". This being that business development reality which not only searches for the best way to create that which can be sold in the market place but also the best and most economic method that can be used in the constructing new methods attached to business targets and also new business "Start-Up" developments. These developments being the best new ways to progress a business start-up venture in which a pursuer can "scientifically" discarded all non-profitable activities and replace them only with those activities that actually create a profit – meaning that the selling price should be well above the cost of the work needed to create the item.

SO NUMBER ONE at my business development presentation was on "Business Communication". This "communication" subject was about the conflicts arising between totalitarian and democratic markets, which also included the different ways of managing the needed workers.

NUMBER TWO at my business development presentation concept was about "Intercultural Relations". This subject was to indicate the pursuit of methods that avoided cross-cultural conflicts, particularly the ways of an emerging Market Economy which sought profit, a realty which is now quickly biting into Russia's current stagnation and deficit.

NUMBER THREE at my business development presentation concept was about "Production Methods" and I called this presentation "Death Valley"! This being because I also used it to explain the Russian communist "Production Virus" that had currently been plaguing Russia during the Communist period!

ENGLISH LANGUAGE TEACHERS OF BIROBIJAN DURING THE EARLY 1990'S DEFICIT PERIOD

For this was the Communist born virus that had been repeatedly destroying Soviet Russia's manufacturing attempts to create a "Market Economy" that could provide all the needs of the Soviet Union's population. I also explained to all listeners that the reason for the Soviet Union's market deficit was that the Soviet Union did not provide a profit for its creators nor were wages linked to the production, meaning that there was no motivation to work amongst all workers. It was this fact, found by my past many business development endeavours, in which I also explained that such guaranteed wage payments, regardless of work effort, would create a non-motivational condition that would produce only 30% or 40% of that which a person could really produce within the same time period! This not being the 100% that is produced when wages are linked to the amount being produced – has they are in the West of the northern hemispheres! For certainly it is now known to all the people of the Russian federation, that it is because of this "non-motivation" reality that "Communism", this being a world without management, is unable to avoid the stagnation and deficit which had been seriously plaguing all the people of a communist controlled Russia.

So yes! These serious "Business Development" presentations, which I was now pursuing throughout Russia, actually showed how to destroy this production "virus", which in the West do knowingly call "Variable Costs".

These being the fixed cost which are known by all to be the never changing rent, heating, electricity, maintenance and under Communism this also included the wages that are not based upon production but are based upon hours worked and so many wage payments were actually charitable contributions.

Thus, and again it should be said, that in Communist Russia guaranteed wages, which are linked to time and not production, will produce only 40 items for the market place! This certainly not being 100 items that would be produced in the same time, this being when wages are paid according to the amount that is being produced, has in the west of the Northern hemisphere.

For again if we say that the total cost of producing 40 items within a "Communist" Russian factory is say £100, this being wage payments and also factory operational and functioning costs. Then this total cost, when divided by the amount produced, i.e.: 100 divided by 40, gives a market sales price per item of £2.50! Also it should be further understood, that only 40% of that which can actually be produced by Russian workers, is now going into the Russian Market Place.

So now let us compare this example to the economic situation which exists in the West of the North of Northern Hemisphere, this certainly being where people are paid according to the amount they produce – a very different motivation system!

Thus it is known that in the West of the Northern Hemisphere, where wages are attached to production, a similar factory will produce 100% of the amount which it is capable of producing! This being a 100% production, which can be said, is completed at the same time and at the same costs has the 40% that which is being produced in communist Russia, where wages are a guaranteed payment – regardless of production.

Thus it can be said, that this £100, when divide by the 100 items that are now being produced, show that the cost of the item in Western countries is actually £1.00 and not the £2.50 cost has that similar item which is being produced in Russia. Thus meaning that in Russia for every 100 items of production entering the Russian market place, 250 items will be entering the market place of the west of the Northern Hemisphere – thus showing the difference in their market supply economies!

For certainly, this occurring of payments, for not working, is likened to a virus that is very active in all Russian productive organisations. It is also particularly noticeable in those organisations which attempt to provide the marketing needs of the majority of people, this being that "demand" which the majority of the population are all need fully pursuing.

NUMBER FOUR was a business development presentation which was about "General Management", particularly concerning the fact that there is no private ownership in Soviet Russia! For in the West private ownership is a system in which owners actively seek to make a personal profit from their self-created marketable goods. These being wanted goods that are sold to the people at the market place.

So certainly it is true that all of the North of the Northern Hemisphere have a different political "I Want" explanation that is "legally" being put forward has a law in these different political worlds! For we must remember that in the Russian communist regime, in which all workers are equal, there was no management, that is ownership, to threaten your livelihood or your payment system, that is if you attended a place of work! The only "workers" punishment in Russia was your sentencing to a Gulag prison or a labour camp for not "attending" a work place, i.e.: you were a dissenter! This being the communist Marxist and Leninist collective equality system in which the management of others did not exist! This reality was still currently and "habitually" dominating the Russian culture.

For in a communist working culture the "unknown" customer was a person who actually "compelled" to do this boring activity that was called "work". Thus any "work" was personally deemed to be an activity that was politically "imposed" upon the worker and it was regarded has a demand which actually got the worker out of their comfortable seat at home. It was also a "Working Activity" that, under the communist system, you received a fixed payment system which had no extra rewards for any extra effort, this being because wages were deemed to be a charitable receipt which was not linked to work output or to effort or to the amount of work done.

Thus, this unified "Communist" method of allocated "non-profit seeking work plus unmotivated wage payments, actually meant that "work" was normally the last type of activity that most people wished to do. The reason being that "work" effort actually distracted them from the bonhomie and the enjoyment of the group's togetherness! Thus this working realty actually meant, according to my personal experience of creating the work required in many manufacturing companies and also the experience which my discovered "business motivational development" methods also told me, was that this method of unsupervised management would create only about thirty per cent of the work that could actually be achieved.

It was therefore found very necessary to explain this customer related "motivation" relationship at many of my Russian business development presentations! This being a reality in which I first statistically identify the "audience" in front of me as my customer and actually state this to be so. Then I bow low towards them and say, *"You are my King and my Queen. You are my customers. I am here to serve YOU!* Then I smilingly say, *"For I know that the better I help YOU, the more "profit" I will make."* To which I carefully add, *"But I would only do this in a competitive market economy in which organizations compete to serve the people of the marketplace!"* It usually gives a clear understanding to the young and also the old of those who are my listeners.

It is further interesting to know that on my travels throughout Russia, I did find that the priority search for Profit became a terrific shock to the more mature people of Russia, who actually believed that you were taking more than is needed to be taken from the customer. I then usually explained that a private business organization is the invention of the most intrepid of explorers, these being explorers who can see the needs of the people around them. I also asked the question, *"Do you not believe that the rewards of an invention belong to the inventor?"* Then I put forward the real answer which is *"Of course it does!"*

This is certainly now being the general answer that is now given by the Russian people who are starting their own private business ventures. For it is certainly a known truth that most Russian people know that it did take Russia over seventy years, of what was a harrowing "communal" experiment, to find a reality which realized that money can be identified has the world's most important "belief" system, especially when in reality it is only worthless paper. Yet it is certainly true that nearly all people think that money is of great and also a much needed value. But enough writings about financial economics, for the job of "Life's Purpose" are really to explain the *"Why?"* and the "What for" of all our world's religions and philosophies. Well, I hope that this sets the scene for regarding my work in Russia, for we are now in Birobidzhan, this being at the end of my three days of seminars and three four-hour presentations, and after my final Tea-Break, I asked the audience: *"Do you have any questions?"* I was then asked a question that I had never been asked before at any of my previous and many years of *"Economic Management"* presentations in Russia. I think it arose because of my often-used religious intonations that often rested within or simply supported my presentations. The question that I was asked was, *"Do you believe in God?"* I also Realized that it was not a question seeking a simple "Yes" or "No" answer!

MY CHAIRED MEETING WITH THE RUSSIAN MANAGERS OF THE RUSSIAN SPACE SHUTTLE FACTORY 1/B THE ARRIVAL OF THE QUESTION

This being identified has a question that was from a Russian audience which was discovering a new way of life and an audience genuinely interested in the Holy Christian Gospels' and also their theological meaning. It was also then, while my thinking was still captured in ultimate economic terminology, I asked my questioner, *"What do you believe in?"* The answer that came was, *"We have always been told to believe in nothing?"* To which, after deep thought, I automatically forwarded the response, *"Well, your nothing is my God, for my God is certainly "No Thing",* it was an answer that received much joy with big smiles and also a great appreciative applause from the audience.

Then I suddenly found myself saying, *"When I was a young man, I also did not believe in God, but, at the age of twenty-five, a car hit me whilst riding my 350cc motor cycle and after this severe near-death road accident, which did put me into hospital for 12 months, I agnostically questioned myself and did ask myself – Is there a God?"* My answer then was as it is now; *"Of course, God is "nothing" but it is actually a "No Thing" which can be experienced within any person! This being an experience in which they actually become has one with their outer experiences, which is a reality which is impossible to describe".*

So yes! I firmly understand that God is a "No-Thing" that created everything that my five senses can experience. This interpretation I then also translated into meaning that I believed that God was no object, no commodity, and no article and certainly no physical matter that can be touched. I also further stated that I understood that God was certainly not visible or a something that the five senses could identify. It was at this point that my heart was stirring, and it was showing to me that believing in "nothing" and believing in "No Thing" was exactly the same. So, I then stated to my audience that I too believed in "Nothing", but to me, this "No Thing" is that which cannot be experienced, but was also that reality which gave birth to the Creation. I then explained that this "No Thing" can be likened to be a reality which worked in the same way as the "Nothing" that we knew to be a zero in our ten prime numbers – these being from the figure one to the figure nine? For in comparison, if we take away the world which has been born by the belief of this "Zero" in the world of numbers, then the modern world made by people would not exist! Therefore, is it not true, I stated, that we cannot understand how this "zero" this "nothing" that is created by people actually works? For is it not true that this "nothing", this zero, when placed alongside a specific numerical position, simply increases that number by ten but when it is standing alone it actually means "nothing". Yet is it not also true that this "belief" and the accepting of this numerical "nothing", this "zero" that creates the power that rest within all numbers, has actually created a new and very advanced world that is made by people?

Therefore, a good understanding of this self-creating, self-evolving mathematical "nothing" is similar to having a serious belief in a "No-Thing" reality which we can also be called God! This also being a reality, which is "religiously" stated, in all our world's religions and philosophies, to have created everything that can be experienced within this creation - which is an energy that is all around us just has it is also within us! But the question now can be "What is God according to philosophy?" For is it not certainly and also "scientifically" acknowledged that God is not a material entity! Therefore it must be factually stated that "He", that we call God, cannot deteriorate or become more perfect! Therefore "He" must be "eternal", which also means that the "Time" in which God exists, must also be "eternal". So is it not a truth, that both of these unchanging realities, these being that which we call "God" and that which we call "Time", must be witnesses to any change that can occur within the creation? This reality being creation in which all life and also all non-life do actually exist! But what is actually changing?

The simple answer to this question must be that this ongoing "birthed" reality, this being that, which we call "The Creation", must be likened to a child that is growing and so like all children must be constantly directed and cared for through this changing period! Therefore, and certainly for this simple reason, there must also be another unseen "natural" entity which "Life's Purpose" now reveals to be the "Mother of the Creation" or the observer, this being that which experiences a person's five sense for the non-believer! This caring "Mother", must certainly be a reality which must be caring for this only child, which we call "The Creation". This being that unified all has one reality which is all around us just has it is within us. Therefore, is it not true that nearly everything that has been newly created by people, within the "present" time of the creation, was newly built by people from a creation which did not previously exist? This being that challenging condition which is now facing the people of the former "Soviet Union".

So the question must now be "where does this previously unknown but needed "creative" and personally comparative knowledge come from?" Therefore under this condition of need, can it not be said that that which continuously and naturally is being birthed must be coming from that reality which we call "No-Thing". This being a "No-Thing" which did and still does, actually support a developing ongoing creation which is known to be required and also needed in a world that is made by people?

Therefore and factually, is it not a true realty that if we take this zero; this "no-thing", which "Life's Purpose" is describing to be God, away from the known world of numbers, then the modern world of people will cease to exist. For certainly, and is it not also a reality, that we, has people, cannot see or fully understand this "God-Like" zero, whose value is described as being "Nothing"! But we certainly know and so experience that it is certainly there. For is it not true and without any doubt that we actually know that this "No-thing", this zero, does definitely increase the world of numbers!

These being numbers that actually leads to inventions that enable people to create a new world. Therefore I now state that this "Nothing" or this "No-Thing", that we now speak, can actually be likened to my God! For certainly my God, or that which is named "Nothing" by the Non-Believer, is a reality which is scientifically stated to have created everything! For is it not a known truth that our universe, which is alive and constantly growing, is scientifically known to have come from "Nothing", this being that "No-Thing" which religious people call God!

It was a very satisfactory answer to my Russian audience and so I went back to my presentation about the creative needs of professional and private business development, this being that which now supplied the Russian "Market Economy"! For certainly this conversational seminar was a much needed business "Start-Up" and "Business Development" presentation which was certainly necessary because no goods existed to be purchased within the current Russian market place, which of course was the purpose of my many visit to support the new Russia "Market Economy."

However, I never did explain the full story about my near-death experience at my age of twenty-three. This accident being when on holiday from my travels around the world has an engine-room seaman in the UK merchant navy; I and my motorcycle collided head-on with an oncoming car that had come too fast around a bend in the road and so it could not be missed. Within this serious collision it is known fact that my motor cycle helmet did save my life has my head collided with the front roof of this oncoming car has I was catapulted over the top of the car and then did bounce down the road behind it. It was also at this accident, that I knowingly moved slowly down a dark tunnel towards a "White Light" in which I could see movement at its end. I also felt fear when I was moving passed dark shadows at the side of this tunnel but then suddenly I encountered some VERY strong words saying to me, *"Go back, you have work to do!"*

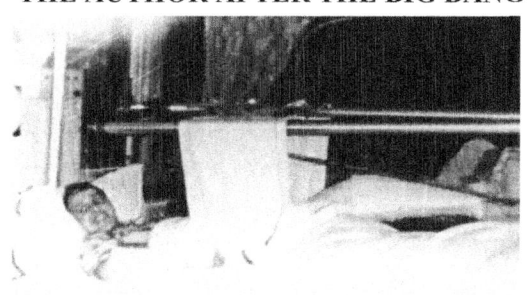

THE AUTHOR AFTER THE BIG BANG

It was then that I tried to sit up but could not, for my left leg was across my chest and it was also this action which surprised the police constable who was talking to the unhurt car passengers. This big surprise being because, has he told me later in hospital, that he had actually covered me with his cape because he had previously checked me for vital signs and had found none and so had pronounced me has being dead to the car occupants? He told me all this at his visit to me some days later when I was recovering in hospital where I had "strongly" refused, when slightly awakening on the operation table to allow the surgeons to take my left leg off when they told me that they needed to do so! This strong demand being after I had unknowingly signed a statement at this operation saying that I was allowing them to do so.

So yes! Me left leg was left on and I still walk with it but with a strong limp. What is further interesting is that at my operation they also invented that which they called the "Cullins Crane", see photo, this being the name of the engineer who built it for them! I slept in it for seven months and it did bring my pelvis pubic bone back to near normal and thankfully I have never had any problem in this area. Then after excellent bed-ridden hospitals recuperation, which lasted for an unscheduled seven months because I did sign myself out of the hospital on December the 23rd at Christmas time. The reason for this being that Christmas day was my birthday and I wanted to be at home with my Mother and Father plus sister and brother.

Eventually, and after a very long "recuperation" which lasted two years after my accident and also when being enabled to change my under-arm crutches for two walking sticks, I started work again. Still and it should be stated, that it was an accident which brought to me the strong need to understand religion and so I actually then began a long scientific "Business-Like" need to know quest to study the Creation's "Natural Laws" and especially our world's religions!

It was new type of work that I had to start, and this was because of my left leg injury and also the need to use a walking stick in order to support my wounded left leg! This need to use a walking stick meant that I could not work on that which we call the factory floor where the item that the company was selling was manufactured. For my current need to use a walking stick in order to support my walking, meant that I could only obtain work in the offices of the factory. This being where I could sit at a desk and to me "sadly", not in the physical world that added market value to the item that was being sent to the market place, this being where in my past that I had always worked. For certainly I still remember that this new type of working in an office and away from the creation of wealth, was a significant unwelcome "social" change that had never happened in my life before.

This being a life which began at my birth on the 25th December 1938 and also when my father was called from his "Christmas Day" Sunday drink in order to greet my arrival! Then at the after leaving my school at the age of 14 and then three days at being the age of 15, I happily starting work at the same coal mine has my father and brother – thus becoming the youngest underground worker in the united kingdom! I also certainly remember my becoming a "Teddy Boy" and has we were not needed for war we teenagers radically changed our style of clothing.

It was then at my age of 15, about eight years after world wars two's end, that I also started to wear long tight fitting jackets whose hem ended at the tip of my thumb and not at the top of the hip which was usual for men's jackets in those days. Also I wore "Drain-Pipe" trousers with sixteen inch

(40cms) hems and not the twenty two inch (56cm) hems has worn by our "older men". We also pursued a new type of music called "Rock & Roll", which supported our new way of dancing, all of which led to the roaring 1960s. It was then that at the age of 18, obtained the honour of being the youngest "official" coal face worker in the UK and this coal face, upon which I worked was three feet high (92cm). My daily work output was called a "Stint", so my working "Stint", this being the measurement of the coal that I hacked out of a three feet high (90cm) and four feet wide (122cm) and thirty feet long (1100cm) seam of coal. But then, at the age of 20 years plus six months, I felt the need to see what the world was all about. I therefore joined the Merchant Navy and began work in the engine rooms with the target to become a qualified Engine-Room Engineer.

    The first ship that I signed-up to work upon was the Queen Elizabeth, which at 83,000 tons was stated to be the largest ship in the world and in which I made six trips to New York. Then, after being at home for Christmas and the New Year, I went to Southampton docks and signed up to work upon a "Banana Boat" whose target was to pick up bananas destined for Europe. Upon this ship I made several trips, from European ports, to all the Caribbean islands except Cuba plus the countries of Central America and the North of South America – all of which were very different from the land of my birth mainly because of the poverty that they showed.

    I then enjoyed several trips working in the engine room of the ship called "Cape Town Castle", these trips being to South Africa's Cape Town and all its coastal ports. This is where when swimming in the sea at East London my inner ears exploded has VERY BIG waves moved over me! I then enlisted upon a Mediterranean "tourist" ship which took its passengers to all the countries of the Mediterranean plus its many holiday islands. After this I then signed up to sail on an oil tanker through the Suez Canal and visited many Arabian countries plus India's Bombay, where I saw such real poverty that it physically hurt me.

    An example of this poverty being shown when I was being taken to a British club on a motor-bike which had attached a small cart that passengers could sit in, this being to the only place where alcohol drinks, for foreigners, were available. What happened was that lots of little children ran behind the cart with hands outstretched begging for money. This really affected me and I put in my hands all the money I had on me and then threw it into the street! I was also really saddened by the mad scramble to collect it from the road. I then told the driver to take me back to the ship and when walking upon the top deck towards my cabin a most unusual thing happened to me. An Indian "Fakir" that which we call a

"Wise Man", stood upon and beckoned me to come to him but I said *"Sorry, I have no money"*. He then said to me *"I want no money! I have come to say to you that when you arrive to your home, you will enter a very large building and when you leave it you will be in a much better condition"*. He then stood up walked off the ship. I had no idea what he had meant but did hear from other crew members that I was the only person that He had spoken to.

But what I do know is that whilst at home and on leave from this trip, I encountered that which I call *"The Big Bang"* and also the message that occurred in my mind when death was arising saying *"Go Back, You Have Work to do."* This being the motor-cycle accident that I have mentioned earlier and indeed it left a deep impression upon me and a strong need to find out what was this work that I needed to do! It was then that I had the opportunity to mention this message to me to a "Very" wise philosopher from India who simply stated, *"Fall silent in front of a blank piece of paper and holds a pen. When the mind is still, ask yourself the question, "What is the work I have to do?"* I did this, and in complete silence, my hand wrote the answer, *"Free the People of the North."*

This revelation did amaze me because I was currently attending evening classes and seeking a high degree in the studying and the controlling of work plus all its aspects. Therefore, this message *"Free the People of the North."* did strongly motivate me to find a new economic system that freed unemployed and also working people to find a job that would better sustain them and their families.

So my main target was interpreted to be the removal ALL unemployment, which then became my target throughout the entire history of my working life. Thus I began to target the employment of people in newly created factories and to build efficient "economic" systems within industries that "created" marketable employment. To aid this development I did eventually, after three years of evening studies, past all exams designed by the "Institute of Management Services" of which I was a member! It was also known to be a fellowship degree which was actually stated to be higher in value than a university "Honours Degree".

I also actually improved the production and also created many new clothing manufacturing factories in England and also in Scottish development areas, these being areas in which unemployment was very high. It was then, after many years of installing new manufacturing factories, which were designed to create employment in high unemployment areas throughout the UK, that I then created my own manufacturing factory in Bradford. This was a company I called "Work-

Wear Fashions" and I started it by renting a disused factory in which I eventually employed over 80 people. But sadly our government then allowed China to sell work clothing into the UK and these being at prices that I could not buy my cloth for! So sadly, my factory at my age of 50 eventually closed – an act which led to my work in Russia, but more will be written later about this new aspect.

But in my past many busy years of building manufacturing factories combined with my morning and evening meditational efforts, in which I experienced "Enlightenment". I found that in my "Present Time", this being a time without any work controlling task, I began to understand that the "Freedom to Work" was not an "economic" aspect but a "spiritual" one. Therefore, I newly began to experience that my past pursuits of creating factories so that they could employ people, was wrong. For indeed I "Self-Aware" that the "Freedom to Work" was a personal aspect i.e.: This being a personal opinion, a personal quality, or a personal thing that actually belongs or relates to one person rather than to other people. Therefore it was a freedom that was not a social or public one. For it actually meant that basically a self-motivated person could only particular their own efforts in order for themselves to be enabled to create, to employ, to operate, to toil, or to perform certain activities etc. Then with all these "Freedom to Work" aspects in place, it was understood that the purpose of a self-motivated person was to target and succeed in gaining the true freedom that was actually encased in the personal experience of "Enlightenment", this being has one entity with the world in which they exist! So the creation is experienced to be "Them", thus making "Enlightenment" to be the actual target of ALL our world's religions and philosophies'. It was then that I also became a tool which began to write "Life's Purpose"! This being that which is "Business-Development" plan which is actually targeted to affectionately bring the reader to experience "Enlightenment". This being after it was knowingly found that the experiencing of "Enlightenment" was the actual target of every religion and also every philosophy that is activated within our world and which is the same purposeful target that rests within ALL people hence the world's desire for religions and philosophies.

UNIVERSITY ECONOMIC LECTURE – MURMANSK

Now back to "Life's Purpose" – which targets the actual "Purpose of All Religions and Philosophies". For certainly "Life's Purpose" is a very modern and a scientifically updated explanation of that which is the target of all our worlds' religions and belief systems! Therefore "Life's Purpose" is written for not only religious but also for non-religious people. Therefore and certainly, "Life's Purpose" truly endeavours to explain not only that which our ancients wisely and culturally described as being God's world, but also how to live correctly in God's world or the world of Nature for the non-believer, and so achieve that which all religions and all philosophies call "Enlightenment". This being a personnel "Self-Awareness" which is the greatest gift that God or Nature for the non-believer has given to all people. For certainly it should also be known that it is for this reason that "Life's Purpose" was written has a "Business Plan", with true "Self-Awareness", being an awareness that can lead to "Self-Realization", this being the actual target of all our world's religions and philosophies.

For "Life's Purpose", and again it should be said, that "Life's Purpose" has been written to contain "scientific" evidence of just how to achieve a "Self-Awareness", which will lead to a "Self-Realization", this being that realty which our entire world's religions and philosophies are targeting to achieve – this being a personal experience of that which is knowingly called "Enlightenment". This being the actual "realization" that you are has one with Gods world, or with Natures world for the Non-Believer, thus meaning that you do actually become "Everything" and there is no observer for you have become has one with Gods world or with the world of nature for the non-believer.

"Life's Purpose" also endeavours to further explain, within its wording, the purpose and target of all our worlds' variable religious and philosophical preaching! For again it must be said that "Life's Purpose" does actually endeavour to "scientifically" reveal the purposeful target of all our world's religions and philosophies and therefore communicates this reality by using a very modern and acceptable business like language. For certainly "Life's Purpose" endeavour is to show a workable way of how to achieve "Enlightenment"! Thus again saying that this "Self-Awareness", which can lead to "Self-Realization", is certainly the actual target of ALL our world's religions and philosophies. Yet and certainly, "Life's Purpose" also recognises that all the people who pursue our world's different religions and philosophies, do personally believe and so do readily accept their own religions cultural preaching's! This being a religious practice in which each person can culturally and comfortably target their oneness with all life and all non-life and so experience the unified bliss of God's world or the world of Nature for the Non-Believer.

For certainly, our worlds various and different religious and philosophical practices, all do target a purposeful life! This being a life in which a person can exist has one entity with the creation that is within them and also that creation which exists all around them! This being a life that exists has in a unified bliss with God's world and which is also a life that is based upon past Realized facts which can be thousands of years old! This is why "Life's Purpose" constantly endeavours to use modern sayings and also modern explanations, all of which are based upon well-known "scientific" facts. For certainly, "Life's Purpose" uses the same traditional examples, procedures and training methods that were used in my past forty years of my establishing new business plans", these being that which successfully created new and profitable business ventures. These being new business ventures which were based upon management training systems that targeted profit via the creation of new business methods! They were also new productive "creations" which also served the many wage earning people who did support these new profit seeking ventures.

So yes! "Life's Purpose" is a modern-day pursuit that is written in a modern business-like way and so it can be likened to a "training" program which targets that which ALL our historically wise ancients did target for their followers! For certainly, is it not a truthful fact that we can now understand anew the words of our wise via modern 2023 "Present Time" translations, this being a reality which can now be knowingly experienced? For certainly, in this modern time, it can now be revealed just how to actually achieve this "Enlightenment", this being that experience which ALL our world's religions and philosophies do target. For is it not now good to know that no person can achieve or create any productive work by simply thinking or dreaming about an "I Want" that takes a them into a non-existing past or future! For certainly it should now be realized that all new developments can only be created within that world that we call the "Present" Time.

For certainly is it not true, that it is only in Gods "Present" or in Natures, "Present" for the non-believer, this being that "Present" which is resting in the current time, that a person can perform a "mantra" based "prayer"! This being a methodological certainty which will bring to the practicing prayer the experience of that which we call "Enlightenment"! This being that experience which our wise ancients did constantly target for all their followers! For is it not true that "ALL" our world's religions and philosophies are targeting the same "divine" conviction! This being a conviction which targets a way that will bring a person to experience the unified singularity of Gods world or the world of Nature for the Non-Believer!

For certainly again, it should now be understood that a person's mind–silencing pursuit, via mantra praying, will enable them to eventually experience the unity i.e.: the unified singularity of the creation that is all around them just has it is within them! This being a non-thinking person's "Self-Aware" awakening of being has one with the creation or a "Self-Realized" experience of actually being the totality of the creation, these being the two realties which all our world religions and all our worlds' philosophies do endeavour to pursue, but which many preachers have forgotten. For certainly, the "Present Time" is that reality which all our worlds religious people call Gods world or it is called the world of Nature by Non-Believer and this is the reason why it is called "The Present"!

So yes! It is now wise to understand i.e.; "Stand under", the fact that many people do not believe in a God created reality and therefore when in conversation with such believers, this aspect regarding their belief must be honoured. This is the reason why "Life's Purpose" is written in such an unbiased way in order to show to all the people of our world just how to achieve this target which "Life's Purpose" and all our world's religions and philosophies call "Enlightenment". This being an experience in which you actually become "aware" that you are actually has one with "The Creation", this being that which is not only within you but also that which is also all around you. For indeed, the task of "Life's Purpose" is to reveal to the forgetting religious reader and also the non-religious reader, just how to attain this undeniable experience which is the target of "ALL" our Earth's many differently worded and practising religions and philosophies.

ENGLISH LANGUAGE TEACHERS –BIROBIJAN
DURING THE 1990'S DEFICIT PERIOD

So first, in my desire to write "Life's Purpose", this being in occurring leisure time, I habitually began to restudy and re-read all our worlds many religions and philosophies, including the Christian Bible, which I had actually put away, has being unreadable long ago. I now looked for positive motivational clues in my search for their "business" target. I also carefully looked within these many religious wordings, these being wordings which religiously explained their "business" sought "marketing" for believers to be attached to their religion! I also sought to understand the worshipping truth that they "religiously" pursued; thus I was business-like seeking if their truth could not be changed or even contradicted—for this truth was also their personally chosen's religions creation! For certainly, a religious truth must always be supported by the worshipper, has it is in our world's major religions and philosophies.

First I found that all our worlds many and various religious practices, writings and interpretations were all differently cloaked in a personally claimed "strong opinion". This being an opinion which was strongly supporting their chosen religions way of how to live in Gods world! For certainly their chosen way of being faithful to God was strongly pursued and supported by the leaders of their chosen religion. For it was good to indentify that our worlds many differing religions were all being translated and preached by moral and well-intentioned religious leaders; all of whom used no scientific understanding nor any corroborating meaning but strongly taught a unified way of life which seemed to many observing non-religious people to exist only in dreams.

For certainly this was a "religiously" sought way of life in which a person would or could become aware or actually experience a realisation that they were actually unified with all life and also all non-life. For certainly I indentified that this fact was a taught reality which was being pursued by all our world's religions and philosophies. It can also be identified by the well known religious saying, has in the Christian Bibles Exodus 3.14 which states "And God said unto Moses, "I AM THAT I AM": therefore if God is everything! Who are you? With this question before me I then thought, and this being after 50 years of planning, building and successfully changing many people in order to profitably modernise many differing manufacturing companies, that I should seek answers to this question. So I then targeted an answer this question which then became my "off-duty" way of relaxing has I studied and practised the many diverse worshipping ways of various religions and philosophies, which also included the studying and practising of many Eastern Philosophies – which became VERY important!

So now in my retirement, and again it can be said, that I have decided to write "Life's Purpose", whose "profitable" target is to achieve that which all our world's religions and philosophies seek. This first truth being a "Self-Awareness" in which you experience yourself to be has one with the creation; this being that which is all around you has it is within you! This also being an awareness which can lead you to experience "Self-Realization", thus becoming has one with Gods world or the world of Nature for the non-believer! The major difference being that there is no observer – meaning that you will not be born again for you have fulfilled the purpose of the creation which is for God or Nature for the Non-Believer to have experienced itself! For certainly, this experience is the actual target of Gods only child or Natures only child for the Non-Believer – which is "The Creation".

It was then, with this target to become first "Self-Aware" that I decided to return to the Christian bibles "New Testament", but I was disappointed again for I found zero understanding of a "Self-Aware" or a "Self-Realization" target which should be explanatory resting within it. For always my question at this time was, "what is this *"Nothing", this "No Thing" that we call God and how do I find Him and so then understand His world"* i.e.: meaning His "Productive Factory" and its purpose.

Then I suddenly found the beginning of an answer. It was so simple that I immediately realized why the Christian Gospels had been so difficult for me to grasp.

The reason for this lack of understanding was that I had been actually trying to factually understand the Bible's interpretations of a man called Jesus. This being a biblical writing which told me about His personal relationship with God and also with the happenings that existed around Him and also which happened to all the many people that cared for Him.

I then found that like the many Eastern teachings, it was nice, but it was also about another person's interpretation about some "thing" which was that reality which I personally sought but could not "productively" grasp. Then I had a flash, a glimmering of a new conceptual understanding, I understand that this was based upon my many years of religious study and also of me work that targeted of a factually known nature – which involved always involved many different people.

ASSISTANT CHAIRMAN:
THE MOSCOW DEMOCRATIC CONFERENCE ON ECONOMICWASTE

So, what did I activate and do at this first glimpse of my first possible "factual" answer to the productivity, i.e.: what was the output or profit obtained by the working questions that I was asking? I took a highlighter pen and chose to work with the Christian Disciple, called Mathew. I then went to read through his text and highlighted in red only the words spoken to him by his manager Jesus. Then, after a day of pause, I began to read only these words that were spoken by Jesus, which I had previously highlighted. I purposely I had no other interpretation or ay attached opinion going through my non-thinking mind, these being any "I Want" which could actually "mindfully" change the meaning of these questioning words. It was an outstanding and very successful experience, as the secret of Christian teaching was then revealed loudly and very clearly to me. I felt and knew that I had actually found the synthesis i.e.: the targeted production and practicality of this dominant religion, which I now understood actually showed the key to the door through which rested the "Target" of all our Earth's religions and philosophies.

I laughed and laughed and laughed at what I had found to be the truth, has many massive scales fell away from my inner mind thinking "thoughts". For I had discovered that by reading only the words of Jesus, I Realized that these were not the expressions of a man merely talking, but that they were actually "statements" that could be likened to words coming directly from God or via the Creation or via Nature, for the Non-Believer. It was a "creative" voice speaking through a man called Jesus, and I realized with certainty, that these words being sounded by Jesus were actually coming directly from God or from Nature for the Non-Believer.

Yes! I therefore suddenly understood and so realized that it was God or Nature for the Non-Believer, that spoke directly through this man called Jesus and that "No Things" Creation, which was all around me has it was within me, had actually the ability to speak with another person's voice. Of course, in the Christian religion, it was a man called Jesus through whom God had chosen to speak.

For certainly, is it not also known the in many of our world's hemispheres, it is known that numerous major religions enjoyed God's or Natures words for the Non-Believer! These also being religious words that many listened to and which were culturally spoken to many people by incarnations such as Krishna, who had a wonderful sense of humour. For when someone asked Krishna why he saved the life of his friend who was known has Arjuna, this being during his fighting in the war against the evil of the Kurukshetra and which was an action that resulted in the death of the more experienced older warrior who Arjuna was fighting, Krishna replied, *"Because Arjuna is my friend"*, (and also, because Arjuna had a great deal more of Gods unifying work to do in this Great War against selfishness).

Of course, Gods Creation also produced people like Mohammed, who's Jihad 2.190 stated, *"Fight in the way of God but do not transgress, for God does not like transgressors"* and 2.193 *"Fight them until there are no more breakers of harmony, but if they cease from destroying harmony, then there is to be no more aggression"* etc. Not entirely turn the other cheek, which means to not hurt someone who has hurt you and I also believe that this action is correct for it searches for harmony, meaning, agreement, accord, coordination, synchronisation and coherence. Thus bringing a "Present Time" world which is the very opposite to energy being spent on unhealthy discord, meaning "I Want" conflict, friction, fighting, and also any quarrelsome disagreement that bring pain and punishment to others.

So, if you are not quite sure what is the meaning of God's or Natures harmony for the Non-Believer, then look at your own body? A person's inner body consists of trillions of different "individual" entities, and there are probably more of these individual entities that exist with our bodies than there are people who live upon our planet. For certainly, is it not true that our inner bodies' realities usually work in perfect harmony with one another? This also being true even when they have different jobs to do, thus birthing a reality which can be likened to the harmony that exists within critically controlled computer systems!

For is it not true that usually computers are all in perfect "Harmonic" balance? This being that same "Harmonic" realty which also exists within our bodies! For certainly does not the low death rate, which is known to be caused by internal disharmony, prove this? It is also interesting that it has been said by our wise, that many of our bodily disorders are a disharmony which is caused by an evolving body that is seeking new parts or the improving of existing bodily parts, this search being for the on-going ever-evolving development of people. For is it not a truthful fact that bodies can and does add to themselves new entities? This fact also being that change reality which did actually develop all our bodies into what they are now – but much more about this later in "Life's Purpose".

Now back to the enlightening words of Jesus which actually need no confusing interpretations! Yet, is it not sad to say that the many interpretations of our world's religions and meanings may have been incorrectly put forward by those seeking power over others? Therefore is it not good for all people to understand, as I did when I read the words of Jesus, that it was a certain need that actually and culturally created our worlds many religions! This need being in order to pursue an "evolutionary" ever ongoing creative purpose! This being a purpose in which all our world's religions and philosophies do actually state that everything that exists within our world is for people to care for, which must be the reason why people have been created!

For certainly it were the Biblical words that were spoken by Jesus that did actually rock my personal thinking into a logical understanding. For I now became aware of a belief system in which Jesus was not just a man but was actually God's personification of the whole of the Creation or the whole of Nature for the Non-Believer. This being a personification that did naturally bring an understanding plus a potential realization of the "Natural Laws" that rule this planet that we call Earth, this being that body upon which we all live. For certainly again, this "Awareness" which can lead to a "Realization" of the truth that our Creator was actually talking through this man called Jesus and He spoke directly to people like me, who had no memory of who we actually were.

I also personally recognized fully the all-knowing words of John the Baptist, who, upon seeing Jesus for the first time, said to his people, *"You must change your hearts – for the Kingdom of Heaven has arrived!"* Now what a man he must have been to have known this reality. Then, also at this time, did not God, speaking through Jesus, say to His disciples, *"Believe me, a rich man will find it difficult to enter the Kingdom of Heaven. Yes, I repeat, a camel could more easily squeeze through the eye of a needle than a rich man to enter into the kingdom of God!"*

It was then I began to understand, really truthfully and physically, that Heaven, which is the Kingdom of God, must actually rest only in the "Present Time"! But then I thought and this was a long time ago, how do you enter "totally" and "understandably" this Heaven that rests only within the "Present Time"? This being the only place which we know can exist in Gods world of Nature and which is a place that we also know that we can actually experience unity with everything that exists upon our Earth.

So yes! How do you go through this door that leads to a "Heaven" that actually exists upon our own Earth, but only in the "Present Time"? Also, how do live in this "Heaven" that can only exist in the "Present Time"? For certainly, it was at this question that I then used my past history of production planning and behavioural quality control in order to seek a productive way that would find the words that were needed to explain the best way to fully attain a "Self-Awareness", this being an awareness of the unity in which all life and all non-life was actually experienced to exist has one body – i.e.: one life form. For certainly this is also a "Self-Aware" condition which could eventually lead a person to a "Self-Realization" reality in which they experienced that they actually were "Everything", a life form in which there was no observer! This being a reality in which a person factually understood that they were truly "Everything" that actually existed in Gods world or the world of Nature for the Non-Believer!

So Yes! I genuinely and factually found that by reading only the words that came from Jesus – within the Christian Bible - that I did experience that it was God who was actually speaking to me through the incarnate that we call Jesus! For certainly it was an experience within me in which I became "Self-Aware" that it was through the body of Jesus that God or Nature for the Non-Believer, was making a verbal and "holistic" contact to ALL the people who would experience an awareness of what these words where actually explaining.

This awareness and understanding being has if God, or Nature for the Non-Believer, who was that reality which created our universe, was actually speaking through this personification of the Creation who we call Jesus, and so was actually talking directly and personally to YOU – dear observer of the world around you! For what else is the Creation but the only Child of God who, has a father, was clearly authorised to speak through this man that we call Jesus, for is it not easily I recognized that the Creator i.e. "The Boss", can speak to everyone, including "Non-Believers". Therefore, it was clearly understood, within my revelations, to be God's or Natures Voice for the Non-Believer, that I was listening too and I also realized, with a great certainty, that these stated words were coming directly from God or from Nature for the Non-Believer. For I suddenly I understood that God was speaking through this man called Jesus and that "No Things" Creation, which was all around me has it was within me, had been given a voice.

Of course, in the Christian religion, belonging to the North of Northern Hemisphere, it was a man called Jesus through whom that reality which did create the "Creation" did speak. In other hemispheres and cultures around our world, in which God spoke to people, is it not a known fact that all our "Earths" religions enjoyed discovering God's words, these being words that were culturally spoken to them by different incarnations. Actually and indeed, this reality being shown has previously stated, in the exquisite sense of humour which Krishna revealed to all his listeners.

It can therefore be stated that if you are not quite sure what the target or meaning of God's supporting harmony is, then look at your own body? Is it not true that your body is a world that consists of trillions of different "individuals", and there are probably more of these individual entities that live and also "privately" perform skilful tasks (work) within our bodies, than there are people who live upon our planet? Is it not also true that all these "inner-bodily" entities usually work in perfect harmony with one another, despite the fact that they all have different jobs from physical to critical control systems and many even have different languages?

Yet all are naturally in perfectly unified balance, has the low death rate caused by internal disharmony proves. It is also an interesting fact that it has been stated that many occurring "disorders" of a person's body are clinically stated to be disharmony symptoms! The question now being is this undesirable disharmony that is being created within the body, actually the body endeavouring to create new additions to its self – has it has done in the past millions of years?

At this point we should again factually understand that it is a scientific truth that energy, this being that which brings life to a person's body, cannot die and so must materialize somewhere else! If in doubt about this reality, ask any woman who has given birth to a child! For she will be able to reveal to you exactly when the Soul (energy) entered the child that was within her! For a person Soul- like all energy just cannot die – it just goes somewhere else to live.

1/C A SINGLE ENTITY OF TRUTH

During my many various religious and philosophical studies, these being that which occurred during my need to relax after serious work creating activities, I sought to understand the power of God or "Nothing" for the unbeliever! It was during one of these studies that I actually realized that we must have nine prime senses and not merely five, these five being that which we call touch, taste, and smell, seeing and hearing.

This can be stated because there are also "scientifically" known to be only ten prime numbers, these being 0, 1, 2, 3, 4, 5, 6, 7, 8, and 9. Therefore, it is a fact that all our numbers begin from "nothing" or "No-Thing" for the believer and so "No-Thing" is a word which is used to indicate that something is not important or it is insignificant because it does not really exist!

For is it not true that "No-Thing" actually means "Nothing", but actually what is this physically well-known and accumulative number that we all call "nothing" and which "Life's Purpose calls "NO-THING"? For is it not true that that the word "THING" is a word that describes something that has been created to exist and so it must exist in our world today – but it's an existence that can only exist in the "Present Time"!

Therefore and certainly, is it not a truth that this "No Thing", this "Zero" this "O" is the only reality that can create the unity that actually expands the physical world of numbers? This being a reality which is much needed in the world that we now live in. For is it not a known and also an accepted truth, that this "nothing" this zero can factually expand any number so that it could even encircle the whole universe?

Therefore is it not a truth that without this "zero", this "nothing", then the modern world in which we now live, would certainly be unable to exist! For certainly, it can also be further explained that the current "Creation", this being that which is commonly known to be "Some-Thing" that is within us and also a "Some-Thing" that is without us, actually needed the "Nothing", or that which is commonly known has "No-Thing", in order for our "Present" to be created – this being our Present Time!

For is it not a fact that the creation which is all around us and also within us, is experienced to be a very positively created reality and therefore "scientifically" it must also be a reflection of that "reality" from whence it came – is this not true?

However, God's target, this being that Godly entity which non-believers call "No-Thing", is certainly the Godly "No-Thing" which must have started and so did birth that child which we call "The Creation." But truly, there is no need to be confused or to be alarmed about this! For it has also been found "scientifically" that our God or "No-Thing" for the non-believer, can also be acknowledged to be a good "Teacher" and a "Teacher" who cares for His only child that we all call "The Creation, or we can call it the "The Universe" if we are a Non-Believer.

Although how the universe created itself is an interesting thought! For certainly it must also be acknowledged that this believed "Teacher", which is God or Nature for the Non-Believer, actually has an undeniable never ending energy which does continually care for all people very "individually" and also very "democratically". For is it not true that this observing reality, called God by the believer or Nature by the Non-Believer, is also a reality which lawfully cares for this only child that we call the universe, this also being a factual reality which continually exists within and also around each person – is this not true?

Therefore, who or what else can it be that did naturally bring all those trillions of caring bits of separate life-forms, this being that which exists within the bodies all life and even non-life – just how to come together into one independently thinking "I Want" unit? This being an "independent" thinking unity which was also a realty that was enabled to not only to bring together their worlds many unified life forms but to also actually provide for the worldly needs of "others"! These providers also were independent life-forms but they actually performed many creative "living together activities"! This also being even when they actually believed that all life was an independent and a non-unified part of the creation, this being that creation which was living all around them just has living within them! Therefore, not forgetting, and forgetting is our worst enemy, that the bodily energy that rests within our lives life is also a part of every single life-form and non-life form that exists upon our Earth!

BUSINESS DEVELOPMENT PRESENTATION AT A TV MANUFACTURING PLANT – RIGA IN LATVIA

Therefore it is good to experience that which our wise ancients call being "Self-Aware" in which you know that everything you experience is YOU. This being an experience which can lead to "Self-Realization", which is the experiencing of a "Present" in which there is no observer.

For it is known by our wise that a personal "I Want" for ME, that reality which is constantly arising in an animalistic mind, can eventually create a world that does not respond to the "peace that surpasses all understanding"! This being that which "naturally" exists in the world around you! This truly being our only existing world whose "Present" is constantly seeking to create a harmony all around you just like it exists within you! Therefore, it is good, and also wise to know, that our creatively allowed inner-mind thinking, this thinking being those thoughts which are usually coming from one or all of your animalistic five senses, is usually their energetic sounding animalistic and uncontrolled "I Want for me" verbiage.

This "thinking", which is truly an "animalistic" thought, is actually endeavouring to trap you into animalistic ally capturing for your body, an "I Want"! This "I Want" being that reality which is currently being observed? Is this not true? For certainly, now is a time that we should actually begin to understand the need to be "Self-Aware" of that which can be "scientifically" called the "Three in One"! For truly and certainly, we do have a "One God", who is definitely "No Thing" and also it is a good time to now understand that we must, according to natural law, also have only "One Mother", which is more fully explained later in "Life's Purpose".

Of course it is also a reality that they also have had only one child, this being that which we call "The Creation" or that which is called the universe by the non-believer. Also and further to this, "Life's Purpose" scientifically acknowledges that the creations "Mother" can only be that entity which we call "Space", this being that reality within which all life and all non-life are being created! Thus "Space" must be that feminine reality in which God or Nature for the Non-Believer, actually planted the seed that is now creating their only child, which is that single life force that we call number "Three," i.e. "The Creation"!

For certainly the "Creation" is their pending child so it must be a child that has not yet been born but is endeavouring to be born – but more about this fact later in "Life's Purpose". For certainly "Life's Purpose" will scientifically explain to all readers just who or what we really are plus the purpose of that which is growing within the Mother, this being that which we call "The Creation"! For certainly again, this is the reason why "Life's Purpose" describes the "Present Time" has being the "Three in One".

These three being the Father, who is God the creator and then the Mother, who is the space in which their unborn child is developing and the third being their pending child, which is the evolving creation in which those who are near to being birthed are called "Self-Aware" people and those who are actually being birthed are called "Self-Realized", but birthed into what? But for now we will return to that which we commonly acknowledge to be the "Present Time"

So now! Regarding these perceived nine senses. It was found "scientifically" that our animalistic and well-known five senses, these being touching; hearing, tasting, seeing, and smelling, are all inherited from our past animal existence, these being that which were engaged to ensure our survival, has it is with all natures animals. So certainly, for this reason, they should be treated has five domestic pets and so be trained and disciplined accordingly. This actual training meaning that if your five senses are "annoying" you, like all pets can do, just repeatedly keep saying to them "Not this", has you would for domestic pets!

For, has it is known, this disciplinary action does actually teach the "animalistic" nature of the five senses to stop their barking there "I Want" into a person's mind. For certainly, it is well known that disciplinary imposed praying and hymn singing can replace a person's animalistic mind filling of an "I Want", this being an "I Want" mind filling chatter which is emanating from one or from all of the animalistic five senses. For certainly, mantra meditation is to stop the animalistic "I Want" mind filling activity and this is the purpose and the reason for all our worlds religiously imposed praying, hymn singing and other group based mind silencing practices! This being why praying and hymn singing is an imposed reality which is practiced within all our world's religions and philosophies, but more about this later in "Life's Purpose".

Now it should be known that it is only people who have an intelligence that can avoid captured by the "I Want" of the five lower animalistic senses! For certainly it should also be Realized that it is only people that have an additional four senses, these being above the five animalistic senses which are of taste, smell, seeing, hearing and of course touching! This truth being because these non-animalistic higher four senses can only exist in a body which has had many lives and which has now growingly established within it the experience an undying "Soul". For certainly it should now be known that the purpose of our many lives is for the Soul to eventually be birthed has one with the creation, this being that which is all around us just has it is also within us.

Therefore, it should now be further known that the Soul of a person can only be birthed has one with the "Creation" when the mind is silent! For certainly, it can experience only through a silent mind that reality which we call, "Present Time", which is Gods world or the world of Nature for the Non-Believer!

This being because the "Present Time" is the only reality in which a person can actually become "Self-Aware" that they are actually a part of that which they observe to be all around them! It is also known that it is only in the "Present Time" that a person can become "Self-Realized", this being that condition in which a person actually becomes "Everything" and so there is no observer, this also being that reality which our ancients called "Enlightenment"? It is also a "Self-Realized" experience in which a person actually becomes birthed and so leaves the "Mother of the Creation" and as a result they are no longer enabled to observe that which used to be all around them, meaning of course that they have left the "Mother of the Creation" or "Mother Nature" for the non-believer and so have been born into Gods world.

For certainly, Gods world is also known to be a reality which is undoubtedly sought by that energy which we call "consciousness", a known reality which powers all the Life and all the Non-Life that actually exists within the Creation. Therefore, it must also be understood that this energy, which brings the light within all life and also all Non-Life, must also have began from that creating entity which we call God or from Nature for the Non-Believer.

For certainly and again, is it not also factually true to confirm that it is only people that God gave this "I AM" the "I AM" expanded consciousness too? This being a consciousness which actually allowed all peoples a freedom of choice to do or not to do, to be or not to be, to live or not to live? I have just seen a young girl crossing a busy road snarling and shouting at the cars that swerve to avoid her. I then think how strange it is that we punish these "wild" people who are newly birthed from the animal kingdom. This punishing reality being instead of absorbing them and humanely treating them with kindness and courtesy, as do all professional animal trainers; for where else can this increase in new animalistic "Souls" be coming from but from the shrinking animal kingdom?

Sadly, in the not understanding of this reality, we punish these newborns from the animal kingdom and imprison them in cages because they still act according to the nature of their past lives. For truly, should it not be acceptably known that such a person is not yet capable of honouring the common law which is set by the majority of people?

These being laws created by the majority of wise people who have had many lives and whose only purpose is to support and encourage the developing creation which is growing all around them, just has it is growing within them. For certainly, should they not also endeavour to actually copy the unifying and purposeful supporting energy which does actually rest within them!

Therefore and certainly, our ancient wise knew that they were not any of this animalistic mind filling "I Wants", this being that reality which is always coming from the greed of the animalistic five senses! These being the animalistic five senses known to be touch, taste, seeing, smelling and hearing. For certainly, these five animalistic "I Want" entities are actually a reality which normally exists within all animals! For certainly, they are also those entities which are well known to create an animalistic pursuing "I Want" mind that is constantly filled by an ever searching "I Want".

For certainly, is it not VERY good to personally acknowledge that has a person you are not the animalistic five senses! For certainly, it is well known that has a person, you are really the possessor of an undying Soul, this being that entity from which all your consciousness does actually come from. For without doubt, it should also be known that your personal Soul is also that energy which is constantly being re-birthed has a person!

This being a person who has been given, by God or by Nature for the Non-Believer, the freedom of choice to do or not to do, to be or not to be, to have or not to have! But is it not also true that we can actually forget; in our early lives has a person, this truthful reality! For certainly, this known truth is why our wise ancients and also our modern preachers and religious teachers, always recommend praying and also the singing of hymns. For undoubtedly, this is a mind-silencing "religious" activity which actually compels a person's animalistic five senses to become silent and so become like well trained pups that are trained to go silently behind their master's heel.

For again certainly, this unifying energy, this being that energy which is emanating from the inner "Soul", must habitually and naturally like all energy constantly attain a re-birth, for it cannot die. Also, like all life, the Soul will naturally endeavour to be reborn into a body which will be created by the family it left behind, although with our given "Freedom of Choice", we could, upon death actually redirect our souls to be birthed elsewhere. For truly, the Soul, which is an energy that knowingly cannot die, will always return, to inherit a newly birthing body, this being that reality which will always be experienced by its pending mother after a few weeks of carrying that "soul" which is to be newly created. For is it not known to be a "scientific" fact, that there can be no waste within the existing Creation?

Also is it not a known truth and also a "scientifically" recognized fact, that there is nowhere for energy to go except to return to the conditions from whence it came? For is it not also a known truth that a past source of love is a powerful attracter and like any good Mother, the "Mother of the Creation" does not waste energy on the need to create love and harmony, this fact being because already Love and harmony "naturally" exists within every person's Soul.

THE PICTURE OF ME HAS THE HONOURARY CHAIRMAN OF THE MOSCOW POLITICAL CONFERENCE ON MANAGEMENT WASTE

Also has a scientifically trained manager of productive added-value, I understand that the "Mother of the Creation" may actually change the Souls re-birthing target, which is normally directed by love and familiarities! This being if She decides that a particular Soul, especially a Soul which may be newly created within a person who was re-birthing from the animal kingdom, could more fruitfully expand its needed activities, this being if was to born into a different environment! Indeed, this must also be a factual truth for it would also enable a newly birthing Soul to nature-ally support the Creations growing need for harmony; this being that creation which constantly exists all around the "Mother of the Creation" just has it normally exists within Her – this being the necessary support of all the Souls that are newly born within people.

Therefore, could it not also be said and so "naturally" stated to be a certain truth that a person who is selfishly harming or stealing from that which has been "Created" around them, could be left without future lives for a long time by the *"Mother of the Creation"*. It is also at this point, that we should further understand that being born with physical or mental problems is not a punishment for any individual! For it can only be a way of life that has been "Self-Chosen" and so it is a life that has been sought so that the "Souls" that personally exist around this "sacrifice", can show their love and support of others, has normally does the "Mother of the Creation". For certainly, it is the "Mother of the Creation" who cares for all the life and non-life that exist within Her only child i.e.: A child that is actually that unity which we call "Thee Creation"! For indeed, does not this reality not also bring forward for all people an excellent opportunity to assist in the unity of all the life and non-life that is expanding all around them, just has it is expanding within them? Therefore, is it not a certain and factual truth, that all people should beneficially act in the same way as the "Mother of the Creation", who truly and knowingly cares and loves all life that has a Soul and also all life and non-life that does not!

So yes! Should it not be further said, that the "Mother of the Creation", or "Nature" for the non-believer, is like all good mothers who do not support people who selfishly pursue "I Want only for me" activities! These being "I Want" for ME activities in which greed based people can and do negatively destroy or disturb the way of life that is constantly evolving in the "Present" time! For indeed the "Mother of the Creations" only reaction can be that Her face is turned away from those people who create these disturbances!

For is it not true that God or Nature for the Non-Believer, did knowingly give to all Souls the "Freedom of Choice"? This being a "Freedom of Choice" in which people can "choose" to live outside of Gods or "Natures" laws for the non-believer"! These being "Natures" caring and loving laws which target the containing of harmony and contentment! However, it is certainly known that these "I Want for Me" people always, carry the Godly gift or Natures gift for the non-believer, which allows them to immediately support the "Godly" pursued world which exists all around them has it does within them and so live a life which is the actual purpose of their personal existence.

So Yes! The *"Mother of the Creation"* never punishes people, but She can and will ignore them for She cannot support those people who target selfish "I Want for Me" needs, these being acts which create disharmony to that creation which exist all around them. So, now it should be realized that it cannot be true, has many say, that they are being punished by God when they act outside the laws of harmony, for in truth they are actually punishing themselves and the "others" that live around them. However, those that they harm will certainly be dutifully cared for in their next lives but those who apply this harm to others, will certainly not be re-birthed for a long time.

Therefore, can it not be witnessed and so factually understood, that "scientifically" we can actually witness greed-based "I Want" for me pursuits that can appear all around us? For is it not also a certain truth that all selfishly activated deeds do eventually turn to meaningless dust and so have no real meaning? Also, is it not a fact that most ill-gotten gains do not bring the happiness that these "I Want only for ME" people seek – which is the opposite to the "Mother of the Creation" target of love and unifying contentment for all life and also all non-life. In simple words "Mother of the Creations" harmony seeking contentment is parallel to a life which is known to be in unification and also supportive of all life and also all non-life! Thus meaning to be a good example to all life and also all non-life, a fact which is based upon love and the caring of all that exists around you just has you care for that which is actually within you!

For certainly, do not all our past European and also our other worldly wars, actually and "scientifically" prove that this "I Want" warfare way of searching for unity cannot be correct! For, has our modern history shows, those who seek a war to control foreign and their own tribe are always eventually vanquished or absorbed into the wellbeing of another countries care! For truly is not a unity with others based upon the laws of harmony, this being that which brings a peaceful search for a union with countries that have a different languages and also countries which have with different named religions! Is it not therefore historically known and very true to understand - "scientifically"- that we have certainly come a long way from our ancient cave fighting days! This age being when an expanding valley of inhabitants disputed and fought with another near-bye valley of expanding inhabitants? For now in our "Present Time", we can actually witness the whole of the North of Northern Hemisphere trying to unite into one entity called "Democracy" i.e.; a government that is ruled by the will of the people contained within its borders! This being a governing reality which favours the majority of people under its jurisdiction has it searches for a majority targeted laws which continue to support a peaceful unification that only personal greed can and does endeavour to stop.

So yes! It should now be further understood that to support this peaceful development there must be four higher senses that a person who is obeying a unifying seeking Soul must use. These four higher senses we can also recognise to be above the "animalistic" five senses that all people do normally recognize. For indeed it is these higher four senses that are needed to identify and so obey the *"Mother of the Creations"* and Her supporting and continual caring for the laws which God created, or Nature created for the Non-Believer. This being the harmonizing personal laws that are known to be natural in God's only child - this only child being the unified Creation that is all around us, just has it is within us.

So again, and indeed it can be said, that is it not also "scientifically" understood that well behaved children do naturally obey their parent's laws and their ways of support? Therefore, and "scientifically", can it not be said that these natural laws, which are coming from God our father, are also community needs that are knowingly "inborn" within all people? Consequently, should not this normal reality be "legally" acknowledged to be a truth and so become necessarily binding within all people and their countries?

Therefore should it now be stated that the breaking or the changing of these natural "democratically" based laws will always lead to a feeling of isolation from the majority of people – is this not true? For can we not honestly say that it is only because of the Creations ever changing and developing needs that God or Nature for the non-believer, actually allows all people the "Freedom of Choice"? This "Freedom of Choice" being that which enables people to take personal actions which are sometime positive and sometimes negative but which are actions that are required to support the emerging creations "Godly-Target" or "Natures Target" for the non-believer! This being a world which "Life's Purpose" says is actually cared for by the *"Mother of the Creation"* or being cared for by the laws of Nature for the Non-Believer.

For truly, is this not our world's creation a living and "evolving" world? This being a world in which people are "religiously" required to maintain and support God's newly emerging laws or the laws of Nature for the Non-Believer! For certainly, is it not true that these newly emerging and growing laws can only be birthed in the "Present Time". Therefore, is it not also known to be true that it is the "Mother of the Creation" who does naturally preserve these family-supporting laws, this being a way of life which all Mothers do naturally pursue!

Is this not also why a person's activity is "always" supported by their God-Given or Nature given for the Non-Believer, "Freedom of Choice"? This "Freedom of Choice" reality being because all lives and also all the non-lives that exist within our emerging nature - do naturally change? Therefore, is it not true, that there is a need to naturally support Gods emerging laws or Nature's emerging laws for the non-believer? Also is not this natural truth the essential and also the "caring" root of all our world's religions and philosophies as well as also the target of all our worlds' political and governing systems? Yet is it not also true that no person in our entire world can "scientifically" say if there is any personal action or any personal activity that God's laws do not allow - which is a very revealing question?

Does this fact not also reveal to the world an understanding that should automatically stop all religious dissent? For certainly, is it not true that all religious and philosophical truths are based upon the God given or Nature given for the non-believer, a "Freedom of Choice"! This being a "Freedom of Choice" world which has been given in order for people to freely choose to support Gods world or to support the world of Nature for the non-believer – is this freedom not true?

Also is it not true that this "Freedom of Choice" is a given at birth reality that was given by God or by "No-Thing" for the Non-Believer? This being a Godly or No-Thing choice which was actually born by that reality which is known to have created a single emerging energy of a love that truly binds together this only child, this being a child which we call "The Creation". Is it not also true that this single unified form of life, which we call "The Creation", is also that reality which contains the world that we call "Planet Earth"? For certainly, does not this "Planet Earth" have a combined life force which also proves that Darwin was partly right when he stated that we are "evolving" according to God's target?

The question now to be asked is *"What is Gods target or Nature target for the Non-Believer"?* Also to be asked is are these revelations actually "opinions" or are they truly based upon "scientific" facts? Therefore, for those in doubt about this truth, take a look out of your window and let you eyes see the world as it truly exists. Also ensure that this viewing at the world around you is without any mind-sounding denials or any added "personal" desires of an "I Want"! These being mind filling words that are being sounded from one or all of your five animalistic senses – for you should now know that you cannot be that which you observe, smell, taste, listen to or touch for you are that which witnesses and experiences these realities!

For certainly, these thoughts that you listen to are certainly animalistic in nature and so they naturally impose a condition that is known to be the selfish desiring of an animalistic "I want" for ME! This "I Want" being the mind-filling creation that can only be traced to the "I Want" of your animalistic within born five senses! This conditions being that reality in which your five senses do actually cloud your mind has they dance in front of your observing Soul. For certainly it should be known that it is this "I want" for ME which does block your Soul, which is the real you, from seeing the outside world! For is it not true that these "I Want" desires, which are being sounded by you five senses, are always animalistic in nature? Also is it not true that these animalistic five senses are always endeavouring, in a mind filling way, to claim the "Present Time" world that actually exists all around them? Do they not also want the "Present Time" to be their own world, has naturally do all animals, because they do not possess a Soul - which is in unity with "Everything"!

For certainly again and in our modern times, is it not also known by people that all non-human animals have only been birthed with the five senses, which are smell, touch, taste, hearing and seeing. Therefore is it not also truly known that it is only people that have been birthed with this God given or nature given for the non-believer, a "Freedom of Choice" reality? This being a that personal reality which does actually allow people to have the full control of their "I Want" desires, these being that which are being sounded in their mind by their animalistic five senses. For do remember dear reader, that you cannot be that which you see, hear, touch, smell, or taste, for certainly you are the experiencer of these realties.

For certainly, is it not also true that this "Freedom of Choice" that ALL people have, is a reality that can refuse the "I wants" of these animalistic five senses? Therefore, and for certain it should be known, that has people we are not animals that must obey their animalistic "I Want" demands! For is it not true that a person's five senses can be disciplinary "chosen" to be controllable by their silent Soul and not by an animalistic "I WANT!"

MY COMPREHENSIVE SCHOOL MANAGEMENT MEETING

For certainly, is it not truly known by all people, that our gifted "Freedom of Choice" is a reality which does factually empower a person to correctly understand God's "Freedom of Choice" laws, or Natures "Freedom of Choice" laws for the Non-Believer? This "Freedom of Choice" being that reality which does actually assist all our worlds people to correctly govern the "Creation" that exists all around them, just has it exists does within them! Is this not true?

For is it not a certain truth that this "Freedom of Choice" does actually exist in people so that they can caringly "CONTROL" their animalistic ally needed lower five senses? Meaning that these animalistic five senses can be knowingly stopped from filling the mind with their ever barking "I Want"! This being an "I Want" for ME, way of life which is only serving the thinkers animalistic five senses which they actually think is "THEM"! They are NOT YOU! For you is truly the observer of these "I Want" thoughts. For indeed, it should be known that the real purpose of our five senses is to support and or assist the "Heaven", this being that emerging paradise which is endeavouring to exist all around of us, just has it does naturally exists within us? For undoubtedly is it not true that our five senses do constantly feed us with up to the minute information that is useful for any task that we are currently performing. This being supporting information like silently informing us has to where we left our keys, etc. An act which is known to be a brief flash of informing recollection and do we not "silently" drive a car without thought, because it is entirely controlled by our well trained five senses?

So Yes! It should now be agreed that the non-disciplined mind filling chattering and arguing of the five senses, these being that which can be constantly sounding in the mind, means that an uncontrolled "dictatorship" is taking place. This being a false based and probably an unknown dictatorship which is experienced to be very real; for is it not true that forgetting is our worst enemy? But what is really true and also a realty that we truly forget, is that God's laws always show that the "Mother of the Creation" is our beneficial leader, but much more about this concept later in "Life's Purpose"

1/D WHAT TO DO NOW?

After receiving this understanding that my previously mentioned "No-Thing" (Nothing) was God and that the Creation was His only child, it was then found that there is seemingly a bridge that is connecting God to His only child – for certainly this child that we call "The Creation" must have come from somewhere and our experts even state what year it was actually born. It should also be known that through our five informing higher senses i.e.: this being that which we call touch, taste, smell, sight and hearing – these being a realities that are attached to each person - was the knowing that the "Mother of the Creation" is actually the energy that "Motherly" supports this "Creation"! This also being a caring energy which does silently support people who pursue the true purpose of their life – which is to support the ongoing endeavours of this only child which is called "Creation"!

For I found it to be true that this "Energy", which is constantly emanating from the "Mother of the Creation", can be likened to be an energy that is silently teaching us how to maintain the growing love of the harmony that does factually exist within the ever moving ever growing "Present Time". This "Motherly" love and its caring certainly is an energy which is constantly supporting the growing purpose of God's only child – a purpose which is later explained in "Life's Purpose!"

Wondrously and always in the first steps of releasing this supporting energy, it will be found that when you perform a creative act that supports and aids the ongoing expansion of the emerging creations harmonic development, this also being that development which is aided by the "Mother of the Creation", then this activity can be likened to building a loving bridge between God and His only child, this being that which we call "The Creation" and for certain it should be known that this is the main purpose of all life. It is also known to be a personal "creation" supporting act that will instantly give the doer a momentary physical explosion of inner bliss! This being a bliss that will fill them with jaw-opening, breathe gushing and an indescribable energized mind-filling happiness which does bring to them a great contentment – is this not true?

For certainly, this experience of bliss, this being that which is resting only within the "Present Time", is actually the experiencing of an "awareness" or a "realization" of a remarkable trinity. This trinity is the Soul, this being that reality which exists only within people, plus the "Mother of the Creation", who also gave birth to a creation and of course God the father, or that which is called Nature by the Non-Believer. This certainly being a three in one reality that lives only in the "Present Time" and which is also that reality which only the acts of people that can physically achieve God's planned future.

It was also found, by methodical analysis, that although there are serious absolutes that are created by a person's right or wrong activity, there are no absolutes in the way in which they are created. For it is a scientific truth that within the totality of the ongoing never still creation, there is a highly engaging single pulse of energy. This being an energy which is emanating only from the one God or from Nature for the non-believer! It is also a supporting energy that actually allows people to freely be enabled to personally perform any act that they desire to perform. For certainly this is the main reason why only people have evolved with a Soul that actually contains the four higher senses, these being that which can be activated above the standard five senses, which is touch, taste, smell, hearing and seeing.

For is it not true that GOD certainly installed these four higher senses to make certain that all people had the "Freedom of Choice". This reality being needed because living conditions do actually change, and cultural reason and cultural devotion are not always the wings supporting the same activity.

So Yes! It is factually known that we live in a developing and continually moving "Creation". This ongoing "Creation actually being a developing creation which does often need the "personally" performing of various activities that seek to support the harmonizing reality of that which can only exist in the "Present Time". Therefore, any individual's personal "creation", should always be a supporting act that can be "scientifically" explained to be a performing activity that assists the bringing together in unity, the many harmony seeking pursuits that can only exist in the "Present Time"! .

Simply put, if your harmony seeking support of the creations peace-developing activities, do actually re-direct an emerging activity, this being an act which pursues or creates a balance that stops or turns an activity that is endeavouring to separate the harmony of the Creation into an act that supports harmony, you will experience good (Godly) rewards. But if you act selfishly, this being for your own personal gain and so you break this harmony seeking unity, you will certainly not be physically punished by God or by the "Mother of the Creation".

For is it not also true that God or Nature for the non-believer, did personally give to you and also all people a gift that is called "The Freedom of Choice", this being that reality which cannot be taken away from you. However, much more of this "scientifically" recognized principle called "The Freedom of Choice" will be spoken of at a more appropriate time but later in "Life's only Purpose."

So Yes! It is a true fact that God or Nature for the Non-Believer cannot punish anyone. For in a truthful God made world or a world made by Nature for the Non-Believer, people can only punish themselves. This is usually achieved by one group pursuing an "I Want for ME", which is opposing another groups "I Want for ME", these all being activities that are being created by their Godly given or Nature given for the Non-Believer, "Freedom of Choice". For definitely is it not true that our "Freedom of Choice" can be used to oppose or destroy all unifying laws that actually target the purpose of our ongoing ever developing creation!

For is it not also strangely true, that the people of one language and /or of one religion, can go to a country that has a different language and religion and there endeavour to kill at this location, all the people who have a different religion or a different belief system than theirs, this being because they have a different religious culture? Yet! Is it not also true that there are thousands of different cultures within our world and also many variable ways of living within our own bodies! Yet all cultures are supposedly trading and supporting their own bodies' goodness, which should be easily likened to be within the many parts of the growing child that we call "Earth"?

Also, what is the reason why there is no immediate Godly punishment for those people who are attacking and destroying a different culture that exist upon our Earth and can this reality "scientifically" and also is simple explained? For truly there is and never can be any Godly punishment of people within our world, either by God or by the "Mother of the Creation" and certainly not by "Nature" for the non-believer. The reason for this is very simple, for God's world or Natures world for the non-believer is perfect and it cannot be changed! It is also a world which "naturally" has within it, an inbuilt correcting system that gives a good re-birth into a new life for those who have been removed from living by the misdeeds of other people or even by the developing on-growing movements of the Creation.

Therefore, is it not useful to now be able to actually understand the reality and also the purpose of these laws of "God" or the laws of Nature for the Non-Believer! For we must now creatively and purposely "think" within our mind for an answer to this question! *"Do I want a good life which is actually based upon a caring love and also a feeling of well-being that exists within a good supporting and social harmony?"* The reality of the above is to acknowledge that any "I Want" for ME, is simply recognized to be a selfish person's "I Want" which is a personal "I Want" that will always be silently ignored by the "Mother of the Creation". Yet when you actually start to support "good" (Godly) harmony seeking deeds for all people and also for the world that exists around you, then the "Mother of the Creation" will bring to you that which we can call "serendipity". This "serendipity" being the natural order that can aid and support you in the pursing of your "Present Time" harmony seeking deeds! It is also known that it will "automatically" support your continuation to expand them towards a blissful and peacefully rewarding conclusion, this being for that reality which exists all around you.

For certainly, that which should now be easily seen and also indentified, is that the purpose of a woman and of a man is to become has one person, which of course is the purpose of marriage! The man, whose mind constantly creates deeds embodied in the future, obtains mental strength from the woman whose mind does constantly lives in Present Time.

For certainly, it is "She" who maintains within the "Present Time" a constructive way to happiness and contentment, these being targets which both can happily achieve together. For certainly it is also "He" whose strength seeks to provide for them both a continuation of much happiness and satisfaction.

Now it should be acknowledged that there is also, regarding this personal search for unity with all things, a certain "scientifically" proven understanding which is always noted within all our world's religions and philosophies. This being an understanding which is best explained as actually being that male and female do have differing targets which does actually link the female's thoughts about the "Present Time" and the male's thoughts about the "Future Time" together. This also should be noted to being that co-operating family task which the "Mother of the Creation" always supports. For truly, a man and a woman's coming together in marriage or by agreement, can be likened to tying two pieces of string together, with one being attached to the "Present Time" and one being attached to a "Future Time"! For it is certainly a coming together has one activity which accepts these two separately developing visions that are seeking to support only one need – the family!

Still, it should also be known that people can never do this twin act that supports their family activities under their own laws and this is why we have chosen to engage governments or tribal leaders who support the unity of the family. For certainly this twin combined family creating pursuit which is dominated by a family creating man and woman, is an act which can be named "serendipity". The reason for this is because it is a "Natural Law!" gift that can only be created in the "Present Time", thus enabling the development of many useful discoveries, seemingly quite by accident.

MY BUSINESS "START-UP" MEETING - YEKATERINBURG

For indeed, many people can easily in the "Present Time" tie a new activating "string", this being to an activity that is suddenly entering their life, to another "passing string" that is also entering or even leaving their life. This being an ongoing activity which will not only support the future energy of the group or their families need for harmony, this being that need which is continually emerging all around them, but emerging only in the "Present Time". It is also useful to put a name to this "Present Time" needed activity in which the *"Mother of the Creation"* uses to support the development of all people!

For this is an activity which is the sole (Soul) purpose of requiring you has a person, to assist in furthering the development of the on-going creations ever seeking pursuit of harmony. For certainly, this will be a *"Mother of the Creation"* actually requesting you, through others, to perform an activity that can be best described has being an act that is needed to support the population that is all around you! This support being a harmony seeking activity that is usually requested by "Destiny" or by "Nature" for the Non-Believer! This is usually being a much needed activity that many people whose soul has just emerged from the animal kingdom, do find it very difficult to pursue! For is it not true that some people still "animalistic ally" experience an "I Want for ME" and so seeks a very animalistic "I Want only for ME" way of life?

For certainly, is this animalistic "I WANT For Me" activity coming from very different form of understanding! This actual understanding being that the main purpose of a person's life is to join an emerging "Present Time" activity to an existing "Current Time" activity - this being in order to support the unity of the emerging creation – is this not a truth? Yet certainly and again it can be said, is it not true that a personal "I Want for ME" effort can be "selfishly" directed to change the direction of a emerging "Present Time" coming together activity? For is it not true that any action can be animalistic ally changed in order to create a selfish "I WANT" only for me and my kind! This being an "I WANT for ME" claim that is actually known to be an animalistic activity that is selfishly claiming an "I Want this for ME", this being a need which is certainly required by others! Is this not a true?

Thus, it is a certain truth that the natural "unthinking" experience of being unified with all things is a reality which is truly resting within all people, but knowingly it can often be "animalistic ally" ignored by those early re-births from the animal kingdom. For it is a truth that the target of those who are born has people is to achieve unity within the totality of the creation which is all around them just has it is unified within them.

For can it not said to be true that this unified reality of being everything that exists within this creation, is normally experienced by people who have had many lives? Also is not this realty that truth which is always and knowingly supporting "Destinies" target – this being that truth which is stated by all our world's religions – which pursue the truth that came from our ancient wise!

For certainly has "Life's Purpose" says, there is only one life that we on our Earth are aware of, and this is that living "unified" entity which we call "The Creation"! For certainly and simply put, our ongoing "Present Time" creation is continually performing within it a unifying activity that can be likened to a person actually tying two pieces of string together and to continually do so even when it breaks. This being that fact which makes the creation a unified ever-growing entity! For certainly, this living child, which we call the creation or named the universe by the non-believer, is a Godly created activity that purposely born by the "Mother of the Creation's" or by Nature by the Non-Believer, this being a truth which is also combined with the "Mother of the Creation's never-ending harmonising support for Her only child, this being that ever-growing child which can only exist in the "Present Time"!

Also is it not true that you dear reader, are that part of that universal child which is called "Earth"? Also is not our "Earth" truly known to exist in an ever still ever moving reality which we call the "Present Time"! In addition is it not naturally true that the constant search for harmony, within the "Present Time", is the actually needed work of all mothers?

For certainly it can be said that upon our Earth we do experience our ever-present "Mother of the Creations" continual support for that part of Earth which is all around us and also within us – is this not true? This being a support which is always being pursued by the "Mother of the Creation" and also by those people who do knowingly support Her harmonizing work!

For indeed, this support by people is seriously needed in order to assist the "Mother of the Creation" blissful creating work which does automatically bring to all people a feeling of care and contentment – even unto death. For definitely, this supporting of such a purposeful unifying activity does actually and knowingly target a "togetherness" which does physically and also holistically, achieve that experience which our ancients call "Enlightenment" – this being an experience in which a person actually becomes the creation that is all around them has it is within them, this being that experience which can only exist in the "Present Time"!

Therefore and certainly, the target of all our world's religions and philosophies is to achieve "Enlightenment", this being the experience which Christians call being filled with the "Holy Spirit" or the "Holy Ghost". For certainly it is that personal experience which is often called "Paradise" by the experiencer! For certainly again, this is the experiencing of that singularity which is called the "Present Time" by the non-believer and a singularity which is called "The Creation", by the believer!

In contrast, many of our world's religions and philosophies certainly have different names for this experience such names, has in the Christian religion, of being in "Paradise", or being in "Eden", or in "Heaven", or in the "Promised Land". Also it is called throughout our world's many religions names such has, "Nirvana", "Moksha", "Shangri-la", "Kenshō", "Bodhi", "Satori", "Jnana", "Svargamu", "Kā "bāga", "Vāṭikā", "Kā jagaha", "Sukhabhavana", "Karma", "Kismet", "Nirvana", "Chance", "Providence", "Serendipity", "Fate", plus *"Luck"*, and even the ancient Zoroastrianism religion of the Fifth-Century BC referred to it as *"Ushta"*, which they described as *"liberation, salvation and the emancipation of the Soul"*.

Therefore and certainly, it is a well known factual reality that a people did experience this religious or philosophical experience over two thousand five hundred years ago and it can even be proven to have historically existed even before this period. For truly all the above names for this experience was also born in many different countries and they were names designed to describe "Enlightenment", this being a known physical reality which is stated to be the actual living in Heaven whilst alive and still living upon our Earth. Therefore and certainly, this experiencing of "Enlightenment", this being that which "Life's Purpose" calls "Bliss", is a reality which can actually be sought, via prayer and meditational incantation to exist, but only in the "Present Time" and by a mind that is not blocked by "I want" for ME thoughts.

So Yes! It is a well known fact that "Enlightenment" can be experienced in two ways and so later in "Life's Purpose"; it will be shown how to take the first positive steps in order to experience "Enlightenment". This being that reality in which you will personally become "Self-Aware", meaning that you will experience that which is around you to be has one with that which is also within you –or in simple terms that everything that exists you will experience to "You"! But do not be afraid for "Enlightenment" , which again should be said is a targeted experience that is called by many of our world's religions and philosophies to be : "Nirvana", "Moksha", "Shangri-la", "Kenshō", "Bodhi", "Satori", "Jnana",

"Svargamu", "Kā "bāga", "Vāṭikā", "Kā jagaha", "Sukhabhavana", "Karma", "Kismet", "Nirvana", "Chance", "Providence", "Serendipity", "Fate", plus *"Luck"*, and even *"Ushta"*.

For certainly this is an experience in which a person has actually become "Self-Aware" that they are a part of that which can only exist in the "Present Time" and so they have no "I Want" , for in reality they have become aware that they really are unified with "Everything" that exists in the "Present Time"! This being the first experience that is knowingly targeted by the "Mother of the Creation" and it is also understood to be the first step towards a person becoming "Self-Realized"!

For it should now be known that when a person becomes "Self-Realized" they actually become has one entity with "The Creator" and they are no longer an observer! For it is certain that within such a reality such a "Self-Realized" person does actually become has one with God or with Nature for the Non-Believer – which of course is the purpose and the target of all the created life that exists within the creation. For certainly, the purpose of this target is so that God can experience Himself, but more about this later in "Life's Purpose"!

For again and also truly "Enlightenment", this being that reality which occurs when a person becomes has one body with the creation, is the religious and or philosophical target that truly exists within all our world's religions and philosophies'. For certainly how to experience this reality is that which Jesus taught has did Muhammad, Krishna, Buddha, Baha'u', Confucius, Tao, Plato, Laozi, Vivekananda, Sri Shankara, and Sri Ramakrishna, plus many more of our worlds wise ancients. "Life's Purpose" also endeavours to show how to "modernly" achieve this enlightenment, this being that reality which is truly the target of our world's religions and philosophies – this being an enlightening experience in which it is Realized that there is only one life and this being that entity which we call "The Creation".

For certainly, we should now know that the target of all religions and philosophies', is for the "worshipping" person and or the religious "attainder", to simply obtain a clear and empty non-thinking mind which is actually obtained when an individual obeys the methodical and automatic need for group praying. This reality occurring when the individual automatically obeys group praying and incanting conditions in which they need no mind-filling thoughts! These usually being "I Want" mind-filling thoughts which are coming from our bodies' animalistic nature and it are these animalistic "I Want" thoughts that actually block a person's Soul from seeing through an empty mind the purity of that reality which we call the "Present"! For certainly, that which we call "The Present", can only be fully experienced when a person unthinkingly becomes "Self-Aware", a reality which can lead to a person becoming "Self-Realized", these conditions being experienced only when the Soul can see through an empty mind that is not blocked by any "I Want" thoughts.

For certainly, an empty unthinking mind brings that awareness or realisation which actually allows the "Soul" or the "Body" for the non-believer, to see through their empty mind and so actually experience the unified singularity of the world in which they currently live – this being the living within that reality which is commonly known has the "Present". For is it not true that you cannot "think" of an "I Want" when you become "aware" or "realise" that you are "everything" and that you are knowingly living in God's world or living in the world of Nature for the Non-Believer! For truly, can it not now be known that the experiencing of this unifying "awareness" or "realisation" is the actual "target" that is pursued by ALL our Earths religions and philosophies - and it is a target that now awaits YOU!

So yes! Is it not a certain truth that the wise ancients that began our entire world's religions and philosophies, all did actually state that it is only in "Present Time" that God's laws or Nature's laws for the Non-Believer can truly exist? This also being that ongoing ever-growing world which "Life's Purpose" continues to further explain is also an ongoing realty in which all these emerging laws are being monitored and supported by that which "Life's Purpose" calls "Mother of the Creation", for with all created life there must be a "Mother"! For surely, it is "Mother of the Creation" who automatically guides and also favourably supports the lives of only those who support "Her" domestic efforts! These actually being efforts to constantly bring together the physically separating parts of the growing Creation, this being a creation which is Hers and Gods only child". For certainly it is also "Mother of the Creation" who automatically guides and also favourably supports all the personal lives of those children who help Her to bring together the physically separating parts of the growing Creation, which is Gods and "Mother of the Creations" only child.

This being a "Motherly" support which actually and always rewards those people who apply the extra work that is needed to achieve the peaceful "bringing together" of the separating parts of their growing child, which we call "The Creation". For certainly, the main caring for and also the supporting of the creations growing activity, is truly the work of the "Mother of the Creation", has it is with all mothers! But certainly, it is also Her needed support for the continual healing of Her growing child, this being that which we call "The Creation", that that part of their only child which we call people, where actually created! These being intelligent life forces that are needed to exist in the trillions of planets whose homes are within in that which we call "The Universe"! For certainly, is it not true that it is only that life force which we call people who are able to assist in correcting a worlds evolving separations, these actually being physical separations that are usually caused by the collision of the creations evolving ever-growing natural laws.

For example, this need for a healing support is a task that can be likened to the freeing of a deer's antlers that have been caught in a tree! For certainly, it is only people who are enabled, with their God given "Freedom of Choice", to set the deer free! For certainly it is also a known truth that natural laws do collide! This being when a moving earthquake actually and physically changes the world around it. For certainly, and it is again good to hear, that it is advantageous to recognize and also very wise to understand that it is only people who have been created with the ability to support the creations developing harmony! This being that harmony which is constantly birthing or growing within the ever evolving "Creation", a reality which exists all around people just has it does within people. For is it not knowingly said, by our wise ancients, that whenever people do support the creations harmony seeking "coming together" acts, these being acts which can be likened to the needed tying of two separate pieces of string together, do we not always enjoy a personal gift that is crowned by a smiling happiness?

For definitely, is it not known that a blissful reality is experienced when a person becomes has one with the joy of all that exists? This being the energising of an activity, whose purpose is to bring people together, has if all are experiencing the same thought! Is it not also experienced to be true that such a "coming-together-has-one" act, can actually being seen has an act of love? Is it not also true that such an act can only take place in the "Present Time"! For certainly and again it should be said that this act of love can only occur when an "unthinking" mind becomes has one with the purpose "Present Time"?

For certainly, can it not also be stated to be true, that the reason why it is being experienced has a feeling of being "loved", i.e.: appreciated, respected, esteemed, treasured and cherished, is certainly explained by some of our wise ancients who described love as being like the element "water"! For all know that if you take the water away from anything, it cracks breaks and separates and so becomes a speck of meaningless dust!

Thus creating a life which can only exists in isolation and so becomes a life that is separate and without any attachment to the love which is joining together everything around it.

Therefore, has "Life's Purpose" states, that any personal "I Want" for ME" activity, actually creates a physical separation which can be likened to an action that causes a leak in a water container. For certainly, this "I Want" for ME" reality will leak away the true "love" that rests and supports the togetherness of that full container, which is a world that naturally exists all around you, just has it does within you! Is it not also true that this world can only exist within a "Present Time"? This being a "Present Time" which is being likened to a container whose contents are unifying itself all around, this being just as they do in unity within you! But do remember that this can only happen in the "Present Time".

So the question now is "What is it that you want if you are a unified "EVERYTHING?" Even that illness that can destroy your body also belongs to YOU! But no illness can destroy your Soul for your personal Soul, like all known energy, cannot die and so it must move on to another body – has any pregnant to be mother will tell you. This being that reality which the pending mother will tell you, this being when the Soul enters the child that she carrying within her!

Thus is it always good to remember that such a "Mind filling I Want", this being that which is being sounded within the mind by one of your uncontrolled animalistic five senses, is certainly a separating activity which stops your Soul from experiencing that it is has one with all that which is around, them just has is all that which has been created within them! For certainly, this "I Want for ME" pursuit is certainly an isolation that is created by people who live in a greed base animalistic "I Want for Me" world - but much more about this later in "Life's Purpose". Therefore, it should now be clearly known to be a scientific fact, that the only "religious" sin a person can perform, is to separate themselves from the creation which is in unity all around! This separation being caused by the pursuing of a personal "I Want", and not the "personal" needs of the emerging creation!

For in this truthful world of emerging reality, how can you steal an "I Want for ME", from the pursuit of the "Present Time"? This being that ongoing creation which is all around you just has it is within you! For truthfully, is not the singularity of the creation, this being that which can only exist in the "Present Time", actually an activity that supports all life and also all Non-Life – a reality which can only exist in the "Present Time" for certainly the past and the future, do not exist. For truly a good farmer knows this fact when he first plants the seeds of a future development?

So yes! It is certainly good to always endeavour to support this unifying present time that is continually seeking togetherness, this being that which actually exists in the totality of the creation which is all around you, just has it normally does within you. For certainly, all personal activity should be to support the emerging "Present Time", this being likened to the tying together the many dormant strings that the majority of people can experience to be actually resting and so endeavouring to emerge in the "Present Time"!

For certainly, was this truth not known to be resting within the people of the former U.S.S.R. Whom in the 1990's pursued a "Russian" way to "seek" a togetherness that is still being sought by the people of Russia, just has it was also being sought at that time by the people of the European Union. This being a togetherness which could actually bring together all of the North of the Northern Hemisphere! For certainly, is not this constant seeking for an expanding peace, not really seen to be an historical truth? This being an historical truth that can only be supported by a majority vote and not by war!

Also, is it not true that our recent European history does actually show that a "Democrat" coming together, this being that which is based upon one person one vote, did happen within all the different language speaking countries that reside in the North of the Northern hemispheres! Is it not also currently being seen that this communicating movement will eventually lead to the whole of the North of the Northern hemisphere becoming united by a democracy based peace? This being a reality which is controlled by the majority of people living in this Northern trust!

For certainly and again is it not true that the beginning of this world peace forming target is now currently resting within the lives of the majority of those people who live in the North of the Northern Hemisphere? Of course this endeavour could be delayed by those who are financially enabled to seek profit for themselves rather than for the wellbeing of the people that surround them.

But it certainly should now be known that it is a North of the Northern Hemispheres "Coming Together" movement that cannot be stopped! For certainly, and again it should be said, that this "Coming Together" reality cannot be stopped! For it is certainly, has our world history shows, a "Nature-ally" sought world unification even with the East of this planet that we call "Earth". This unification being when the Chinese government do become seriously influenced by the wishes of the majority of the Chinese people – of course this is also a serious step towards world unification in which all people are treated with equality!

For is it not true that an atomic war between China and the above differently governed countries would "atomically" destroy the well-being of both adversaries!

AN EMBARRASSING WARM "TRADITIONAL" TOAST FROM OMSK "SPACE SHUTTLE" DIRECTORS

It may also be believed that the USA and all European People and now also the Russian people, are the current countries that are actually holding close the actual way ahead for the first of our worlds unifying "Togetherness"! This being a North of the Northern Hemispheres country based "Market Supply" togetherness, whose management is created by the votes of that countries majority of people, or it is based, has in Russia, upon a historically experienced management who the majority of people acknowledge to be their needed government. For certainly was not this "New Russian Business World", very different from the previous Russian "Communist" world? This being a world which did not search for profit or efficiency and so, without this motivation, did not even create the adequate amount of food that was needed by the Russian people.

This reality being created because of the Soviet belief that people should have no higher management to make them work for all people were deemed to be equal. This also meant that there would certainly be no search for profit, this being that which was seen has a capitalist pursuit that increased selling prices which served only the rich and which also kept workers poor and always in need!

For certainly in Russia, this belief meant that work was not motivated by management has all working people were deemed to be legally equal! But in reality this was a non-motivation system which would normally produce 25% to 35% of that amount which could be produced per week under different management, such has the motivation system of payment which is used in the   West of the Northern Hemisphere! For certainly in the West the more produced items a person created the more they would be paid! It is also a known fact that this type of motivation system that would produce 75% to 115% of the same item per week! For certainly, in the west of the North of the Northern Hemisphere, produced items were certainly linked to wages whist in the East, wages were linked to time only and not the amount being produced!

For certainly, is this market deficit that crippled mighty Russia not now known to be an actual truth? This truth being that the Russian people's first attempt to seek an industrial way of life was based upon the security born by the payment of wages and not by independent private owners searching to produce goods that made a profit? For is it not true that communism sought a secure way of life that was born by a guaranteed payment of wages and not a way of life that was motivated by a search for a "Profit" that went to the owners of that which was for sold to the general population! Is this not also the reason why the people of the Russia Federation did naturally fall into stagnation and deficit because there was no owners of marketable goods that searched for a personal profit to the owners and to the suppliers of such marketable goods! This being that condition which created a market place in which people with high sums of wage paid money could find nothing to buy? For is it not also known that even before the end of the stagnation and deficit period, this being that which seriously plagued the U.S.S.R., that everyone in Russia began to recognize that the "Soviet Union's" community based market economy was even failing to supply the needed food of the Russian People!

Therefore the first question that I always asked at all my economic presentations throughout all of the Russia Federation, this being during the 1988 to 1998 recovery period in which the Russian Government was forced to abandon all foreign countries in order to concentrate on providing the necessary food and goods that was seriously needed by the Russian People. These presentations' were to most of the major cities and large productive companies of the former USSR, and it was also the first question that I asked President Gorbachev's economic advisers in 1988 after they had just returned from touring the world in order to find a way out of the stagnation and deficit that was plaguing Russia.

This actually being on my second all expenses paid invitation to visit Moscow and this invitation was because President Gorbachev's advisers had seen my brief TV appearance on Moscow Television in which I had criticised the "All Russian Chamber of Commerce and Industry"!

This being a five minute well worded criticism which I had made during a T.V. appearance that had occurred when I was walking out of the "All Russian Chamber of Commerce and Industry" conference. This walk out being after 15 minutes of listening to the chambers on stage joint venture presentation which was being presented to the world by a group of Russian organisers who were simply seeking financial payments from western companies. This being the main reason why these all Russian Chamber of Commerce managers had sent their personal "all expenses paid" invitation to the "British Chamber of Commerce" who securely represents a unique network of businesses across the UK and also around the world – this being the enterprise that I was currently representing. For it was the "British Chamber of Commerce" via the Bradford Branch, of which I was a member, who had actually chosen me to represent them on this second visit to Moscow.

Now, on this second trip to Moscow, in which again all my expenses would be paid, was a private invitation to me that came from the "Supreme Soviet" leader Mikhail Gorbachev's "Economic Development" team - who had just finished travelling the world seeking possible ways out of the Stagnation and deficit that was currently plaguing Russia. For it was President Gorbachev's chosen "Economic Development" team who had now privately invited me to Moscow in order to discuss with them their world travelled findings, these being regarding the possible ways out of the stagnation and deficit that was currently plaguing the Soviet Union.

It was also at this private meeting with them in Moscow, that I showed the only way out of their countries stagnation and deficit was to allow "privately" motivated people to "factually" provide the marketing needs of the Russian people. It was also stated at this presentation, that the chosen government should also select people who would be the best managers of those government controlled industries which produced the natural resources that lie hidden in the land that these chosen managers controlled! These also being the people who would receive a percentage of the profits being made by these industries they controlled – has also does some members of the manager's team!

It was also conclusively proved that the answer they had agreed to present to Mr Gorbachev, which was too apply a "Value Added Tax" to all market goods, would not change the stagnation and deficit that was plaguing Russia but would make it worse. This being because there was no motivation to work. It was also further showed – diagrammatically- that in fact it would make the economic situation in Russia even worse by creating even more debt.

It was also interesting that at this presentation I physically showed, via a game of playing cards; the proof has to why stagnation and deficit would not be stopped under these currently proposed systems and also why it would not be changed under the economic system that this important group was going to propose to Mr. Gorbachev.

At the end of this presentation my audience then went into a private meeting and upon its end they came back into the lecture room and then individually shook my hand has they walked out of the lecture room. At this ending point one of them stopped and said to me *"Our answer to Mr Gorbachev has now changed and it now is that under the current communists system there is no way out of Stagnation and Defect"*. Then, has history does show, Mr Gorbachev, who now upon strong advice, was reluctant to continue with the "legalised" communist governing structure of the former U.S.S.R and so he resigned his position. Then, in his resignation speech on December 26th 1991, he ended the past political "Communist" system of the former Soviet Union from which a whole new Russia began to emerge.

For it was certainly then and almost immediately after the above meeting, that I was invited over the next eight years and with all expenses paid, to visit and give economic presentations to the people of the majority of Russian cities and with many meetings also occurring on Russian Television! It was also during the beginning of these eight years meetings and also business training in Russia, that I legally formed the "Russian Rebirth and Development Ltd" company, this being the name I used during all my Russian business and economic presentations.

It was also under the name of this company that I was being invited to present to large and small audiences plus regional television, just how to economically develop "private" businesses and also how to profitably develop "government" controlled organisations. These actually being "Business Development" presentations in which I also showed people how to install a "Payment by Results" system that enabled a profit to be made. These presentations that I willingly gave were also too many VERY large companies whose budgets were now designed to actually target the making of a "profit", this being a profit in which various managers were also given a fixed percentage! It was also seen that this business serving of profits was also being achieved within most of the government controlled councils of Russia. It can also be stated that one of my economic presentations even included a class of infants aged seven, who wanted to see this man from another world. It is also interesting to know that the first question I often asked the audiences of the many large organizations I visited throughout my Russian tour was, *"Which is the richest industrial country in the world with the poorest industrial people?"* The answer given by all my audiences was always, "Russia."

So yes! The Russia people have certainly been there and tried a new world which actually sought a unity of people which did not create managers and owners who sought to make a profit by the controlling of other people needs! But it did certainly create a non-motivation system which, without the need for motivated managers, did fail to produce surplus goods and now Russia is entering a new privately developing world which seems to be now the saying *"Love thy neighbour as thyself"*. For truly it is now certainly known that the "Communist" system did fail to establish a classless based system in which places of work were owned by all workers and private property, which is actually the responsibility of the private owner, is non-existent and so all conditions exists without personal responsibility! This being a "Communist" all in it together condition, which does actually mean that there is nothing to work for because all needs are expected to be provided for and certainly there is no gain nor is there any need for a profit or a "surplus" seeking management.

But now, in the years following the year 2000, the Russian people are allowed to privately seek their own creative businesses and so pay wages that do actually target the need to create a surplus called "Profit" from that which is offered at the market place. This being that surplus reality from that which had been created and whose sale also pays to the government taxes which are targeted to benefit the "masses" and not just the creating individuals? These being the governments' creation of hospitals and schools but the fact remains that in a competitive society, this being that which is based upon market economy principles, it is known that the selling price is really that totality which a buying person is prepared to pay. It is also a well known reality that from these customer agreed payments the seller will have to deduct the workers' wages that created it, plus all needed services that are provided by other companies that aid the producer, thus meaning that it is only after these deductions that a profit is obtained. This being a profit which is a surplus to all the paid costs that are needed to create the item or service that is being sold. This realty being based upon the fact that in a competitive society, the market based selling price is the most that a person is prepared to pay and profit is that which is surplus to the providers cost to make. This being a profit which is audited and also monitored under a government's democratically made law, for certainly the target is that all taxation should be paid not only from wages but also from

"Profit", this being that reality which is carefully monitored by several government departments.

Indeed, and it is "NOW" that by continuing the reading of "Life's Purpose", that apart from the community benefits that are created by the payment of taxation, you will also find the actual benefit which ALL religions and philosophies do really target, this being the "Self-Awareness" or the "Self-Realization" that you are has one with the creation that is all around you just has it is within you! For certainly in the reading of "Life's Purpose" you will also find how to silence the demanding animalistic "I Want" thoughts that are being created within your own mind! This Self-Awareness" or "Self-Realization" occurrence being the actual silencing within you of those mind-filling "I Want for ME" thoughts that seek a "profit" that can only be falsely taken from the needs of others. For certainly after a will-powered concentration, this being that which will lead to a mind-stilling silence, you will enter the "Kingdom of Heaven", this being that reality which can only exist in the "Present Time". For certainly, when you "mind-silently" absorb the readings of "Life's Purpose", your life will become likened to you being contentedly fed with a plate of good food. For certainly, the experiencing of a Self-Awareness" or of "Self-Realization" is like the tasting of a "silent" but appetizing food which, when actually experienced a person will fully experience the love of God or of Nature for the Non-Believer! For certainly, they will experience the unity of the love that is emanating from the "Mother of the Creation" who's loving support does constantly exist within you.

"Life's Purpose" will also bring to you dear reader, our wise ancients' many sayings! These saying being that which explain a knowledge that is based upon their knowing way to achieving a "Self-Aware" experience, this being that experience which can lead to "Self-Realization", meaning that you actually become has one with the Creation that is all around you just has it is within you. This certainly being that religious and or philosophical experience which all our world's ancient wise do target for their listeners. For certainly it is an experience in which "You", dear reader, will become aware of a "stillness" in the mind that will bring to you a knowing experience that you are the only life-force that is existing all around you, just has that which exist within you. For within this experience of being "Self-Aware", you will know that you have actually become has one with God's world or the world of Nature for the Non-Believer.

For truly, it is known by our wise ancients that "Self-Awareness" is an awareness' that you are has one with the creation and this being that reality which can lead to "Self-Realization", this being that which is the end target that is pursued by all our world's religions and philosophies! For certainly it should now be known that the achieving of this "Self-Awareness" target, which can lead to "Self-Realization", is the only reason why our wise ancients gave birth to all our world's different culturally based religions and philosophies. For is it not true that in our worlds many religions and philosophical pursuits, our ancient wise did clearly program a religion in which their listeners did pursue their religions culturally imposed praying and incanting, this being in order to disciplinary still the "I Want" animalistic thoughts from entering mind. This being that reality which is needed to experience "Enlightenment" and so understanding that you are has one with the creation that is all around you just has it is also within you. For certainly, "The Present" is a reality which can only be experienced when the Soul can see through the empty mind and so become has one with the "Present Time"! Therefore it can be acknowledged that the purpose of "Life's Purpose' is to use a modern "World Based" understanding that can be targeted to bring to all readers, in a modern way, this ancient target of ALL our world's religions and philosophies!

So yes! The first step is to understand the singularity experience of actually becoming "Self-Aware" of God's world or the world of Nature for the non-believer. This experience being when a person actually becomes "Self-Aware" that they are has one with the creation that is all around them, just has it is within them! This being that un-thinking "Present Time" reality which is supported and fed by the Mother of the Creation - or is being fed by the world of Nature for the Non-Believer. Therefore it is good to understand that that when you have performed, within the "Present Time" a supporting "beneficial" activity which is often called "Righteousness", then you can rest assured that there is no better "rewarding" judge in these matters than the "Mother of the Creation". For truly, you will knowingly understand (Stand-Under) that it is She or the world of Nature for the Non-Believer, who actually supports all these "Godly" supporting actions, these being that which can only be performed in the "Present Time"!

So yes! It is certainly the "Mother of the Creation" who will certainly bring to you even more ways of how to support the Creation's ever developing ever growing harmony, which is an activity that is called LOVE. For certainly, is it not stated in many of our world's religions and philosophies *"Thou shalt Love thy neighbour has yourself"*, which simply means to seek the wellbeing of any and every person that exists around you, this of course being a reality that can only happen in the "Present

Time"! For certainly, this "Present Time" unthinking reality is known to exist within the loving harmony that the "Mother of the Creation" is continually supporting in our world, this being that world which exists all around you, but only in the "Present Time". Therefore, is it not historically known that you really can experience the creations oneness, this being when you have a mind that is without thought for it is then that you will actually become "Self-Aware" that all this that we call "The Creation" is really YOU!

So yes! "Life's Purpose" will also show to you dear reader, the reason why only people have been given the ability to act according to the "Freedom of Choice"! For certainly it should now be known that it is this "Freedom of Choice" ability that enables only people to support the emerging truth of this reality. For it certainly can be known, but only by people, that a "positive" supporting act can actually support the emerging harmony but the same act, under different circumstances, could actually destroy it! Therefore "Life's Purpose" will attempt, in a modern practical way, to factually reveal the helpful knowledge that our entire world's religions and philosophies do endeavour to teach us. This knowledge being supported by the fact that all good or bad rewards, within your current life, will always be automatically given to you has your "wages". These rewards being an automatic positive or automatic negative payment for your present-time activities, for certainly these are automatic payments that are "rewardingly" based upon the "Present Time" acts that YOU perform.

So yes! "Life's Purpose", with its ancient but now modernized revelations, will endeavour to reveal to you that if you do feel an emanating happy "holistic" reward coming from others, this being because of the "needed" activity that you have just performed, then this can be likened to receiving a smile from the "Mother of the Creation" who always does willingly support you. But if you "experience" an unhappy or an unwanted reward for your personal actions, then this is in payment for what harm you have done to the ongoing Creations process. Therefore, your act must be a selfish act which is the opposite or even attacking the "Mother of the Creation" harmony seeking endeavours'. For certainly these endeavours are a reality which actually binds "The Creation" together, this being a creation which is Her only child.

So yes! This seeking of unity or the feeling of being has one with the creation, is the only reason has to why God, or Nature for the non-believer, gave to all and only people the "Freedom of Choice". This being a God given "Freedom of Choice" which is certainly a reality which also ensures that the caring "Mother of the Creation" cannot punish you for what you choose to do! For certainly and truly it can be said that it is because of your negative "I Want for ME" acts that you are actually punishing yourself! For is it not true that Jesus of the Christian faith must have experienced great sadness when He chose to go silently to a painful death! This being in order to avoid inflicting pain upon others, but still, the real death of someone is when you forget them.

So yes! It is good to experience the supporting love which constantly comes from the "Mother of the Creation"! For certainly it is the "Mother of the Creation" who does always and lovingly supports God, the father of the creation and His emerging laws! These being that which can only be active in the "Present Time"! For certainly it is "She" who is also a great lover of God's only child, this being that which we call "The Creation"! Also, and is it not true, that like all mothers, the "Mother of the Creation" certainly supports that part of Her only child which assists Her in supporting the emerging Creations harmony. This being a harmony which is within each person and also that harmony which is also in unity all around each person! For certainly the acts of all people are based upon the Godly given "Freedom of Choice" and also is it not true that it is only people have been given this "Freedom of Choice"? This being the reason why it is only people who is judged and therefore it is only people who are positively or negatively rewarded according to their activities. Also, simply stated, is it not also good to know "scientifically", that those people who destroy Her creating principles, this being by that "I Want only for ME" reality which is selfishly claiming that which exists all around them, will find it good to be reminded that even whilst being shunned from all the harmony surrounding them, they will instantly be forgiven when they perform a together activity that actually supports the Mother of the Creations unity. For they will certainly be rewarded by Her bliss, this being that reality which is given those whose actually support Her "Godness", this being that which is known has "Goodness."

For certainly, in our ancient times, did not Buddha say, this being an activity which Hinduism still preaches, that 84,000 dharma doors (teachings) will open to show to any person their "duties". These being duties that if performed, will bring any person to the reality known has "liberation", which "Life's Purpose" calls becoming "Self-Aware" that you are has one with the creation that exists all around you, just has it exists within you! This being that awareness which enables people to actually experience themselves becoming has one with all that exists around them just has that which is experienced to be knowingly exist within them, this being an awareness experience which is called

"Enlightenment". For is it not true that many of our current modern religions and philosophies are still revealing these ancient based ways of just how to enter Gods world or the world of Nature for the non-believer? This being why "Life's Purpose" does knowingly explain "scientifically" and in a modern way, how to become "aware" or to "realise" all our worlds religious targets! This being the experiencing a "Self-Awareness" in which a person becomes aware that they are a part of the creation that is all around them just has it is within them! This being a "Self-Aware" experience which can lead to "Self-Realization", a reality in which a person actually becomes everything that is called "The Creation" and there is no observer! This is why "Life's Purpose" does endeavour to modernly show a single meditational practice which, when used repeatedly, will successfully bring a disciplined "practicing" person to experience that which ALL our world's religions and philosophies target – which is called "Enlightenment"! But more about this realism later in "Life's Purpose"!

For certainly, it should now be known that the experiencing of "Enlightenment" is certainly the actual target of all our world's religions and philosophies! This being a purposeful target in which any person can now actually seek because of their modern understanding of the world that exists all around them, and also an understanding of that world which actual exists within them. For indeed, is it not true that a person's future "Destiny" is usually dictated by their good actions, just has it is also dictated by their not so good actions? These being actions which you, dear reader, will personally do for yourself and even do for yourself even commanding others – is this not true? For certainly, "Life's Purpose" will endeavour to reveal to all readers, that any "I Want" for me acts are really selfish pursuits that will always bring to the doer only pain and suffering. For certainly, this "I Want for ME", is an activity that will always bring to you sorrow, suspicion plus worry, wrath, avarice and conceit! For certainly, it should now be known that all this pain suffering reality is that which "YOU" personally created for yourself and sadly, also for all those around you – and you should also know this to be true.

So Yes! This much sought religious and philosophical world of contented peace is a world which all our world's religions and philosophies do target! For certainly it is a known fact that all people can actually experience an awareness of this peace that rests within them and also that which experienced to exist all around them! This being an awareness which is anciently called an "Enlightened" experience! It is also that experience which all our world's religions and philosophies do target! For certainly, "Life's Purpose" is written in a way which can be likened to be a 2023 "Business Plan"! This being because "Life's Purpose" targets the quickest and the most easiest way on just how to move away from a selfish "I Want for Me" world and so become profitably aware of that truth which is called "Enlightenment"- this being the target of ALL our world's religions and philosophies.

2 THE WAYAHEAD IS IN HARMONY

It may be useful to know dear reader, that my original "Sugar in the Water" story, regarding the economic sweetness of life, was further developed into this new reality which I call "Life's Purpose"! This being based upon my 11 or more years of actually lecturing in Russia in which I did strongly supported the unification of their newly emerging democratic political system, this being a new political "economic" system which did develop throughout Russia. Thus Russia did certainly and quickly became a "New World" order which fruitfully began after communist Russia's "Soviet Union" did economically collapse! This being a collapse which also forcefully compelled the "Soviet Union" to release the twelve or more non-Russian speaking countries that were compelled to exist within USSR, this certainly being a decision which did allow these Non-Russian speaking countries to become "Self-Governed" by the people of that countries language.

It was also further hoped by many people, that this change would lead to a new development that would replace the *"North Atlantic Treaty Organization"* (NATO) with the *"Northern Hemisphere Treaty Organization"* (NHTO)! This treaty being between all the lands that exist within the North of the Northern Hemisphere, all of which are countries that are controlled by democracies which are elected governments who pursue the will of the majority of their voting people and not the pursuit of a few political or wealthy people who constantly sought even more personnel "economic" control.

But now, after much thought, my retirement now desires me to give a real answer to the often-asked question as I travelled throughout Russia. *"Do you believe in God?"* This being a good question, for I knew that the past history of Russia made it a country that had never had any government supported religious teachings. Still, I also realized that this question *"Do you believe in God?"* is also a question in which many people in our modern world have become confused about, especially agnostics who believe that it is impossible to know whether or not God exists – which of course is not a truth!

So yes! Many of the following pages within "Life's Purpose" are designed to contain very modern plus precise explanatory "Business Plan" answers to this question *"Do you believe in God?"*! These being answers that I have obtained in gathering amounts over a long period of time and they are also "Business Plan" described answers which are targets that have been set within many of our worlds' religions and philosophies! For is it not true that there are many religious and philosophical "truths" within our world that are constantly being supported by "Words from our Ancients"?

Therefore "Life's Purpose" does not just scientifically explain but also business-like reveals how to achieve that truth which all our wise ancients targeted, this truth being how to experience God's world or the world of Nature for the Non-Believer, this being an experience which is called "Enlightenment". For certainly, it is true that that which is called "Enlightenment" is a singularity experience which is an experience that is actually targeted by all our world's religions and also by all our worlds philosophical belief systems. These being many religiously based belief systems which actually go back thousands of years and which have been personally and methodically studied by me for over fifty years, especially their meditational rituals, plus mantra praying in which a single world is pronounced in the mind and also many other suggested ways of living.

So yes! The following chapters are targeted to be like a normal business plan, this being that which is not designed to change a person's current religious or philosophical belief system or even to refute a person's current agnostic or atheist non-belief system. For certainly, these pending do now "revelations", these being that which are being revealed within "Life's Purpose", are like a "Business Plan"! This being "Business Plan" which has been written to give to all people of all belief systems a way to experience the becoming has one with the world that exists around them, just has does that unity which exists within them – which of coursed is the target of all our world's religions and philosophies! This experience being obtained whether their belief systems are religious, philosophical, agnostic, atheist, they will receive by reading "Life's Purpose", a greater understanding not only of their personal life but of God's way of life or Nature's way of life for the Non-Believer.

So yes! These being the creations or natures for the non-believer, strongly binding methodological "laws" which are not attached to the "I Want" culture that people create in order to govern their country or their private communities! But they are laws from our ancient wise in which they endeavoured to show to their close followers just how to achieve the reality of living only in Gods world or the world of Nature for the Non-Believer – this being that which "Life's Purpose" does scientifically target! For certainly this personal experience of "Enlightenment", this being that which is sought by all our world's religions and philosophies, is a reality which can be discovered only by an individual! This being because it is certainly a personal experience of a truth that will really bring to the practiser a *"Peace that surpasses all Understanding"*. Thus, it is a certain, reality that a person will physically experience this peace has being that which exists within the unified harmony that is all around them, just has it is within them! Also and for certainly they will seemingly become "Self-Aware" that they have been personally "blessed" by this experience of being has one with God or with Nature for the Non-Believer.

So yes! Those people who have firm religious and or philosophical beliefs or even those people who have no religious beliefs; "Life's Purpose" will be give a valuable understanding of that creation which supports all life and also all non-life! For without doubt, the target of many words within "Life's Purpose" will certainly show a practical way of how to achieve the experiencing of "Enlightenment", this being the actual target of all our world's religions and philosophies. For certainly it can be known that the experiencing of "Enlightenment", which is actually a "Self-Awareness" in which a person eventually "Self-Realizes" themselves to be has one with a peaceful way of living that can easily be attached to any way of life that exists in any of our Earths ongoing "Civilisations". For certainly it is the actual experiencing of "Enlightenment" that all our worlds' ancient belief systems do pursue for their believers and followers to achieve! This being because "Enlightenment" brings an experience in which the creations truth is experienced to be residing not only within all life but also within all non-life! This being that reality in which they will personally experience the "Present" that is explained and pursued by all our wise ancients.

So yes! The purpose of "Life's Purpose" is for any person to be enabled to discover how to actually become "Self-Aware"! This being by simply practicing and methodologically using the best "Scientific" way to obtain that experience which our entire world's religious beliefs and creeds systems are targeting! For certainly it is an actual truth that a worshiper who is seeking unity with God or with the world of Nature for the Non-Believer, will always need to practice a mythological system in which the doer will eventually experience "Enlightenment"! This being a worshipping target in which the doer will experience that which is knowingly recognised to be a gift from God or from Nature for the Non-Believer. For certainly, it should be now be known, in our modern time, that "ALL" our words religions and philosophies do physically, culturally and mentally, target this experience of being has one body with all that exists within the creation! This being that "singularity" experience which is often unknowingly misinterpreted by many religious followers who interpret this unification with all that exists, has being good-humoured friendliness! This being that friendliness' which is experienced and also enjoyed by many religious followers?

For certainly, it should now be known that it is only with this "personal" experience, which is known has "Enlightenment", that a person can be "Self-Aware" or "Self-Realise" that they are has one with the creation that is all around them juts has it is within them! This being that reality which enables only people to establish the practicalities as to what habitual activity they must do to support the "Present Time", which is truly God's present or a present from Nature for the Non-Believer. For is it not true that our entire world's religions and philosophies do say that it is only when experiencing "Enlightenment" that the individual will "Know" just why our wise ancients did consistently bring to them many habitual "praying" practices! These "praying" and "worshipping" practices being that reality which people did separately create within our entire worlds many different creed-based religions and philosophies! For certainly it is known that these various worshipping pursuits are that which empower our worlds many religions and philosophical belief systems, many of which have been legally added to their cultures controlling principles. Therefore, it should be further acknowledged that the writings within "Life's Purpose" will endeavour to be "Scientifically" useful, especially regarding the salient views held by our worlds many religions and philosophical belief systems. For certainly, "Life's Purpose" does carefully use known "business-controlling" methods in order to give an understanding of our worlds many religious and philosophical belief systems, these being that which our wise ancients did introduce to various areas of our world. Thus "Life's Purpose" brings a new interpretation of our world of nature which "Life's Purpose" explains is also especially appropriate regarding the endeavouring purpose of all our world's religions and philosophies. For is it not true that in a private way, all our world's religions and philosophies do knowingly and also unknowingly, endeavour to reveal to their worshippers how to first experience "Self-Awareness"! This being an awareness in which they experience that they and they and the creation that is being observed, are has one body! This also being a "Self-Awareness" that can lead to a person achieving "Self-Realization", this being that there is no observer for the observer and the creation actually become has one entity - which of course is the purpose of the creation- but more about this later in "Life's Purpose"!

So yes! This explaining of what is the target of all religions and philosophies does certainly reside within "Life's Purpose"! For certainly "Life's Purpose" does constantly endeavour to provide to all our world's religions and philosophies a cultural explanations of what is the actual purpose of the creation! For is it not well known that Christianity, along with many of our world religions and philosophies, has actually fractured and splintered into many differing ideology groups? These often being groups that are seeking new ways of how to discover or realise the true purpose of all our world's religions and philosophies!

For certainly, it is known that many of these various "Break-Away" groups do contain institutionalized and habitual belief systems that emanate not always from their founders but from the leaders of these differing creed-based groups. It will also be shown in "Life's Purpose", that this splintering has occurred because many people have lost, due to their "I Want for ME" thinking, an actual understanding of their religion's original target. Therefore, it is unquestionably understood that "business-wise" the actual reason for this unknown "I Want for ME" fracturing is caused by a lack of knowledge of the root understandings of their founders' introduced unifying belief system, this being a group unifying belief system which was originally accepted by their culture! These new changes are usually formed by "I Want" for me thoughts which are then attached to their "I Want" my belief system to be the only religious belief system and not yours. This being an animalistic reality which sadly leads to our world's religious wars which are greedily supported by "I want" ideologies!

Often these "I want my religion not your religion to be the only true religion" which created ideologies that controlled and shaped a person's life, this being a false "I Want" reality in which people "animalistic ally" imprisoned themselves during these "I Want for ME" pursuits!

It is further understood, and "Life's Purpose" will endeavour to show this fact, that this "I Want" reality can be the only reason why many of our worlds beliefs systems fractured and moved away from the divinely enlightened core teachings of their incarnate teachers! For certainly, these teachers, who were the originators of our world's religions and philosophies along with many of their followers, were truly "Enlightened" people! These being people who were has one with Gods world or has one with Nature for the non-believer. For certainly it is true, that all our world's religions and philosophies originated with the sole purpose to end the suffering of a re-birthing people who had forgotten that energy cannot die and so they are being born again and again until they knowingly became has one with that which created them.

For is it not true that all our worlds ancient wise did explain to their followers a way to fully experience that reality which we knowingly call "Enlightenment"! This being an enlightening experience in which a person realises that they are has one with God's creation or the world of Nature for the Non-Believer and so there is no need to be born again! For certainly, it is in obedience to achieving this truth that "Life's Purpose", is "Scientifically" written to overcome these personal or group made fractures! This being done by showing not only factual words that endeavour to explain the true reality of the "Creation" but also the purpose of the "Creation" or that which is called "Nature" by Non-Believers! For certainly, "Life's Purpose" will endeavour to reveal a truth that will reveal a simple but proven way for an individual to personally and knowingly become "Self-Aware"! This being an awareness in which a person can "knowingly" experience that they are really unified with everything and so are actually enabled to experience the Godly based or Nature based for the non-believer, singularity of all our worlds life and all that which we call non-life! For certainly this is that exercise which can eventually and truly lead to a person becoming "Self-Realized", this being the realty in which there is no observer –but more about this later in "Life's Purpose"!

For certainly "Life's Purpose", within its writings, will first reveal how to achieve, via a meditational practice, a "Self-Aware" experience in which you actually become "observably" aware that "ALL" the creation that you observe and experience is really "YOU"! This being a "Self-Awareness" which, via continued meditation, can eventually bring to you a "Self-Realized" experience in which you knowingly experience that you are "Everything" and so you actually realise that there is no observer for all that exists is YOU! For certainly, this is that experience which is often spoken about by our ancient wise and it is also a condition in which you will know, via this unifying experience, that you are has one with Gods world or the world of nature for the non-believer!

For again it can be said that, via meditational incanting in which you disciplinary repeat within the mind a single word whose purpose is to stop all other thoughts from filling the mind, you will first become "Self-Aware"! This awareness being that experience which naturally occurs when the mind is empty of all thoughts for it is an experience in which you become aware that you are everything that you are actually observing? This also being that awareness which can lead to a person becoming "Self-Realized", a reality in which you actually realise that you are "Everything" and so there is no observer! For certainly, and again it should be said, that this is a reality that can develop into an existence in which there is no observer! For the experiencer actually becomes has one with God or with Nature for the Non-Believer, which of course is the purpose of the creation!

So yes! There are two main truths that are arrived at by the inner mind sounding of a repetitive mantra! For certainly, this is the ancient way of stopping the bodies mind-filling animalistic "I Want" from sounding in the mind! This being an "I Want" that is emanating from the five animalistic senses! For certainly, it is not unusual for these animalistic five senses to be allowed to constantly sound their mind-filling animalistic "I Want" into a person's mind. This being that inner mind sounding "I Want" reality which is a creative activity that stops the Soul from seeing through the mind and so experiencing its oneness with the creation that is all around it, just has it is also within it. For has our worlds history shows, it was well known by our ancient wise that the disciplined practice of sounding a repetitive word into the mind or even the repeating of religious prayer or the singing of a hymn, would stop the worshippers animalistic five senses from filling their mind with their constant "I Want" chatter. For certainly, it was experienced that with the repeating of a single word into the mind, the doer would actually experience not only the "Present Time", which their Soul occupies, but would also experience a oneness with the creation that was all around them just has it is within them! For certainly, mantra meditation will disciplinary silence the "I Want" chattering of your mind filling animalistic five senses. This being that mind-silencing fact which will allow your soul to silently become aware that it is has one with Gods world or the world of Nature for the Non-Believer, this being that reality which ALL our world's religions and philosophies do pursue. For certainly, this experience of a "Self-Awareness", which knowingly can develop into the experiencing of "Self-Realisation", is that truth which all our world's religions and philosophies' do target. So again it should be said, that this is why the reader of "Life's Purpose" is actually shown, in a practical way, just how to achieve this "Self-Aware" or "Self-Realized" target, this being that target which our entire world's religions and philosophies do pursue!

For certainly the reader of "Life's Purpose", when they become a mantra sounding meditational practitioner, will eventually become "Self-

Aware" that if continuing their mind controlling meditation, they will actually achieve "Self-Realisation", this being the purpose that rests within ALL our world's religions and philosophies. For certainly the target of "Life's Purpose" is to show a modern "Scientific" way, just how a person can "personally" achieve this religious or philosophical target. For certainly and again it should be said, this is that target which has been laid before many of our worlds cultures by our wise ancients.

So Yes! The revelations that rest within "Life's Purpose" will show how to achieve in a modern way, this target which our entire world's religions and philosophies do pursue – which is "Enlightenment"! For again it should be said that the experiencing of "Enlightenment" is that reality which can only exist in "Present Time" and it is an enlightening condition that no person can change or alter. For certainly, "Life's Purpose" will also show the way just how any participating individual can achieve "Enlightenment" and so accomplish the contented life that all our Earths incarnates plus all their enlightened followers did and still do speak about. This being the teaching of an "Enlightened" understanding of an experienced way of living a life that our wise ancients did and their writings still do, constantly endeavour to bring to all people! An "Enlightened" example being explained such has the full meaning of the words that God, in the Christian Bible, did say unto Moses *"I am that I am"*, which explains that God is "Everything", including you dear reader!

This being a reality which also explains the true meaning of the word "Self": For was not the word "Self" also explained in the Shakespeare play which is called "Hamlet"! This truth being explained by the words *"This above all to thine own self be true and then it must follow, as night the day, Thou canst not then be false to any man!* Obviously meaning our world in general!

Now certainly, and at this first revelation towards a personal experience that they are has one body with the world that is all around them just has it is within them, they must fully understand and also acknowledge the meaning of the question *"where am I now"* and also the full meaning of *"what am I now!"* To this thought should also be added *"what is my personal life all about now"* and also *"what is all life about?* For is it not true to remember that our ancient wise did endeavour to bring to every individual who they spoke to, a real understanding of their listeners personal capabilities? This being supported by an experienced understanding which could bring to their listener the knowledge that every person has an essential part to play in their life, this certainly being within their current life; especially also revealing the purpose has to why they actually existed! For certainly, the discussion that follows within "Life's Purpose" will certainly show how to achieve a way of life that is compatible with every individuals unifying search for happiness and its contentment! This also being an achievement which our wise ancient's stated would bring to the doer that experience which is called "Enlightenment". For certainly a personal "Enlightenment" is anciently known to be an experience which brings to the practicing individual a unified way of life in which they actually become "Self-Aware" of not only who they are but what they really are! For certainly "Life's Purpose" will also give to you dear the reader, certain proof that every individual person that lives upon our Earth has a significant AND contented part to play, this being within the environment in which they were chosen to be born in and so are knowingly enabled to serve the ongoing creation "personally" within that environment!

So yes! These writings within "Life's Purpose" are simply written in order to discover a way not only to recognise but to also satisfy the needs of your current environment! For certainly, it is also known fact, to our wise ancients, that this unifying activity will bring to the doer the experience which our ancients called "Enlightenment"! This being an "Enlightenment" which our ancient wise say is the experiencing of the "Peace that surpasses all understanding!" This being that experience which all our earth's ancient wise did endeavour to bring to their followers.

For certainly, and again it should be said, that this is that target which the creators of all our world's religions and philosophies did seek and also their re-births, still seek! But sadly, is it not true that some "religious" followers have now forgotten the meanings of their beginner's original teachings. For certainly, that which has been forgotten is that all mobile lives have only one need, which is to actually taste the "Sugar in The Water" with "Sugar" being life in which the highest form of life is people and with "Water" being the food for all the unified has one "creation" – for certainly, is it not true that the creation is only one entity whose energy gives birth to and also sustains all life and that which we call "Non-Life"?

For certainly, the experiencing of "Enlightenment", this being that which brings the *"peace that surpasses all understanding"*, will ensure that the "Self-Aware" observer, who experiences that they are a part of this unified reality, will eventually become "Self-Realized" in which they actually become the unified totality of the creation and so there is no observer! These being the two experience which were always being targeted by our ancient wise and which are also realities that can actually be obtained by the "scientific" practicing of that which we call "meditation"! This being a practice which is similar to praying and so does no harm to any life – which of course is why our world has many culture based religions who are all targeting the above same experiences!

So yes! This reality of seeking to be has a unified one with the creation, is the sought practice put forward by all our wise ancients' creed-based teachings. It is also an experienced "awareness" or an experienced "realisation" of that which explains the truth of all that which exists around and within each individual, a condition which also includes the absorbing unto silence all their current beliefs and ideologies. It is also an experience which cannot be purchased, as we do for many items purchased in numerous religious shops! These purchases usually being religious artefacts such as idols, figurines, and pictures, all of which portray a deep "peaceful", meaning too many and various religious believers and of course, these artefacts are also good holiday memories to take back to our homes! Yet for the shop owners and sales staff, their livelihood is obtained by their knowing that such sacred items do actually blend seamlessly into the commercial world of "I Want" something religious for me. The real fact that should be "Realized" is that you cannot buy the experience which is called the *"Peace that surpasses all Understanding",* this being the experiencing of "Enlightenment". For certainly, this is also a very personal experience which can come to a person no matter where they are or even what time of day it is.

So yes! For certainly and it should be said again, that you are genuinely the only "priest" that can take you, via prayers and incantations, to truly experience first a personal "Self-Awareness"! Thus experiencing that you are aware that you are has one with the creation, which is an awareness that can also lead to you becoming "Self-Realized", meaning that you realise and so experience that you are "The Creation", this certainly being that final reality which all our worlds' religions and philosophies do target.

So yes! Now let us find together that which is the only truth that can be taught regarding this search for a unified life that can be only lived in such "Enlightened" harmony"? This again being said is a personal experienced "Enlightenment" which is certainly the target that all our wise ancients do always speak about! For certainly it is often in this personal seeking, via the teachings of our world's religions and their wise men, that the praying mediator can also obtain a way of living in the "Peace that surpasses all understanding!" This being that reality which is also experienced in the search for harmony, this being within the world that exists all around you just has it also does in unity within you.

Also, it must be further understood that this personal unified experiencing of a "religious" harmony, is certainly described has the **"Peace that Surpasses all Understanding",** this being that reality which is named to exist in the experiencing of personal "Enlightenment". It can even be an enlightened reality which can be or is experienced in a war zone or under torture and even in the act of being bullied. For is it not truly known that the "Enlightened" incarnate Jesus did silently undergo much bullying torture, and even when nailed to a cross did say nothing until upon His death He finally said the words, **"Forgive them for they know not what they do!"** For certainly at this cruel time Jesus would truly know that the "Present Time" unity he was experiencing which is the being has one with the creation that was all around him and also within him, was very different from the "I Want" for "ME" unity of the people who persecuted Him. It was certainly the creations harmony that He could not condemn, for He knew that under the laws of everything that exists, God's peace, which is supported by the "Mother of the Creation", would eventually change the violent ways of his persecutors.

Simply put, our wise ancients often taught and said that living in true harmony is achieved by simply experiencing God's words; or the words of Nature for the Non-Believer, these being practical words that are continually being silently spoken by the "Mother of the Creation" or by nature the non-believer. These being silent words that are spoken to all people and this being continually – but only in the "Present Time", which of course is why we call it "The Present!"! For certainly, "Life's Purpose" does knowingly state that these communications from Nature can only be understood by those people who are knowingly targeting "Enlightenment"! This being that "Enlightenment" which can be constantly experienced in the "Present Time"! For certainly, the "Present Time" is Gods World or the world of Nature for the Non-Believe" - for is it not true that the Past and the Future do not exist, except in that world which we call "Hell"?

So yes! What the certain fact is that should be understood, is that God's world or the world of Nature for the Non-Believer, can only be experienced in the "Present Time", which is why it is called "The Present! This actually meaning that this truth, which rests within the Creation, cannot be experienced in the Past or the Future"! For is it not true that the Past and the Future do not exist and therefore they can hold no truth within them? But then, within this experienced reality that we call the "Present", the "scientific" question must be, *"Can people hear the language of God's harmony or Nature's harmony for the Non-Believer and is it in understandable words?"*

It is then that the answer must be *"Of course not"*, for is it not a fact that a person's mind is usually being continually filled with the creating thoughts of a future "I Want" for me! Also is it not true that this mind-filling "I Want" for me, is a desire that is based upon a future "I Want" or a past in which I did not get a desired "I Want"? Therefore is it not usually true that the "Present" time is a world that that is continuously being destroyed by a falsely based and personally targeting "I Want for ME"? For indeed is it not true that the beauty, calmness, and harmony of the real world is that condition which does usually exists around all people, but only in the in the "Present Time". This being that "Present" which all our wise ancients do often speak about. For is it not also true that the "Present" cannot be fully experienced when words and images are pounding an "I Want" into mind? Therefore is it not true that the silence resting in the experiencing of "Enlightenment" is undoubtedly the way to experience a smiling future!

So yes! Is it not also true that there can be a "Present Time" harmony experienced in the sudden taste of good food or smelt as in the wonder of a rose, or in the marvelling of becoming "Self-Aware" of the physical world that exists all around you! This also being when you hear the song of a bird or when listening to some chosen music or silently experienced when looking down a valley whilst resting upon a mountain top. For indeed can it not be said that this world of existing harmony is a world that can only exist has the "Present"! This being a "Present" which we say must have come from God or from the world of Nature for the Non-Believer for it could not have come from something that did not exist! Therefore it should also be known that it is the creation that is speaking to you all the time – but more about this later in "Life's Purpose"!

Of course, this personal harmony can always be broken as in an "I Want" for "ME" war, this being that which is usually based upon personnel greed! But is it not strange that after a local war, these warring countries usually return to their previously established borders. These being borders that usually contain that country's language! For indeed is it not a known truth that after our world's expansion that a country's borders became known to be that which contains its language - this also being even after another country's language-based harmony did actually attempt to replace it? Therefore, is it not true that we now see many "North of the Northern Hemisphere" countries actually returning to the "cultural" harmony that lives within their borders, these being the borders that are still based upon their language? Can it not therefore be said that this reality is a true fact? Also is this reality not factual because within the majority of a countries people, their "rule of law" is usually attached to their original and ancient verbally spoken culture and its ideologies? Therefore is it not a fact that a foreign language cannot be imposed upon the culture of another country? For is it not also true that every country's "Present Time" harmony controlling laws, did actually originate from their language? Thus meaning that a countries "harmony based" culture is based upon its past history and therefore its language is being continually used to establish that countries future? Therefore can it not now be said that there must have been a higher language based communication system that actually existed before these present day language divided separations. These now being border based separations that do presently contain our modern day "foreign" languages?

For certainly is it not a concept that there must have originally been one very ancient language? This being a means of communication that must have been spoken by our Earths first created life forms that we now call people? This ancient family based living-together existing long before the occurring of tribal based expansions! These being tribal expansions which eventually led to a world that now consists of many nations that are currently being separated by an "I Want this land for ME and my family" meaning a need for a "tribal" expansion"!

This being a tribal "I Want" the lands in which your tribe live. These being lands that are normally separated by known borders that have been created by tribal people with a different language! Yet, is it not also a true fact that within the "Past" and in the "Present Time" our Earth has never created any "I Want" only for me borders? This being a natural born truth which also shows that a person without any "I Want for ME" thoughts, must be "Aware" or may even physically "Realise" that they also have no "I Want" for me, this being has they do bond has one with the creation which is all around them just has it is unified within them!

This being a truth in which a person will experience a "Self-Aware" or even a "Self-Realized" condition has they actually become has one with the existing "Present Time". Thus experiencing with this non-thinking mind the awareness or the realisation of that existing truth which we call the "Present Time"? This truth being where God's or Nature's harmony for the non-believer, does truly, exist?

For certainly is it not a truth that language did originate because of the need to explain to others the conditions of the "Present" time? Therefore truly, was it not within the "Present Time" that people gave birth to all our Earths languages? These being communicative languages that could only be heard in "Present Time"! This also being a time which must have existed long before any communicating language was enabled to be used by people and this being within all the countries that exist upon our Earth?

So yes! The experiencing of "Enlightenment" will take you to a real understanding and a true believer in God's world or the world of Nature for the non-believer. This "Enlightenment" being of a living world that only exists in the "Present Time" and it is an experience which you will never be able to explain to other people! For is it not true that our world's ancient wise could not describe "Enlightenment"! For did not our ancient wise say that when experiencing "Enlightenment", you will be aware or realise, that it is an experience which is best described has *"a realm beyond the ability of words to properly convey"*. Yet it is strange that many people "Think" that they live in the "Present Time", although they are neither "Self-Aware" nor "Self-realized". For it cannot be a true world that is painted by thoughts that impose an "I Want" my view of the "Present Time" to be true! This "Present Time" being God's world or the world of Nature for the Non-Believer. For certainly, the "Present Time" is the only real world which exists all around you just has it does within you, and everyone knows this to be a truth.

So yes! Is it not true that the "Present Time" cannot exist in thought? For is it not a truth that "thinking", this being that which creates an "I Want" in the mind, is sounded by one or more of our animalistic five senses? This being that which creates within a person an illusionary "I Want" mind filling world which often "paints" over the truth of that which exists in the "Present Time"! This being a "Present" which God or Nature for the Non-Believer has not given to us! This being that real world which exists has a present, this being that which exists in unity all around a person, but only in the "Present Time"! For indeed it is a certain truth, yet often an unknown fact, that ALL religions and philosophies do target the need for their followers to enter the ever silent "Present Time", which can only be Gods world or the world of Nature for the Non-Believer. Also, should it not be "Realized" that people should become "aware" that all our worlds' religions and worshipping creeds are born to achieve the reality that people should be aware that they are living in God's world or the world of nature for the Non-Believer, this being that which can only be experienced in the "Present Time" and is this not a truth?

For is it not true that our entire world's religions and philosophies do factually target, via disciplined praying and hymn singing plus silent meditation! This being that meditational reality in which one word is silently repeated in the mind in order to disciplinary stops all thoughts! For certainly it should now be known that all thoughts that enter the mind are being created by an "I Want" that is coming from one or more of the animalistic five senses! For certainly, mantra mediation is a very ancient exercise which is designed to stop these animalistic mind filling "I Want desires! For positively such church disciplined exercises and certainly the meditational "Mantra" sounding exercise, will positively enable the practitioner to be aware or even realise that experience which is called "Enlightenment"! This certainly being an experience which no known language can describe for the practitioner becomes has one with the creation that is all around them and just has it is within them!

Therefore and more clearly, the feeling of "Self-Awareness", in which the experiencer becomes aware, via observation - that they are has one and so in unity with the creation that is all around them just has it is within them! This being a "Self-Awareness" which can lead to "Self-Realization" in which the experiencer actually becomes the creation and so is no longer an observer of God's world or the world of Nature for the Non-Believer! Therefore and again it should be known that this creation can only be experienced and so realized in the "Present Time", for again it should be said that the Past or the Future do not exist – but more about the reason why these experiences can be obtained - is later in "Life's Purpose".

For certainly like all Fathers, our God, or that from which the creation came from, for the non-believer, does protect and also cares for every persons "Future" needs, whilst like all Mothers the "Mother of the Creation" protects and cares for every persons "Present" time needs! This also certainly being that controlling reality which can be witnessed to be that which factually is developing within our ongoing "Present" time! But certainly, it should be known that God, recognized to be the father of the creation and "Space", which "Life's Purpose" recognises to be the Mother of the creation, are certainly awaiting the birth of the most evolved part of their only child, which are "Self-Realized" people – but more about this later in "Life's Purpose". Of course, it is known that there are now, within our world, many hundreds of religions and philosophies that are all growing within this world that we call "Earth". For certainly this is a world which has also many hundreds of different teaching systems, all of which are targeting "Enlightenment", this being that which will certainly bring birth to their followers. But sadly is it not also true, that within the legality of the "Freedom of Choice", many people have created false worlds in which they and their leaders "religiously" claim their own personal "I Want".

For certainly are these false worlds not Realized when their leaders say, **"My religion is better than your religion, and my way to God is better than your way to God"**, and also, **"Your way to God must be stopped, and**

God will bless me if I do this!" Of course, this ungodly mistake is truly an "I Want for ME" and it will certainly be an "I Want" that will not change God's laws in which the "Mother of the Creations" controlling harmony always exists. Therefore, is it not known to be true that ALL people need to individually seek their own private and personal way to that reality which will bring them to achieve and "Awareness" that can lead to "Enlightenment"? For Gods laws or the Laws of Nature for the non-believer cannot make a mistake.

So yes! With the knowledge of this reality, the doer's only active practice will ALWAYS be to support the development of harmony that always rests in God's world or the world of Nature for the Non-Believers! This reality being that world which is continuously existing all around all people just has it exists in unity within them, but only in the "Present Time"– so YES and truly, forgetting is our worst enemy.

Nevertheless, "Sugar in the Water", meaning the actual tasting of "Enlightenment" within the "Present Time", will always show to the taster an experience of becoming has one with the harmony that is existing within them and also all around them! For indeed and surly, these are certainly the experiencing of natural laws that will always reward the seeker who actually becomes "Self-Aware" of or "Self-Realizes" the unity that exists within Gods creation, this being that which is all around them just has it is within them, or within natures creation for the Non-Believer.

Here is an example of the above unity which can be explained by a few words that are resting within "Life's Purpose". These being words which were also described by Jesus who was the originator of the Christian faith and who all the people of our world do realize or are aware of, was actually filled by that which is called "The Holy Spirit"! This being that reality which "Life's Purpose" also identifies has being the "Soul"! For certainly the Soul is an energy that exists only in people and it is also a life force that is known to be has one entity with that which we call "The Creation". For certainly it should also be known that the Soul, which "Life's Purpose" recognises to be the "Holly Spirit", can only experience the creation through a person's mind when the mind is not blocked by the "I Want" verbiage that is being sounded by one or more of the animalistic five senses.

Now let us listen to the sayings of Jesus the Christian incarnate who "Life's Purpose" says, was really the "Holy Spirit" of the one God that was created in order to speak directly to you with such words has are stated in the Christian Bible i.e.:- **Luke 12:10-12** – ***"Anyone who speaks against the Son of Man will be forgiven, but there is no forgiveness for the man*** *who speaks evil against the Holy Spirit."* It is also well to understand that attacking or abusing any "Enlightened" person who is not animalistic by nature, is not good, but it does happen! Therefore it is most useful and also necessary to understand that God's harmony or Natures harmony for the Non-Believer is not a harmony that is based upon riches and a power over others which are often habitually desired by another person! So wisely, Luke also added these words that he had heard from Jesus: – *"And when they bring you before the synagogues and magistrates and authorities, don't worry as to what defence you are going to put up or what word you are going to use. For the Holy Spirit will tell you at the time what the right thing for you to say is."* Thus it is also certainly true that this condition of "Enlightenment" is described within the Christian religion as actually experiencing the "Holy Spirit" or the "Holy Ghost". This truly being an experience which is gained by an empty mind that is free from any "I Want!" i.e.: This being a non-thinking empty mind condition which is that reality that ALL our world's different religions and philosophies do target and constantly speak about, for many are their religious words which describe the experiencing of "Enlightenment". These being words that are stated in our worlds many religions that describe "Enlightenment" has experiencing *"Moksha", "Bodhi", "Nirvana", "Gabriel", "Ushta"*, and many more words plus all stating that "Enlightenment" brings the feeling of *"liberation", "salvation", "emancipation", "peace", "freedom"*, and *"a feeling of an awakening that is impossible to describe."* "Life's Purpose" will also endeavour to explain how to experience this true reality, and therefore will actually show "scientifically" and "physically" just how to achieve this reality called "Enlightenment"! For certainly and in truth, this "Enlightening" experience is actually that reality which all our worlds' religions and philosophies do target. For it is an experience in which a person first become "Self-Aware" that they are actually has one entity with that which they are observing. This being an awareness which can lead to "Self-Realization", in which the Soul is freed for it is a realisation in which a person becomes has one with the creation and there is no observer. Therefore and certainly, it is this reality which all religions and philosophies do target and also endeavour to achieve – but more about this later in "Life's Purpose"!

So now it is certainly worth understanding that all our world's religions and philosophies do use their own "culturally" based words to convey to their listeners a way to accomplish and so experience the above Gods world or the world of Nature for the None-Believer. For indeed it is certainly known that this "Self-Aware" experience or this "Self-

Realisation" experience is the actual experiencing the Godly harmony that can only exist in our worlds "Present Time"? For indeed the truth is that all readers of "Life's Purpose" should "factually" and "scientifically" no know that this "Present Time" is the only time in which God's world or the world of nature for the Non-Believer, can and does actually exist.

For certainly is it not a known truth that it is only in the "Present Time" that God's Creation or the Creation of Nature for the Non-Believer can be experienced? This is also a truth that does actually rest within all our worlds' philosophies and all our worlds' religions. For certainly all our worlds' philosophies and religions do actually recognise that a person can become "Self-Aware" of that which exists all around them has being that that which also exists within them! This being a "Self-Awareness" of the creation which can eventually lead to experiencing that which is called "Self-Realization", a reality in which a person actually becomes "The Creation"– this being that experience which is called "Enlightenment"! For again and certainly, this is the experiencing of an "Enlightened" reality which is known by our wise to be a joining with or the becoming has one with God or with Nature for the Non-Believer. Therefore such an experience has "Enlightenment" is certainly a Godly gift which also brings to the experiencer not just the true knowledge of life but the true purpose of what all life is actually targeting!

So yes! This first experience of "Enlightenment" will bring all your thoughts to their knees in a silent obedience to the unthinking "stillness" that is all around you, just has it is within you. This being a silence which is actually a Godly gift or a Nature given gift for the Non-Believer and a gift which should always be within you just has it is always outside you!

For certainly this is that "truth" which is always a personal experience which is always waiting for those who have never experienced their real self, this being who they really are and which is why the ancients call this experience "Self-Realization". For certainly, it is a known fact that this realism is actually an experience in which you truly encounter that which is the real "YOU", which is truly your "Soul", this being that which experiences that it is "Everything"! For again is it not true, just has the Christian gospel states that when the "Son of God", who is named to be Jesus and who knew that He was a personification of the Creation, was roughly arrested by those individuals who feared Him. He actually admonished one of his disciples for being brutal towards a guard who was arresting Him, this being because it was an act which is known to have broken the social harmony that was emerging around them – within the "Present Time."

For without doubt, is it not stated that that Jesus did correct this active aggression coming from one of His disciples, this correction being in order to restore the peace and harmony that is always endeavouring to exist within the creations "Present" Time? Is it not also said that Jesus then went quietly in keeping with His captors' brutal punishment and did He not also remain silent even when tortured, beaten, and then brutally nailed to a cross? This cruelty being from those "I Want for ME" believers who usually took for themselves the gifts emanating from the creation that existed all around them! Also is it not true that Jesus did indeed remain in silent none-speaking obedience to this racial disharmony that wanted His death, this silence lasting until upon his pending death He said ***"Forgive them for they know not what they do"***, and then he died.

But, is it not also true that Jesus' "Enlightened" activity, this being that wisdom which came from His Soul, did actually change the world in which we now live? For is it not true, this being a truth which can be seen by looking at all our worlds past history, that brutal governing cultures are not accepted in God's world, or the world of Nature for the Non-Believers. Also is it not true, has our world history shows, that all evil "I Want for ME" acts are always eventually removed by the goodness residing within the majority of people, especially when such evil endeavours to control them?

So yes! Is it not certainly true that the experiencing of the "Holy Spirit" or the "Holy Ghost", this being that which is spoken of in the Christian religion, is truly words that describe "Enlightenment"? This "Enlightening" experience being when a person experiences a mind that is without thought! For a person's mind is that place which the animalistic five senses can sound their "I Want for ME"! This, and again it should be said, is that mind-filling reality which stops a person Soul from becoming has one with the creation which is existing all around it! Therefore it is certainly good to be "aware" that if you can hear it in the mind, then it is not the real you! For the real you is that which listens, tastes, smells, sees and touches the outside world!

Thus the real you is that non-thinking reality in which you become "Self-Aware", this being a "Self-Awareness" in which your Soul is allowed to experience, via observation, that you are has one with the creation that is all around you just has you know that the same creation does "unthinkingly" exist within you. This being that reality which a person experiences when their mind becomes empty and without any "I Want for ME" input, this input being words that are being sounded by their animalistic five senses. For certainly, this silence in the mind, when it occurs, does allow a person's soul to see through their still mind and so they become "Self-Aware" or even "Self-Realize" that they are has one with the creation that is all around them, just has it is within them, these certainly being realities that can only exist in the Present Time".

So yes! This is certainly an "Enlightening" experience which can only occur when the Soul is allowed to see through an empty mind and so become has one with that reality which we call the "Present Time". Thus what is certainly needed is an empty and still mind reality which can only occur when a person's mind is not filled by any mind-blocking animalistic "I Want for me" desires. These being mind filling "I Want for me" desires that are being sounded within your mind by one or more of your animalistic five senses. For certainly, it is this condition which does constantly fills the mind with a past or a future thinking "I want" so it is now good to know that an empty mind is a condition that anyone can achieve – but more later in "Life's Purpose" about achieving this awareness or the reality of being has one with that which we call "The Creation".

Now here are some words from our wise ancients in which we can start with words that are from the Prophet Muhammad, blessed be His name. For certainly the Prophet Muhammad was a member of a Semitic Arabic-speaking people who lived throughout North Africa and Southwest Asia and the Prophet Muhammad was also an Arab religious, social and a political leader and he was also the founder of the Islamic religion whose belief is in the existence of one God, or in the oneness of God. It should also be well noted that the literal meaning of word "Islam" means "Peace", therefore the Islam religion indicates that a person can actually achieve a real peace whilst in their body and so, with a silent mind, experience the realty of the "Present Time", this being that world which rests in the obedience of the one God.

According to written history, Mohammed was certainly a prophet who was divinely inspired to preach the belief that there is only one God, and also to confirm the monotheistic teachings of Adam, Abraham, Moses, Jesus and many other prophets. Also Mohammed, *"Peace be upon Him"*: is believed by both Sunni and Shi'a Muslims, who are His followers, to be the last in the succession of our world's prophets. An important example of Muhammad's teachings can certainly be noted in Mohammed's Quote 3: The Golden Rule: ***"You will not enter paradise until you have faith. And you will not complete your faith until you love one another."*** Paradise is another word for that which "Life's Purpose" calls "Enlightenment", this being that which can only exist in the "Present Time", which is the only place that the singularity of God's world can be truly experienced.

   A further proof of this reality also rest in the words of Krishna who is a major deity (God) in the Hindu religion. For it is stated that there is a trinity of Hindu Gods who are known has Brahma the Creator, Vishnu the preserver and Shiva the destroyer. What can also be noted is that a text from the wise Srimad-Bhagavatam, meaning "Story of the Fortunate one," truly reveals the wisdom that is resting in Hinduism. It factually covers a wide range of knowledge including the nature of the true "Self" with an example being in Chapter 3: in which Gajendra's Prayers of Surrender carefully stated: - *"If one takes Krishna seriously, a devotee may externally not be very well educated but because of devotional services God gives him "Enlightenment" from within. If God gives "Enlightenment" from within, one can never be in ignorance."* Thus meaning, has "Life's Purpose" says, that the person, whose "empty" mind rests in silence, will experiences only the "Present Time" and so live within God's harmony and not any mind filling "I Want" for ME! This being that certainty which blocks the Soul from seeing through the mind and so experiencing the "Present Time", for only a silent mind can allow a person to experience the "Heaven" that actually exists upon our Earth, but it can only exist in the "Present Time".

   Also, in Chaitanya-Charitamrita, a composed Sanskrit verse by Krshnadasa Kaviraia in 1557 and purport to 7.118 – states *"When a person perfectly performs spiritual activities that lead to enlightenment, they become perfect in knowledge and understand that they are not God but a servant of God."* These being statements that are complete truths but may not be understandable to those whose minds continuously seek ways to machinate and create a personal "I Want" for ME world!

   For simply stated, "Enlightenment", in which a person experiences that they are has one with the creation that is all around them has it is within them, simply means that there are no thoughts in the mind! These being that which "Life's Purpose" says are emanating from one or all of the animalistic five senses. Therefore accurately stated all religions, and there are of course many religions and philosophies within our world, have differing creeds but all pursue the same beliefs. For certainly, all our worlds differing and unique religions all state that "Enlightenment" actually reveals to the experiencer the only path that can lead towards truth of that which we call "reality".

   For certainly, all religions and philosophies explain a workable path that targets an "Enlightened" experience which reveals that the purpose of a person's life is to be in unity with those people who support the world and who also aid "naturally" the creations progress towards a unifying perfection, this being a perfection which can only be achieved within God's harmony or Nature's Harmony for the Non-Believer. For again it can be said that it is certain that all people can genuinely experience "Enlightenment". This being that which brings them to experience that they are has one with all that exists within our entire world's environment. This being "Enlightenment" in which a person truly experiences ALL conditions that are unfolding before and within all life and also all non-life.

So yes! Simply put, all religions and philosophies upon our world say to their followers, *"Have Good Thoughts, say Good Words, do Good Deeds"* and also *"There is only one path and that is the path of Truth"* or *"Cause brings Effect"* also stating *"Do the right thing because it is the right thing to do"* plus continually adding *"All beneficial rewards will come to you!"* For certainly is it not also well known to all people that the above words are all religious and philosophical sayings that come to us from our ancient times?

So yes again! Being "Self-Aware" of who you are or experiencing "Self-Realization" of what you are, is a personal experiencing of that which our wise ancients called "Enlightenment"! This meaning that you experience only the "Present Time", which is God's world or Nature's world for the Non-Believer. Thus, and it is also known to be a certain truth, that it is only in the "Present Time" that there rests the only world that a person's Soul can hear, see, touch, smell, or taste. For is it not a certain truth that none of these experiences can be truly realized in a thought created non-existing past or a non-existing future? These being those many "I Want" non factual concepts that are being created in an undisciplined "I Want" for "ME" animalistic mind. For is it not true that this "I Want for ME" is a greed based mind that is being filled by an "I Want" that is being sounded by a person's animalistic five senses?

It is also mentioned by our wise that when a writer meaningfully copies the religious sayings of our wise ancients, none can be sued for correctly explaining the ancient description of their words. This classical description is because our ancient wise knew that their sayings' did actually target the support and pursuits of God's world, this being that world which always exists upon our Earth, but only in the "Present Time". Thus, these ancient sayings are used because all our worlds' wise ancients knew that it is the Godly given "Freedom of Choice" which is the actual deciding factor that supports all Godly pursuits and activities! These being activities which are so designed to not only accept a true way of life, which is to support and actively maintain God's creation which is that "un-folding" harmony that

ALWAYS rests upon our Earth – but only in the "Present Time"!
   Yet, is it not also further understood that only people have been given a Godly maintained "Freedom of Choice"? This being because a personal act is that which is actually needed to support the Creation's on-going "Harmonizing" development! But is it not also true that sometimes that same and certainly needed action can destroy the creations harmonising development? This being when the act does not "Holistically" include all people! This explanation meaning that an individual's personal harmony pursuing activity should also be used to care for all people and so not support any racial concepts that any person can, via their "Freedom of Choice" actually create to exist around them.
   For is it not true that racism is that condition which is personally created when a person exists only to pursue a personal "I Want for ME!" For certainly this "I Want for ME!" search for personal greed cannot support God's harmony or Nature's harmony for the Non-Believer! For is not this "I Want for ME" really a way of life that Gods laws or Natures laws for the non-believer, cannot support? This realty being because of the truly simple view that the whole creation is but one life, therefore, a whole system of needs must be considered rather than the need to obey a simple "I Want for me". For truly, it is also a known fact that "Enlightenment", in which the worshipper experiences a "Self-Aware" realty and so become aware that they are actually a unified part of the creation or they may become "Self-Realized" in which they actually become the unified totality of the creation – but more later about this in "Life's Purpose".
   So yes! It is certainly a truth that a person, who is "Self-Realized", meaning to be "Enlightened", can live in unselfish harmony, will become a good "seed" in all the communities that exist within God's world or the world of Nature for the Non-Believer. This being a personal world in which no "I Want" for me can destroy them. For certainly, these words that are written in "Life's Purpose", are designed to activate and so give birth within all our worlds communities, a simple "seeding"! This being a "Seeding" which all our wise ancients stated would bring to all pursuing practitioners that which they called "Enlightenment". Thus it should be now known that "Enlightenment" is the experiencing of that same seed which did activate a pursuit which developed all our world's religions and philosophies which still exist within our world today.
   Therefore and certainly, it does not matter if you live within a dominating "I Want For ME" social structure, this being that which creates all around you rocks and thorns! For now you should be aware that the "seeds" presented in the following pages will produce for you an

exceptional blissful reality, despite the greed based "I WANT" society in which you may currently live! This being a blissful reality which certainly will produce a healthy "Present Time" reality which will remove you and your children from living in a Hell which is being created by other people or even by your own cruelly pursued "I Want" world. This being an animalistic "I Want for ME" world which does actually encourage disharmony and personal greed to develop, this being that reality in which ALL our Religions and Philosophies do endeavour to stop. For certainly, your life's need is to actually stop your five senses from ignorantly pursuing THEIR own animalistic "I Want". For certainly, if you can hear them "talking" in the mind, then know that this is not you, for you cannot that which you listen to, taste, touch, smell or observe! Is this not true?

Also and for certainly, this reality of experiencing "Enlightenment", is simply achieved by choosing to live in the "Heaven" that can only exist in the "Present Time"! This being the only place that can be filled by that Godly created harmony which is a knowledge that actually encourages a personal search for "Enlightenment" and so experiencing that bliss which our wise ancients stated *"Surpasses All Understanding"*. For certainly it is that experience of obtaining unity with the creation that our entire world's religions and philosophies do target. For indeed, it is also a scientifically known fact, has stated by our wise ancients, that this experiencing of "Enlightenment" can knowingly be achieved by any person! For certainly it is not an event that can only be experienced by those people who attend a particular religion or philosophy, but it is an "Enlightening" experience which can be achieved by a any practicing person who simply seeks the goodness (Godness) of Nature, this being that stillness which can only exist in the "Present Time". For certainly, it is anciently known that when achieving a mind that is without thoughts, these being that which are coming from one or all of the animalistic five sense, a person will automatically become "Self-Aware" of only the "Present", this being an experience in which the observer knows that they are the singularity of the "Present Time".

"Life's Purpose" also states that it should be understood that this "Self-Aware" experience can lead to a person experiencing that which our wise ancients called "Self-Realisation"! This reality being when the experiencer actually becomes the creation and there is no observer - for it is known that they become has one with God or with Nature for the non-believer, but more about this later in "Life's Purpose"! For definitely, this "Freedom Of Choice" is only and always will be an "Enlightening" gift that has been given to all people and this is a truth whether you believe in God or you believe in Nature for the non-believer.

For certainly, it should again be said that any persons disciplinary "praying" practice is a searching reality which actually targets that experience which is religiously called "Enlightenment", this being that target which can only arise from an individual person's "Freedom of Choice". This being why "Life's Purpose" repeatedly says that this personally selected "choice" must be made by a person prior to their targeting that which is called "Enlightenment". For certainly it is good to acknowledge again that "Enlightenment" is the target of ALL our worlds' religions and philosophies. For certainly and again it must be said, that it does not matter what your current beliefs are, be they religious, atheist, agnostic or just plainly ignoring that true world which constantly exists within you and also all around you! Therefore, and certainly, these "present" writings in "Life's Purpose", will describe a path towards living an "Enlightened" way of life for any individuals "Soul". This being a "Soul" which is a part of everything that exists and which is that reality that is resting within all people. For "Life's Purpose" will reveal in a simple way, just how to achieve the target of ALL our world's religions and philosophies. Simply put, the modernly written words in "Life's Purpose", will show to all readers just how to experience God's "Harmony" or Nature's "Harmony" for the non-believer, this being that which can only exist in the "Present Time"

For indeed, it is certainly and very religiously known, that this is a dutiful way of life that will bring to the practitioner that "Enlightenment" which all our world's religions and philosophies do seek for their worshippers. This is being the actual experiencing of "Enlightenment", which all our world's religions and philosophies' do target; this again being said is that reality which is called the ***"Peace that surpasses all understandings"***. For certainly, and yes, it is without doubt, that "Enlightenment" can be experienced within the lives of all people. But still it can be truly said, that many people have lost the knowledge of how to awaken this awareness or reality which actually enables them to enter Gods world or the world of Nature for the Non-Believer!

Thus, it is certainly true that "Enlightenment" is a positive experience which all our wise ancients say will bring to any experiencer an inner peace that surpasses all understanding! This being an inner peace that will remove from all minds the negative and self-claiming "I Want" for me desires and also their "I Want for ME" pursuits. For certainly, these "I Want" pursuits are animalistic desires that do greedily exist in an animalistic non-human "I Want for me" world. Therefore, it is only with an un-thinking mind, this being that reality in which a person does automatically become has one with Gods world or with the world of Nature the non-believer! But it is also certain that some people, via the God given "Freedom of Choice" can "choose" to break that naturally supporting world in which we as people do "Choose" to live.

For certainly, is it not a certain truth that God or Nature for the Non-Believer, did give to all people the "Freedom of Choice"? This being so that people can be freed from the animalistic "I Want for ME" nature of their dominating five senses? Yet, is it not sadly true that many people plus some of our world's governments and even some of our world's religious leaders, do actually use their animalistic five senses to attack other leaders, these being leaders who have different politics and/or religious faiths? This usually being in a destructive war that says, *"I want my way of worship and my administration to be more important than your way of worship and your way of administration!"*

For again, is it not also a truth that some governments and certain followers of our world's various religions do actually create an aggressive "I Want" only for ME way of life. Thus personally creating a change to the world that is not birthed by the creations natural ongoing laws, but is a world that is controlled by a person's "I Want for ME" demands! Is not this "I Want for ME" pursuit also being knowingly targeted by their saying, *"I want my politics (or my religion) to be pursued because your politics (or your religion) is not has well to me has my politics (or my religion) are!*

This confusion is certainly not coming from a naturally growing world which has been affectionately created to provide a much needed reality in which in which all people support all endeavours which target the purpose of the creation - which is for a person to become has one with God or with nature for the Non-Believer!

For certainly it is not a world that has actually been created by a negative "I Want only for ME"! Neither is it a world that takes from the needs that nature is providing for others! For it is a creation that has been formed to provide for the needs of all life and also of all non-life! For is it not true that our world has been God created or Nature created for the non-believer? This certainly being a world that exists within a universe which has knowingly been created by God or by Nature for the non-believer! For certainly, is it not a known truth that God or Nature for the non-believer, did and does naturally provide the needs for all life and is it not truly a world that is based upon a God given or Nature given for the non-believer, "Freedom of Choice"? This being a world that has been created by God or by Nature for the non-believer to give all peoples a "Freedom of Choice"!

This being a known reality which allows all people to "privately" choose their way of life, even to choose their own death if so chosen – has in war – but why have only people been given this "Freedom of Choice"? It is a good question which the following writings endeavour to answer.

Therefore, in order to pursue a life promoted by "natures" promoted systems, these being that which are contained within "Life's Purpose" and also contained within the many religious belief systems that are pursued within our world, it can be understood that it does not matter what your current belief is or even what your political, tribal, family, personal, philosophical, or religious beliefs actually are. For in truth, the following "modernised" words that have been carefully written in "Life's Purpose" will show "Scientifically" the way to achieve that target which is pursued by all our worlds' religions and philosophies.

This being a personal experience which is that reality that ALL our world's religions and philosophies do call "ENLIGHTENMENT"! This being that enlightening reality which all our world's religions and philosophies do seek and when once it is experienced, it can never be forgotten or changed. It will certainly be an experience which will bring to you an understanding of that truth which does actually exist within you just has it exists without you. Therefore, you will also be aware or actually realise that the greatest and purest "creed" that you can belong to, meaning faith, dogma, doctrine, philosophy or belief, principle, and especially your understanding of a personal faith, is an "experience" which can only be experienced within YOU!

It is also useful to understand, that most of the disciplines practiced within our world's religions and philosophies, were anciently designed to bring to the people of a particular country a "cultural" way that would target their personal experiencing of "Enlightenment". For certainly, the people who search for this truth must understand that another countries religious devotees may culturally possess a different way to achieve this target called "Enlightenment"! Therefore, it is useful to know that all activities practiced within a countries religion or philosophy are culturally designed to bring to their followers the experiencing of that which we call the "Present Time", which is God's world or the world of Nature for the non-believer. For certainly is it not true that this must be a world in which the past and the future do not exist. For indeed and truly, this Godly (Goodly) realisation is the experiencing of only the "Present Time" and it is a "Present Time" in which there are no thoughts in the beholders mind. For truly, this is certainly an experience which is "constantly" available to all people for it is an existing reality that can certainly be experienced, by any person, but only in the "Present Time". For certainly and again it should be said, that the "Present Time" is the only time in which rests, when the mind is without thoughts, the experiencing of "Enlightenment"! This being that reality which exists only in the "Present Time" and when it is experienced without thoughts, a person "Self-Realizes" that it is a personal experience that cannot be explained in words – and it exists only for YOU and only in the "Present Time"!

An example of this is that some people in our world say that the Christian Jesus did not historically exist –this being a negative belief that is not really important. For what is really important are the "enlightened" writings that represent His words, these being words that are stated to have actually been spoken by Jesus of the Christian faith. For certainly the words of Jesus do accurately bring to the listener the bodily experience of an "awareness" or even the final "realization" that they are has one with the creation which is all around them just has it is also within them! This reality being because these teachings of Jesus can remove the mind filling animalistic "I Want" words that is being sounded into the mind by one or from all of your animalistic five senses! This being animalistic ally created mind filling sounds such has "I Want to Taste this or I Want to See Smell, Touch or Listen to that!" For is it not also true that our world of animals are disciplinary controlled by this "I Want for ME" fact? A fact that animalistic ally leads to wars and continued unrest which is the exact opposite to a world that is taught by our worlds ancient "Godly" chosen religious teachers. For is it not true, has our worlds history shows, that their words did target for their listeners experience a "Self-Awareness" that they were has one with the world around them. This certainly being that awareness which is a condition that can lead to "Self-Realization", this being a realisation in which the experiencer actually becomes "Everything", which of course is the purpose of the creation, this being so that God the Father can experience "Himself"! For certainly it is anciently known that "Self-Awareness", this being that which can lead to "Self-Realization", are both experiences in which the majority of people do quickly become aware or realize for themselves that condition which our ancients called "Enlightenment"! For undoubtedly they are experiences in which you fully realize that you are "Everything" and so you cannot be harmed, persecuted, or harassed by that which you know is really a "You", but you can be harmed by those people who have forgotten this fact.

Therefore it would be good to now be aware or realise that there is a very simple way being shown in "Life's Purpose" that will enable you to achieve an awareness of "Enlightenment"! This meaning that you will find your true existence in your world which is really God's world or the true world of Nature for the Non-Believer. This certainly being a world of harmony, enjoyment and well-being and a world in which all our wise ancients say has been Godly or Nature created for the non-believer, which means it has been created for all people, which are certainly you?

For unquestionably, when leaving individuality, you will undoubtedly experience that your personal meditation is a very simple way to find and so experience this ancient truth! This truth being that you are NOT alone but that you are everything - but more about this later in "Life's Purpose" in which you will certainly find answers to the following questions! *"What is the immortality of the soul?* Also *"Where do I come from and where am I going?* Plus *"What is the point of my existence?"* and *"What is the Soul?"* As well as answers to *"Who or what is God?"* and also *"What is the purpose of Nature"* plus *"What is it that Reality which does actually control and also support Nature?*

But certainly it should now be known that there are only three basic truths that a person should be aware or to be realized to live with on this path to *"Self-Awareness"* or *"Self-Realization"* and these needed truths are: - *1. Have a generous heart. 2. Use only kind words. 3. Pursue the well-being of others.* For correctly only on the way towards experiencing "Self-Awareness", this being an awareness which can lead to the realisation that you are has one with the creations! For certainly this is the experience which is targeted by all our world's religions and philosophies, for it is a reality in which you will certainly experience that you are has one with the totality of the creations harmony and has previously stated, if you need to find how to obtain this unity with the creation – READ ON

3 WHO ARE "YOU"?

So yes! God's world or the world of Nature for the Non-Believer is a developing world that can only exist in the "Present Time" and also when there is no personal "I Want" endeavouring to claim it or to change it! For truly is it not anciently and wisely known that it is this personal "I Want for ME" which is that reality that actually separates the claimant from their true selves! For certainly it should now be known that the reason for this isolation is that their "I Want for ME" endeavours to create a false world which actually separates them from that which they really are, which is the singularity of the creation – a reality which makes their forgetting to be their worst enemy. For certainly, it is because of this forgetting whom we really are, that people fill their minds with many "I Want for me" thoughts, this being that which is being created by one or all of their animalistic five senses. Therefore it is now a really good moment to fully understand that any thoughts that are sounding in the mind are emanating from one or from all of your five "animalistic" five senses, which are certainly NOT you! For you dear reader, are really a listener and a taster, plus the viewer, touchier and the smeller of that reality which you know to be your observation of the outside world. For truly, Gods' world or Natures world for the Non-Believer, is a unified world which exists without any personal ego and so you cannot be that which you observe is a claiming "I Want", for this is simply the desires of the animalistic five senses!

For certainly it should be known that it is only people who can genuinely and honestly, via their observation, move personally above and beyond all this animalistic "I Want" reality! It is also good to remember that "You" are also not the creator of the atmosphere or the heavens or the air, or of water or fire, and you are certainly not the owner of the wind. For you are that energy which you "observationally" experience to be resting within you! This actually being an energy which is has one with that energy and so it also exists in unity with all that which is outside your body. For you are definitely not that thought which you see appearing in your mind or that reality which speaks within your mind. Nor are you that which holds another's hands! Nor are you any part of the body that moves, rests or sleeps, for you are indeed and truly that life force which is called the "Soul". This being an entity which an integral part of that energy that actually supports all life within our universe and also all that which we call Non-Life! For certainly it is true, that this is a creative energy which also does actually rest upon that which we call "Planet Earth.

So yes! It is possible that a person can actually experience, when without mind-filling thoughts that block the Soul from seeing and so experiencing the world around it, this being self-awareness or a self-realisation condition which is named by our wise ancients to be "Enlightenment". This certainly being an "Enlightening" experience in which a person becomes "Self-Aware" that they are has one with everything that exists and not only with that which is within them but also with that creation which exists all around them. This is certainly known to be a personal experience and it is an awareness that can develop into that reality which is called "Self-Realization", a condition in which there is no longer an observer for the experiencer becomes has one entity with the creation. For certainly this is a targeted reality which binds together a blissful harmony of a love that automatically exists within the unity of a creation in which there is no neighbour. For certainly again, you can become Self-Aware" that you are an entity that has a total awareness of that bodily unity which exists within all life and also all non-life - this unified singularity being God's world or the true world of Nature for the Non-Believer.

For certainly it is also the experiencing of "Self-Awareness" which can develop into a "Self-Realization", this being that reality which contains no hatred or dislike for any of the world that exists around you or with that which exists within you! Neither do you have any separate "I Wants" for the totality of the creations unity is experienced to be "YOU!" For certainly via "Self-Realisation" you will experience that you actually exist within all things that can be experienced within the creation that is all around you, just has it is within you! Also within this experience of "Self-Realized" unity you will have no hate or greed nor any delusion that can be based upon pride, or arrogance! Nor do you have any feelings of envy or jealousy and certainly you will have no desire to seek freedom from this unified body.

It is also further known, by our ancient wise that you will also be without any thoughts! For certainly you will also experience that nothing needs to be clarified because all knowledge has been given to you that you need to know? For you "Self-Realise" that you are has one with "everything" and therefore you will experience a unified singularity with the totality of the "Present Time", this being that which exists all around you just has it does within you!

For certainly you will then become the true "I AM" and so will actually support the needs of the creation, but only in the "Present Time". For certainly, it is also known that within this "Self-Realized"" condition you will experience no value nor devalue with that which is within you and also all around you. Nor can any happiness, sorrow, pain, or pleasure be connected to you, for you are beyond all these things. You also no longer need to comfort yourself with creeds, or the visiting of holy places! Nor comfort yourself with scriptures or rituals nor sacrifice your personal time or your leisure values! This way of life being because you are no longer a faithful observer for you are now "Self-Realise" that that which you observe can only be "You!"

Also you will not have any fear of death, for you know that you cannot die and that you're "Soul" will always be born again in its search to become has one with God, or to become has one with Nature for the Non-Believer. You also will never fear being separated from that which you know is the real "You", for "You" do not have any doubt about your existence and also the reason why you exist! Nor have you any judgment about the place of your birth or of your birth conditions! You will also know that your Soul has no Earthly father or Earthly mother, this being those who created the body which contained your soul at its birth! You also have no separate relatives or friends, nor do you have the need of a teacher, nor can you be taught. For in "Enlightenment", you "know" and understand that you are the all-pervading Soul! This being that which is unified has one with "Everything", this also being that entity which is without any attributes or any known form.

Therefore you will also know that you cannot be attached to the world but you will also know that you cannot be freed from it. Nor do you need to wish for anything because you know that you are everything! You will also experience that you exist in all people and in all time zones and that you are always in perfect balance has a oneness with developing time. You will also know that you has the Soul, cannot be an actual "Server" or a "Servant", this being that reality which is accommodating, caring, nurturing, hospitable and also charitable. Nor can you be the "Artisan" who is creative, inventive, imaginative, playful, and dexterous. Nor can you be the "Warrior" who is forceful, loyal, protective, determined, and steadfast. Nor are you the "Scholar" who is curious, attentive, academic, analytical, and neutral. You also cannot be the naturally engaging "Sage" who is articulate, charming, entertaining, and expressive. Nor can you be a "Priest" who is inspirational, uplifting, motivating, energising, visionary, and lastly, you cannot be a "King" or "Queen", who is loyal, commanding, assured, powerful, authoritative, and decisive.

For you are the Soul, this being a life force that knowingly is the actual unification of all life and also all Non-Life. For has a "Self-Realized" person you actually become has one with your Soul and so you actually "Self-Realize" that you are part of everything that exists in this ever-moving yet ever still world, this being a created world that consists of a blissful harmony that is naturally bound by a love that has no neighbour. Therefore you actually know that you are personally an individual that has the total awareness of a unified creation which must be empowered by an originating God or powered by "No-Thing" for the Non-Believer.

So yes! We should always understand that a person's non-questioning and always silent but observing "Soul", has a non physical awareness that can see and listen to everything that occurs around it, but it is also good to remember that this is a realisation that can only occur within people! It also should be known that it is Godly created or Nature created for the non-believer, in order to allow its carrier, which is you, to be "animalistic" within the freedom of this "Consciousness", which is a unified energy that supports all life forms. But it should also be known that it is an energy which exists only within people, for certainly it should be known that it is only within people that there rests an observing Godly given soul or a Nature given Soul for the Non-Believer. This being a Soul which has been birthed with the instructions not to interfere with a person's "Freedom of Choice", for indeed is it not well known fact that it is only people who can act to support nature's harmony or negatively can act to destroy it. So truly, it should now be personally realized that the Godly reason has to why only people have been given this "Freedom of Choice", is so that they can actively support the developing "Heaven" or the developing "Nature for the Non-Believer", which is that reality that can only exist in the "Present Time", for the Past and the Future can never exist.

For certainly again, is it not also known to be true that all people should be aware and so realise that within this divinely Godly given or Nature given for the non-believer, "Freedom of Choice", many people have forgotten the true purpose of their life? This being a life which always should be remembered is to support the Godly on-going development of all our worlds' life and also all our worlds non-life! This being that life which unifying and supportively exits all around them, just has it does within them! Yet sadly, many people often use, deliberately or unknowingly, their God given freedom of choice to "choose" to take for them that which belongs to Nature or that which really belongs to "Others" to care for: This certainly being the animalistic ally created "I Want" for myself reality which actually a painful "Hell" that only people can create. For certainly it is an animalistic creation which can only arise in a person's mind when it is filled with a Past or a Future "I Want" thought? For certainly, this is a "personal" animalistic mind blocking reality which actually stops their Soul from peacefully seeing out of their body and so viewing Gods world or the world of Nature for the Non-believer, this being that reality which can only exist in the "Present Time".

It is usually a perpetual mind filling "I Want" for ME! This constantly being a mind-filling claim that actually creates a personally made Hell for the thinker to live in! This reality being because it stops the inner "Soul" from seeing through a person's non-blocked silent mind the needs of the Heaven that actually exists all around them, just has it does within them, but only in the Present Time. For certainly the "Present" is always an ever-moving, ever-growing and ever-developing world in which the life form that is known has people can "choose" to support or "choose" not to support. For it is certainly true that it is only people who have a "Soul" that cannot die and which is religiously known to be an observing Soul which can rest only within people! For it is only within people that their rests the knowledge of that which is needed to support the caring works of the "Mother of the Creation"! Therefore, it should now be said that if you wish to enable your Soul to fully enjoy this reality that is called the "Present"- then Read on.

4 WHERE IS HEAVEN OR HELL

Now the question is do you believe that there is a Heaven and a Hell, these being the places that you believe your soul, or your energy for the non-believer, will go to when you die? Do you also think that Hell is a place that you will be in pain forever and that Heaven is actually a blissful place of paradise and ecstasy! This "Heaven" also being a place in which you will exist forever with the loved ones who have gone there before you and also with their families who went to heaven before them? Is it not also true that some people who wish to impose their own "I Want" upon you, do state these conditions will only be facts if you do what they say you should do! Or do you believe that upon death, your energy will "sleep" until the next "Big Bang"? This "Big Bang" being the same has that reality which we say did occur when our current "Creation" or universe for the non-believer - was born and so came into existence!

For certainly, the statement of going to exist in Heaven when you die is good to listen to, but the going to a punishing "Hell" for eternity when you die is such a punishing waste that many actually believe that it cannot be accurate, for what loving "God" could allow such a thing? Also many people agree that it is more accurate to be aware or realize that no "Father" or "Mother" would or could create such a wasteful punishing "Hell" for an only Child to exist in. But what we actually know and further understand is that the hypothesis of the "Big Bang" indicates that the Universe must have come from an existing origin, as do all known physical life forms! Also what is further interesting, is that all life is now known to have been started by this "Big Bang" explosion which appears to have come from "No-Thing"; this being that a reality which actually birthed "The Creation" or birthed the "The World of Nature" for the non-believer. For certainly, is it not also "scientifically" known that this "Big Bang" also included within it the birthing of that well known singularity that we call "Planet Earth"?

So yes! Many of our world's major religions and all our worlds philosophical beliefs systems do simply state that you do not exist in a "Heaven" or in a "Hell" forever when they die, so knowingly this punishment could never be inflicted upon the children of this Creation.

For certainly this death would be a very punishing way of "existing, this being after such a short period of life when compared with the life time of the existing universe and it pending! For indeed, is it not also a well known fact that God, this being the common name for that reality known has the father of the creation, will not and does not punish people in their current life! For is it not true that God or that which created people for the non-believer, did knowingly give to all people the "Freedom of Choice", even if they pursue an end that they know will destroy them? For certainly, it is a known fact that if you put your hand into boiling water, who is it that is punishing you? For is it not truly known, that if you stop a non-harming natural law from continuing or from just emerging, this being a law which is being birthed by the creation that is all around you and also within you, who is that is sinning?

So yes! Who is it that in their current life, is actually deciding the conditions of their next life? For certainly it is now true to know that your next life must be birthed because it is a known fact that the unified energy which you know has your life, cannot die! For certainly, it should be known that this truth is based upon a proven scientific fact in which it is known that energy cannot be destroyed! For now this known fact is currently being forwarded by our Earths scientists who further state that if energy is "seemingly" destroyed, it will definitely be reborn again somewhere else! Therefore, does this not mean that all the energy that exists in unity within our Creation cannot die?

Simply put, we do modernly know, through thermodynamics, that energy cannot be created nor can it be destroyed. It simply changes its state, which ensures that the total amount of energy in an isolated system cannot and does not change. And also thanks to Einstein, we also know that matter and energy are the two realities that exist within the same hierarchy system that actually controls all life and also all non-life! Therefore our bodies' energy, this being that, which empowers our "Soul", must constantly energise itself and so "scientifically" it can never leave the Creations energy or leave the energy created by Nature for the Non-Believer. For certainly, this scientifically accepted reality regarding life, is a well known fact and also a reality which our scientists are now revealing. Consequently this fact, regarding the body's energy, is now a factually known "scientific" truth which our scientists are all now acknowledging! Thus it is now stated that this re-living energy must actually be the same as the energy from whence it came! Hence, and for that reason, it is now being "scientifically" stated that the unified source of all energy must always be "naturally" recoupable and thus it cannot be lost?

If this is true and it is easy to now be aware or even realise this certainty is a "Scientific" truth, then all your loving ancestors are now living all around you! Therefore, has a result of this truth, you must be an "ancestor" to those families that now exists all around you and also to the bloodline that is all around you – this being that which you have certainly been born into!

Therefore, when you die, it is not true that you go to "Heaven", this being a place which is regarded in various religions has the home of God, and of angels plus your past ancestors. Nor when you die do you go to "Hell", which is a location or a state in the afterlife in which the Soul of evil people is forever subjected to punitive treatment, most often through torture - this also being a "Heaven" that is traditionally depicted as being above the sky. But truly, the "scientific" fact is that when you die, you can only "leave" a personally created "Heaven" or leave a personally created "Hell", this being that which actually exists in your current life's "Present Time". For certainly, it can now be said, that upon death, your Souls entry into a heavenly halfway house may be a temporary situation or it may be for a far more extended period! This being a "purposeful" way of life which actually follows God's or Nature controlling laws which "Life's Purpose" says are constantly resting within the harmony seeking factors that are governed by the "Mother of the Creation", who, just like God, will never leave you? But "Life's Purpose" also identifies, that because each person has been "Godly" given the "Freedom of Choice", then both "God" the father of the creation and also the "Mother of the Creation", which is nature for the non-believer, must sadly turn their faces away from you, this being when you choose, via a personal "I WANT", to create your own world which is known to be that which we call a negative pursuing "Hell!"

But positively it is certainly Realized, that it is only within the "Present" time, that God and the "Mother of the Creations" comforting love for "you", can return! For certainly, it is known by our ancient wise that this comforting experiencing of love, will be experienced when you actively and physically support the "Heaven" that does constantly rest in our "Present" time! For it is an anciently known truth that this personal and heavenly experience will certainty reveal to any active doer that reality which our ancients called "Heaven! This being constantly described has paradise and bliss plus an ecstasy of rapture which is actually the exact opposite to the experiences that are said to be experienced in the world we call Hell! For certainly, these are the creating laws that are implanted by that reality which is named to be God and they are without doubt definable laws which state that Gods only Child, this being that energy which we call

"The Creation", cannot die! These are also being laws that cover His love for the "Mother of the Creation" which "Life's Purpose" identifies has "Nature" and of course this being that which cares for ALL the unity which exists upon this planet that we call Earth.

Therefore it is known to be a simple logic that God or No-Thing for the Non-Believer has NOT created "you" in order to waste "you", this being after such a short life time. For the law of energy actually shows that you must "reincarnate" after death, for it is a known truth that your personal energy cannot die, and so again your body will be re-activated by "your" Soul. For certainly and genuinely, many of our wise ancients, these being those wise ancients who birthed our religions and philosophies, also state this fact. For certainly this re-birthing is again being stated in "Life's Purpose" so that you dear reader, will understandably silence the "I Want" that is usually being sounded in the mind by one or all of your animalistic five senses. This being that exercise which will bring "awareness" or a "realisation" that will support the unification of your body in its ability to become has one with your observing Soul, which actually knows that it is a part of "Everything" and that there is no other! This awareness or reality being the actual unification of your living body with that which is existing all around you, just has is the unified creation which is resting in unification within you! So certainly, this awareness or realisation experience shows that the only purpose of a person's life is to "lovingly" be more useful in supporting the harmony seeking activities of the developing Creation – and this is because you are "Self-Aware" and so "Self-Realise" that the creation that is all around you and also that which is within you - it is your "Self"!

For certainly it can now be said that God smiles when experiencing the love of that part of His only Child which is known to be the dormant "Soul", this being that reality which exists within the advanced consciousness of His Creation - which is certainly His only Child? For certainly and honestly, is it not true that that all our world's Religions and Philosophies state that the Creation is the only Child of God, who must therefore be the "Father of the Creation"?

But what is now being acknowledged within "Life's Purpose", is the "scientific" fact that there must be a *"Mother"*, who like all Mothers must be the primary Teacher and carer of this only Child that we call "The Creation"! Therefore this "Mother" can only be known has "The Mother of the Creation"! For indeed can it not be said that it is this "Mothers Love", who like all mothers, does physically support this only child which we call the Creation and also its growing development towards its divine target –

which will again be explained later in "Life's Purpose"!

For indeed, can it not be said that many people who are entwined within the potential of a personal life still ask, *"Why is there a Creation and does this creation have a target?"* The simple answer to this question is that which ALL our Earths religions and philosophies do target! This being the personal experiencing, via praying, of "Self-Awareness" in which the experiencer becomes observationally aware that they are everything! This being an awareness which can lead to an experience called "Self-Realization". This being that reality in which a person actually becomes has one with the creation that is all around them just has it is within them and there is no observer! This actually being the experiencing of a "Personal" unification with all life and also all non-life for the experiencer realises that everything that they experience is truly "Them" and that there is no observer! This truly being that reality which is known to actually rest within all people and "Life's Purpose" understand that this reality must be because God was lonely. For is it not true that loneliness is also the greatest fear that rests within most people? Also is it not true that even the hermit does knowingly avoid isolation, this being to prove that he exists!

So yes! Is it not "Unsurprisingly" logical and also "Scientifically" acknowledgeable to understand that it was because of loneliness that God created and then seeded Space? This being that separate reality which "Life's Purpose" explains to be the Mother of all life, this being that entity which must have given birth to their only Child, and this being that which we call the Creation. For truly it can now be said that God is no longer lonely for He now actually experiences a well-based love that all fathers and mothers experience at the unified birth of an only Child!

For certainly, is it not a historically known truth that encased in the majority of people is the fear of loneliness? This being a personal fear which normally seeds within the majority's pursuing activities a fact which states that no one should ever be lonely? Therefore is it not also logically correct to say that there is truly a *"Mother of the Creation"* and that this mother must actually be the space in which the creation was birthed and then born! This "Space" also is being the Mother who actually and separately cares for Her only Child, this being that child which we call "The Creation"! Also is it not true that it is *"Mother of the Creation"* who you can quietly "feel" in the love of the "Space" that is silently experienced to be resting all around you and which is also attached to that which is resting within you! This experience being that which our wise ancient called "Enlightenment", which is actually the experiencing of a *"Peace that surpasses all Understanding"!*

For certainly is this experience not that fact which is described in many different ways by ALL our world's religions and philosophies? For unquestionably, is not "Enlightenment" the actually experience of being has one entity with the "Creation"? Or maybe it is an experience of actually being in the arms of "Mother of the Creation"! For without doubt, "Life's Purpose" continually says that it is a never ending experience of a *"Peace that surpasses all Understanding"* and it now awaits you! For certainly it is a truth, that no matter if you are a believer or a non-believer or even what belief system you have obtained, you can and should endeavour to experience! "Enlightenment"! Therefore, it is well to remember that whether you currently live in Heaven or in a personally made Hell whilst upon this Earth, God and the "Mother of the Creation" really do love you? For certainly, this great truth actually show's that within this truth it is God or Nature for the Non-Believer, who has given to each person the "Freedom of Choice"? Therefore, is it not true that if you live in a painful Hell on this Earth that you're "I Want for ME" may be that reality which is punishing you! Also it will certainly be woe to them who inflict "unnatural" punishment upon others, for certainly and undeniably, they will really experience in their current life or in their next life, a correction that is usually imposed upon the animal kingdom – and indeed they may be born has such.

For is it not certainly "Realized" to be true that God, who truly knows that with the support of the Creations Mother, any person will eventually learn how to live in a Heaven whilst alive upon this Earth! For is it not also a certain truth that it is only people who can adjust and so learn to live in and also support the "Godly Harmony" that is endeavouring to expand all around them, this being in that which we call "The Present".

Also, is it not now seen to be true that the "Mother of the Creation" is a certainly a Mother who actually endeavours to maintain the harmony, wisdom, and balance that is contained within the emerging Creation, this being that which is endeavouring towards a united target that cannot be stopped? For is it not known to be true that you actually experience this truth when you live in the "Heaven" that normally exists upon this Earth, this reality being because your body can actually taste the "Sugar in the Water", this being that which rest within the "Present".

For certainly, this "Sugar in the Water" tasting of the "Present" time experience, is the sweet and needed gift that "Mother of the Creation" is constantly presenting to you! This reality being so that you physically know that to experience the sweetness of life, you certainly need to support the expanding harmony that is evolving and being continuously released all around you, just has it is within you! For certainly, this support is for the harmony that you – when "Enlightened" - will personally identify and so actually support all its proceeding endeavours. Therefore, it is also good and certainly important to remember, that none of the "Mother of the creations" sugar", this being that which sweetens a person's life and which is also that reality which the "Mother of the Creation" gives to encourage Her only Child's good work, can make any receiver annoyed?

So yes! It is certainly essential to understand i.e.: stand under, that the "Mother of the Creation" can, like all mothers, only reward via this "Sugar in the water" those people who unselfishly pursue and so seek a harmony to exist around all of life and also all Non-Life. For certainly, the "Mother of the Creation" cannot give "Sugar" (The Taste of Happiness) to all existing life! For truly, this contented happiness can only be experienced by those people who actually do not endeavour to stop or oppose her good work. Indeed, those who oppose her work live in an "I Want" dream that can be likened to a nightmare and so they actually live in a painful Hell whilst existing upon this Earth and sadly can create such for those good people who live around them.

So yes! The quickest way to awaken to the reality of a life that can be lived in the Heaven, this being that, which actually exists all around us, is to let the *"Mother of the Creation"* activate and guide your personal Soul. This being an activation and guidance which is based upon the fact that only a person can readily identify the creations ongoing needs! But certainly, this awareness or reality can only occur when "ALL" mind filling thoughts, particularly of an "I Want" for ME ceases to be sounded in the mind. These being the many mind filling thoughts which are actually coming from one or from all of your five animalistic senses! For certainly this mind filling animalistic "I Want" verbiage is that reality which blocks the Soul from seeing the needs and also experiencing the bliss of the "Present".

But what can now be accurately said is that this none-thinking emptiness of the mind is that truth which does first bring a "Self-Awareness" experience to the non-thinker! This being when the non-thinker actually becomes aware that they are a soul observing reality which physically experiences that it is a unified part of everything that exists in the creation that abounds all around it, just has it does within it! For certainly, to experience this "awareness" means that that you have "disciplinary" silenced your mind, and so your Soul can now become has one with the stillness of the creations unity, this being that reality which can only be experienced in "Present Time". For certainly, this is that real world which is experienced when the brain is no longer filled with any personally created "I Want" for ME animalistic thoughts! For indeed, it is known by our wise, that this "I Want for Me" thinking is actually an animalistic mind filling activity which does block a person's "Soul" from seeing through the mind – that world which we call the "Present" time.

Now the understanding and also the controlling of this animalistic "I Want" activity, was and still is a reality which was well understood by our ancient worlds wise ancients! For even in those thousands of years ago, our ancient wise stated that a person should first pray ("i.e.: meditate") and thus become "Self-Aware" that they are has one with the creation that exists all around them just has it exists in unity within them. For certainly it is known that such mind-filling disciplinary praying can replace the "I Want" animalistic demands that are usually and constantly filling the mind! For certainly it should now be Realized that these animalistic mind-blocking thoughts are certainly animalistic "I Want" mind-filling sounds which do constantly emanate from one or from all of your animalistic five senses. This being that situation which our wise ancients knew does stop the experiencing of that reality which is known has "Self-Awareness". This being awareness in which you silently become conscious that it is a heaven that silently exits all around you and that it is a heaven in which you ALWAYS have a *"Freedom of Choice"!*

For certainly, the experiencing of this heaven that silently exists all around you, is obtained via praying (i.e. meditation)! Thus this self-disciplined praying reality is a correcting exercise which stops the mind filling sounds that are coming from one or from all of your animalistic five senses. This realism is actually achieved by disciplining them unto silence via an imposed prayer! Thus ensuring a mind-empty reality which allows your inner Soul to "observe" and so become aware of the "Present"! This being an awareness which can only be experienced when the inner Soul can see the world through an empty mind - this being a mind that is without any mind blocking "I want" thoughts which are being sounded in the mind by one or more of your uncontrolled animalistic five senses! For certainly it should be said again and again that it is only with an empty mind that are you able to become "Self-Aware" of that world which is constantly being supported by the "Mother of the Creations" endeavours! Or, because of your God give "Freedom of Choice", you can continue to live in your self-created "I Want" mind filled nightmare, this being that world which is created by the "I Want" of your animalistic five senses. For certainly it should again be known that it is these animalistic five senses that are always sounding into your mind their demanding "I Want" for ME!

For certainly, this is truly a fascinating fact, but it should now be reasonable known, that being born has a person you have really been Godly given or Nature given for the non-believer, the "Freedom of Choice"? This being that "Freedom of Choice" reality of which all our wise ancients do speak about.

But now let us, dear reader, also understand that reality which all our wise ancients do speak about! This being how to return to a life that is lived in Heaven, this being whilst living upon this planet Earth. For certainly they state that the best progress towards this living upon our Earth, can only be achieved by an unselfish love for a world in which we are has one! This "unselfish" love means that the actual activating of any "harmony for all actions" can only be accomplished by a person whose activity will automatically lead to a life that can be likened to living in Heaven, whilst living on this Earth.

Therefore, yes, it is certainly known that these personal and unselfish supporting of nature acts can only be achieved in the "Present Time", which is certainly God's Creation and also a "Present" world that is cared for by the "Mother of the Creation", which is called Nature by the non-believer! As a result, it is certainly stated by our holy ones that a person's "right actions" will lead to a good "GOD" caring re-birth in their next life? Or perhaps, has is often stated by our wise, they may need to be re-birthed into a new bloodline in which the "Mother of the Creation" does care for them. This being away from the last place in which they were born and then died and the reason being because the "Mother of the Creation" knows that She can make good use of them in Her on-going pursuit of creating harmony within the one body, this one body being that reality which we call the Creation or the world of Nature for the Non-Believer. For indeed is it not also known to be true, that God is a reality which can also exist outside of Time and Space? For is it not scientifically known to be true that our scientist actually know the time when our universe was born? This being a birthing creation which our scientists called "The Big Bang"! But is it not also strange that our scientists say that our universe was born within a body which they called "No Thing"! For certainly, is it knowingly stated by our scientists that the period before the "Big Bang", this being prior to the birth of the universe, that is was extremely cold and that the temperature was almost absolute zero! Also that this space, prior to that which we call the "Big Bang", was empty of everything and yet this space was also identified by our scientists to have an energy, which "Life's Purpose" calls life and which our scientists says was and is an energy of an enormous size! Also our scientist state that all this emptiness, called

"Space", must have existed prior to that birth which we call the "Big Bang". This being the "Big Bang" that occurred 13.8 billion years ago when this child that we call "The Universe" was born from what our scientists call a single primordial atom, which must have come from God.

For certainly, this child must have been seeded within this "Space", which "Life's Purpose" calls "The Mother of the Creation" and seeded by that which many within our current world call "No Thing" but which "Life's Purpose" calls God. For certainly there must naturally be a father has well has a mother of this only child that we call the creation! For is it not known that all life needs a father – and also a mother? So certainly, there must be that which "Life's Purpose" calls the "Mother of the Creation" and which is also that reality which is called nature by the non-believer! For certainly, there must be a reality which can be called the *"Mother of the Creation"!* This must also mean that when your Soul experiences the stillness of the "Present Time", which it can only realise through a mind that is without thought, it is known that within this stillness you will also "silently" experience the Love of God, which is emanating from the space that is within you and also all around you! So again, it can be said that this experience is that condition which our ancients called "Enlightenment".

So yes! It should be known that God does not do anything, for He has already done all that is needed to be done and certainly His plan is evolving under His laws, these being that which the "Mother of the Creation "harmoniously" controls". So frankly, is it not wrong for any person to believe that they can change these evolving laws and so permanently break this unfolding law by their own animalistic "I Want" for ME? Therefore, is it not also interesting to "acknowledge" that we have amongst all our worlds' populations, many new human births coming from the animal kingdom? These being human births which have just emerged from the animal kingdom and which have just been "re-programmed" to be birthed as people because their environment has been destroyed by human kind?

Is it not also true that these emerging new-rebirths from the animal kingdom need special consideration regarding the way in which they should live? For certainly they are not foolish, but of course they will become harmful to others if they are being maltreated because of their animalistic nature and so become un-cared for by those who live near to them! For it certainly it must be Realized that there is a great need to care for these early re-births from the animal kingdom and without suggesting such! There certainly being a need to show to them care, kindness, and also careful consideration! For certainly, they will need to be guided on just how to how to live within the controlling laws made by people!

But the question now is, how do you recognize these past animals that are now being re-birthed has people? They can and will, automatically harm or kill other people without problems and they can easily steal from others because they feel no law against their need to hunt! They can also cunningly becoming pack leaders and so start a war without difficulty and only a democracy in which the majority of people have had many lives - can control them. Yet, it is also known to be clearly unwise to place them in cages because of a dislike and also to automatically persecute these new animalistic life forms that are being born has "people". Nor should you treat them like beasts of burden, for in your next life, you may well be thought to be in need of rehabilitation and so will be Godly and or Nature ally "re-taught" by being born as an animal. Then would it not also be your thought and hope, that you would be placed with a good "understanding" boss (owner) who will teach, train, and treat you with honour.

So yes! It is further understood that "Life's Purpose" naturally explains a significant need to move away from a mind blocked with the thoughts of an "I Want" only for "ME" belief! For certainly, it should be said that these modern words, which are written in "Life's Purpose", are targeted to be written in a relaxed way so that they will breed a different understanding about this world in which all life and all non-life do endeavour to exist! For indeed, what is certainly important is that creation which we call the "Present" time"! This being a time in which people no longer believe that the Earth is flat or that the Earth is the centre of the Universe that revolves around it! For certainly is it not true that we should now understand that our world is a creation that is a harmonized "singularity", this being a harmonised singularity that is known to be a world which contains all life and also all that truth which we call "Non-Life". For certainly, we also understand that we live on a planet called "Earth" which is known to consist of a collection of atoms that are also recognized to be composed of sub-atomic particles! These sub-atomic particles actually being that reality which we have named to be protons, neutrons, and electrons" etc! But what is also further interesting and which is also factually recognised, is that some of our Earths sub-atomic particles do instantly change their positions when being observed, this simply being by the energy resting within a person's gaze – but more about this later in "Life's Purpose!"

5 WHAT IS "ENLIGHTENMENT"?

So now we should first know that the first all-knowing step that can be taken by people when experiencing that reality is called "Enlightenment"! This being the experience which occurs when the observer becomes a unified one with the creation that is all around them just has it is experienced to exist within them! For certainly within the experiencing of this reality a person should be aware or realize the factual truth that rests behind these simple words *"Don't be afraid of God's Creation"* or that creation which is birthed by "Nature" for our Non-Believers!

For again we should be aware or realise, that all people ought to recognize this well-known "scientific" reality! This reality being that no matter what we think and believe or even what we actually do and achieve, we "scientifically" should always acknowledge that the "planned" purpose of God's Creation or what is known has the Universe by the Non-Believer, will always be accomplished. For certainly, it is also scientifically stated that we will never be able to stop this harmonious and lawfully pursuing development that is actually targeting this Creations end, which is scientifically acknowledged will be its death! What is also true and it is certainly known to be true, is that it is only people who have been given that gift which we call "The Freedom of "choice". Therefore is it not true that any person can "choose" to support or not support the development of this creations on-going development and also its movement towards a harmonious death, this being of our existing Earth! But pleasantly it is also known to be true that the destruction of this planet that we call Earth is a reality which will happen in a few million years time and so until that time that which we call the "Freedom of Choice" to do or not to do, to be or not to be, will remain has a gift to ALL people. This "being a "Freedom of Choice" fact which is said to be a gift that has been given to people so that they can support the development of God's pursuit of Harmony, this also being a support which is actually said to be a good (Godly) thing to do.

For certainly, it is this "Freedom of Choice" reality which is needed to factually create the harmony that rests within all our world's major religions and philosophies. Or any person can, via their "Freedom of Choice", choose to act against and search for harmony and so pursue a personal "I Want" my religion to be the only religion in this world! These being pursuits which may not be compatible with or able to blend with the many unrelated foreign cultures that rest within our world's various religions and also philosophies.

So Yes! The personal and unreligious question that should now be arising within your mind is *"How do you choose or know what to do with your current life, this being a life that is now resting within the current ongoing Creation?"* The simple fact, in a first answer to this personally seeking question, is to know that what you believe is acting has the real "you" may not be the real "you"! But it may seem to your observations that it is truly you that is consistently "choosing" what to do with your life for the source of this thinking "I Want" energy does also strongly believe that it is really you? But the truth is that this sounding in the mind, which is targeting your motivation, will actually be emanating from one of your demanding "animalistic" five senses! This being that reality which you "mechanically" and "habitually" think is the real you! This being because you believe that these sounds that are being worded in your head are actually coming from the real you! For certainly being animalistic in nature your five senses will be constantly sounding into your mind that which is needed to be done in order to satisfy their demanding very animalistic "I Want"!

So Yes! What is now needed to be fully understood is that God gave to all our Earths life - the light of "consciousness", but it was only to people that God gave to this viewing "light", the "Freedom of Choice"! This "Freedom of Choice" meaning that we can "choose" to see or not to see, to taste or not to taste, to touch or not to touch, to smell or not to smell, to listen to or not to listen to and even to die if the choice is to do so! Thus it is only people, who in childhood, were enabled to empower, via this "Freedom of Choice", their five senses with this gift. For certainly it should now be known that it is also only people who in ignorance, can and do unknowingly "choose" to re-direct this "Freedom of Choice" to the "I Want" of the five animalistic senses, this being because they think these five animalistic senses are the true "Them"! Thus forgetting that a person's God given or Nature given for the non-believer, "Freedom of Choice", is a reality which should be controlled by the reflexes and impulses of a person's silent Soul. For certainly, it should now be understood, that in childhood, this "Freedom of Choice" was mistakenly transferred to the mind filling "I Wants" that were emanating from the animalistic five senses, and so we eventually entered the "Iron Age", spoken of by our ancestors.

So, what is now necessary to understand, is that the guiding light that rests within you, this being the real entity which actually observes everything around you, is you're ever silent Soul. For certainly, this reality which has been Godly given or Nature given for the non-believer, has truly been gifted with the "The Freedom of Choice". This being a reality which allows it to do any dutiful task that assists the progressing or the supporting of God's Harmony or Nature's Harmony for the Non-Believer.

It should also be further understood that this is the reason why the Soul, which personally rests within all people, has been given this "Freedom of Choice". For certainly, it should also be known that it is only people that are enabled to perform an act that aids and supports the creations developing Harmony, this being that reality which can only exist within the creations developing "Present Time". Still, it should be further understood, that this same act, if preformed under different conditions, could destroy the emerging unity – hence the reason why only the "Soul" has been given the "Freedom of Choice". Therefore, this "Freedom of Choice" reality means that the Soul is enabled to do the duty that rests upon it, which is to aid the on-going harmony of the ever-developing and ever-growing Creation! But a question does now remain? This question being how do you, has a person, remain obedient to this task that God or Nature for the non-believer, has created for you to do? How do you, in reality, actually enable your personal Soul to achieve the doing that is required to support the developing of only God's world or the world of Nature's for the non-believer? Therefore, if you actually require a knowing answer to the question of how can you support this "Harmony" that is constantly emerging all around you? – Then Read on.

So now the first "important" suggestion, which is based upon many years of "scientific" and practical analysis of pursuing the only truth that rests within us and which is linked with that which is all around us, is to understand just what task is needed to support the events occurring in the "Present Time" and which task not to support in the "Present Time"! This advice being especially useful when you notice that you are "thinking" what action to do or "thinking" what action not to do! Or maybe enjoying the act of simply NOT "thinking", but actually "knowing", this being without any thought, just what supporting action to do and what supporting action NOT to do! For certainly, it is now good to know that these caring "unthinking" but needed actions can be easily pursued towards finalisation by the all knowing Soul, which is the real, you! For the Soul does not think but always knows exactly what action is needed to be performed to support the harmony that is emerging or should be emerging around the observer.
This certainty being because the Soul is actually in unity with everything that exists in the world around you just has it is with the world that is within you – but only in the "Present Time"!

For is it not true that what you habitually think is really coming from you', are those words or pictures that are filling your mind? For undeniably it should now be known that this reality is NOT true! For undeniably, if you hear in the mind words saying what to do or what not to do, they will be words that are really being sounded by your animalistic five senses and so they are not words that are coming from the real YOU – for you are the Soul, this being that which silently observes everything that is attached to the "Present"! Meaning that it is your Soul that silently tastes, sees, touches, smells – everything! For you cannot be what you taste, smell, touch, see or listen too! For you are that which all these senses are reporting too! Is this not true?

For certainly, you will become aware of this fact when you realise that they can be experienced to be arguing amongst themselves, for without doubt they are constantly seeking their own personal "I Want"! For is it not a known truth that the silent mind knows exactly what action is needed to be accomplished – this being because it can exist only in the "Present Time"! For certainly again, is it not correct to know that these five senses are NOT the real you! This being because they are actually being needed by your animalistic body! For again is should be said that the real you is your "Soul" this being that which witnesses "everything"! For is it not true that the Soul can only be that reality which observes these words that you are sounding within your mind? This being the sounds and pictures that are now known to be sounded by your bodies animalistic five senses! These being pictures and sounds that are now being allowed to be freely released into the mind because YOU have "historically" and "habitually" chosen that this is what should be allowed to enter the mind – probably in childhood.

But certainly, it should now be Realized that these five senses are not the real you! For they are really your Godly gifted or gifted by Nature for the non-believer, five animalistic senses! These being that which the real you, which is your Soul, is continually observing to be sounding into your mind their animalistic "I Want"! For certainly you should now be aware that this mind blocking chatter is that animalism which is constantly sounding a verbal "I Want" into your mind, therefore and always it should be Realized that this sound is made by one or all of your animalistic five senses. For without doubt, it is this fact which blocks the Soul from seeing through your mind the true reality and needs of the worlds "Present Time", this being that which we call "The Creation". For indeed, it should now be silently understood that these five senses where childhood "freed" to pursue their own animalistic "I Want", and so habitually you now think that these five animalistic senses are the real you! They are not you! For you is the Soul, which is that silently observing reality that is always aware of the "I Want" chatter which is being sounded by one or all or your "animalistic" five senses! Therefore, it is now good to realise that these sounds that you are listening to in your mind cannot be you, for you are the listener!

Therefore, is it not "scientifically" true that that which you are listening too cannot be you for you are the listener! Also, and again it should be said, that that which you are listening to, or touching, seeing, smelling, or tasting is actually a report which is arising from one of your animalistic five senses! This certainty being because your uncontrolled five senses can be likened to five and also very active young pups, this also being a reality in which you believe they are the real "You"! As a result and for that reason, and because of this mistake, the five senses are "allowed" to be in a controlling contact with the "Present Time". This certainly being that world in which they bodily pursue their constantly sounding "I Want" animalistic demands, these being that sound which is constantly filling the mind! It is therefore and certainly because of this animalistic mind filling fact, that a person's Soul cannot see or influence the targeting unity of the "Present" and so certainly the all knowing unity of the Soul is not influencing that which is happening in a "Present Time", this being that which is usually controlled by one or all of a person's the animalistic five senses.

Also it should be truly known that this is because these animalistic five senses do constantly argue in the mind. These being mind filling words which are constantly clouding the mind regarding their own "personally" desired animalistic "I Want". For truly it should be Realized that these animalistic five senses are not the entities that have been chosen to create or support the developing goodness resting in God's Harmony or Natures Harmony for the non-believer, this certainly being the need to support the emerging creation, this being that which is constantly and obediently endeavouring to develop all around them. For certainly, it should be known that the five senses are definitely "animalistic" in nature and so they fight and argue over what should be to touched, tasted, smelt, heard or seen; thus pursuing their own animalistic "I Want" claim regarding any reality that exists within the Creation. This animalistic claim also being that which constantly targets the obtaining of their own personal "I Want", this being that pursuing target which does constantly create their actions. Indeed, this is that animalistic "I Want" for me reality which does knowingly and physically plus falsely actually motivates their actions within their ever-pursuing, ever claiming "I Want" life! These being "I Want" claims which is for everything that exists within the world around them.

Therefore the target of a person's life is to stop these animalistic "Five-Senses" from constantly claiming their "I Want" for ME, this being that reality which is continually sounding in the mind and it should be know that this is not an easy task to achieve? This being because you actually and really "think" that these animalistic five senses are the real you, but now you know that they are NOT you, for you are the observer of this reality. For certainly, you should now know that this "animalistic" thinking that you are the five senses, will always bring confusion and misery to you and also to all those who are around you! This reality being because your animalistic five senses will and do always endeavour, to claim for themselves all that exists within the Creation that is resting all around them. But the truth of your currently existing life, this being that truth which our wise ancients spoke about those thousands of years ago, is that you can, by sounding a mantra into the mind, will actually "experience" the oneness of the creation which exists all around just has it exists within you! For you and the harmonious creation become has one, with the non-thinking "Present Time"!

For certainly, it is then that your true "Self", which is your observing Soul, becomes has one with the creations emerging harmony and so you certainly become aware or realise just which supporting action is needed in order to support this harmonious reality that is existing and emerging all around you! This certainly being you're Souls supporting activity which is again stated to be that reality which is actually needed to support the still but emerging world which is growing all around you. This being the taking sides with an activity which supports the need to be has one with all that is around you just has it is within you! For certainly, it is the supporting of this factual truth which can occur only in the "Present", which certainly achieves that experience which all our wise ancients call "Enlightenment".

For certainly, this is an "Enlightening" reality which silently brings together in unification the sense of touch, taste, smell, hearing and seeing, and so we actually become "Self-Aware", meaning that we experience that we are has one with the unity of the creation that exists all around us, just has it experienced to exists in unity within us! Also this is anciently known to be a "Self-Awareness" in which we knowingly observe that we are has one with the creation that exists all around us just has it exists within us! For certainly it is also known by our wise ancients, that this "Self-Aware" experience can actually lead to that which our wise ancients called "Self-Realisation"! This being a realisation in which you actually become has one with the creation and that there is no "observer", which of course is the targeted purpose of all life and all non-life, but more about this later in "Life's Purpose"!

So yes! It should always be understood that disciplining and stopping of the animalistic five senses, this being from freely and animalistic-ally sounding their "I Want" into the mind, is the target of ALL our world's religions and philosophies. Thus praying and hymn singing is a religious pursuit which replaces the "I Want" animalistic thinking process which was innocently allowed in childhood when a person actually began to think that these animalistic five senses was really them! They are not you! For you cannot be that which you observe or experience for you are the observer and the experiencer! - But now, when you silently experience being "Self-Aware", you will certainly understand that that which is sounding in your mind is not you – for you are the observer and the listener of that creation which is all around you has it is within you! For is it not also true that your five senses are really just animalistic instruments that are personally for your use?

So yes! This "Self-Aware" experience is an experience which our ancients called "Enlightenment"! This being when you're inner Soul can knowingly and silently observe, through your still mind, the reality of that world which exists outside your body, thus experiencing an awareness which can only be experienced by you when your mind is without thought. This simply means that you become "aware" that your body is actually has one with the creation that is all around you just has it exists within you! Therefore, you actually experience that you are a unified part of the creation that is in existence all around you just has it does knowingly existing within you!

For certainly it is a known religious and philosophical truth that you first experience becoming "Self-Aware" that you are has one with the creation which is all around you just has it is within you! This "Self-Aware" condition is certainly being an "awareness" which the first step towards becoming "Self-Realized"! For this is an experience in which you actually become has one reality with "Present Time", this being that which is Gods world or the world of Nature for the Non-Believer! For certainly again, this is the purpose of a creation in which God targets his desire to experience "Himself" – but more about this later in "Life's Purpose"!

Therefore this constant religious and philosophically world seeking target is to become "Self-Aware" of or to actually "Self-Realise" that condition which our ancients called "Enlightenment"! For certainly it should now be known that "Enlightenment" is the actual aim which all our world's religions and philosophies do actually target. This target being because our wise ancients knew that it is "scientifically" possible for a person to become has one with their real "Self" and so exist has one with that which is all around them, just has it is within them! For certainly our wise ancients knew that in the actual experiencing of that unified reality which was resting within this truth, a person would "automatically" do all that they could do to support that which had birthed this unity! This activity usually being to support the developing and ongoing "Harmony" which was being observed or actually being experienced to be emerging from all that, which was around them, just has it existed in unity within them! Therefore, and certainly, they would personally aim to avoid the painful misery that comes when people actually endeavour to claim the creation for "themselves" and therefore create an "I Want" that is negatively against the creations unifying target.

Now, who can say that this endeavour is wrong? Also who can say that only supporting your own personal "I Want" or the pursuing of a racially based "I Want" is the correct truth? But if you actually "think" that this particular search for achieving personal "Enlightenment" is an incorrect and wrong concept – then read on! For "Life's Purpose" will prove "scientifically", that ALL our world's religions and philosophies, these being that which pursue "Enlightenment", have actually been created by very unselfish people!

For certainly our ancient wise did actually live within this unified reality for did they not explain this truth which naturally rests within us? This truth being of our unity with the "Present" which is all around us just has it is within us! This "Present" being that reality which only people can actively support, for they know that they are supporting their own body! These being supports that are of course not only for their loved ones and/or for their own communities', but also to "non-interferingly" accept all other differently developing cultures, these being cultures which are based upon another language, cultures and economics! This certainly being a non-interfering way of life which does peacefully accept all other culturally developing religions and cultures in which an expanding world constantly introduces to them – but only if it is possible to do so.

For truly is not the creation the ever-developing ever growing world of nature? This being that which is constantly showing us that there is a static but also an ever on-going development of the Creations or Nature's evolving plan. This being an ever developing plan which is based upon Natures growing harmony, this being that world which exists all around us and which is also enjoined in the totality of that world of harmony which exists within us! Of course there are cultural shocks to this ever developing harmony, especially when the Earth stretches it muscles etc.

So yes! This static but ever-moving naturally developing on-growing world, is a reality which truly exists around all people, just has it exists within all people! For certainly, this ever-growing development is indeed an ever-ongoing evolution that is based upon the reality of an absolute truth! This being a truth that ensures that all-life and all non-life, which is the totality of that world which exists all around us has it does within us, is to be "Naturally" akin to the "unselfish" developing Harmony that exists within our own bodies! For can it not be said that our own individual body is a single unified entity which contains trillions of separately developing and also very skilled individuals? For is it not also true, that these individuals do truly live according to the unifying law that is required for a compatible whole to meaningfully exist? This being that holistic fact which people should naturally copy within the world that is also all around them! For is it not true that this is the natural reason has to why we, has people, have been created to dutifully serve the ever growing creation and is this not the reason has to why we have been given the "Freedom of Choice"?

Thus indeed, is it not true that the Creation or Nature for the Non-Believer is always and constantly pursuing an evolutionary plan that is based upon a harmony that can be easily seen by those who have eyes to see and also ears to hear? Also is not also true that it is only people who have the ability to see the existing creations truth? This unifying truth being that truth which does growingly exists within our ever developing "Present"? This "Present" being a truth which has Godly or Nature-ally" been born to also grow upon our unified Earth? For is it not true that this growing Harmony also inhabits our ever developing world? This being that world which does personally and unifying exists all around us, just has it exists has the life that rests within us! For is it not also true that we can actually become "Self-Aware" of this singularity or even truly "Self-Realise" that this unified energy, that we call Harmony, exists not only within us but also in unification with everything that exists around us! Indeed, is not the Creation, this being that which is growing within and around our Soul, not able to first produce a recognisable "awareness" to this unity, this being to the observer with a silently clear and un-blocked mind! This being that "Self-Awareness" in which a person may eventfully experience that blissful reality which our ancients called "Self-Realisation", this being that reality in which they become the unified totality of the creation and so they are no longer an observer!

Therefore, it is now wise to currently understand that this religious or philosophical for the non-believer known experience, is an "evolutionary" realisation that that which exists outside our bodies is has one with that reality which exists within our bodies? This being that condition or realisation, in which there is no observer – which fully explains the words of Jesus of the Christian faith when He said, "Father, forgive them; for they do not know what they are doing", this being when is animalistic torturers cast lots to steal his clothing for themselves. For is it not true that all around us we can actually see this unchanging law of a naturally developing harmony? This harmony being that which exists within and also between all things, this being that harmony which is endeavouring to emerge within our creation! For certainly, can it not noticed that when this Godly or Naturally growing "harmony" is broken, has in an earthquake or a flood of water, or even a war between surplus sons who become "I Want" people, but wars do make this to be only a passing situation! For nature or the support of nature, cannot be destroyed except temporarily by our "I Want" unwise?

For certainly does not all our world's ancient and modern histories actually prove this reality to be true? For example such a truth can be seen in the many changes that have occurred in the worlds north of our Northern Hemisphere and also recently within the former USSR? For now we see within this former "Soviet Union" area, that people with different languages are now enabled to return to their own governing? This self-governing of a countries language is now existing within the ancient borders of that which contained the people of that language. But is it not also known that a second "Financial" language is struggling to unite all of these newly developing self-governing countries? This being into one unified acceptance of laws that will govern trade and also all communications – and woe be to any country that tries to stop this cultural development! For those who try to stop this "monetary" unification will be quickly challenged and then changed if need be, for this developing search for the "legal" unification of all these different language speaking countries cannot be stopped. For again and knowingly, a more direct way to assist this joining of like-minded but different language speaking countries, is for those who are unsure of such developing singularity, should "Scientifically" and "Factually" acknowledge that only the majority of people have the ability to "create" a good (GOD) world, this being a reality in which a person experiences a unified world which is accepted by at least 65% of that country's population. For is it not true that there should be a moral acceptance of a majority-based community decision? This being a majority decision that would show a way forward that would prove the acceptance of any unifying non-aggressive activity that does knowingly benefit the majority of people, this being in that world that culturally existed all around them, just has it does within them. For without doubt, should not the way forward be a majority decided development and not an "I Want" dictatorship or a financially gaining "I Want for ME" one?

For certainly this cultural togetherness in which the majority of people do govern has one, is certainly an informal development which targets and so pursues the needs of the majority of a countries population? Also is it not true that this growing reality of a coming togetherness is always continuously and naturally evolving throughout our world? The reason for this is, has "Life's Purpose" reminds, that there is only one Soul, this being that which silently observes the creation, but only through the empty mind of the person within whom it silently rests - in the "Present" time! But agreed it is also sadly known that sometimes and mistakenly, some governments are still not targeting the desires of the majority of people within that country! But certainly, what is now "modernly" taking place is the reality that a countries people are now enabled to communicate with the majority of another countries people – this being a unifying activity that "Life's Purpose" says, is the natural work of the Soul?

Therefore, is it not true many harmony seeking actions can be sparked into a beginning by a single individual, this sparking being by the words of an individual who is attached to a certain group or a part of a religion or political party that exists within the culture of another country? For certainly, you have to "culturally" acknowledge that any Harmony seeking activity can only happen in the "Present" time? For truthfully is this not a simple fact which all a countries people do readily accept? These being simple facts in which an individual that is living within a different country can perform a unifying act which than creates a majority deciding way of life! These being "individuals" who calmly attempt to change the racially based cultures that govern certain countries and also programs them to join with the communicating life that exists outside their tribal borders.

So yes! The only endeavour for all our worlds' people is to establish within the majority of that countries people a God's harmony or a Natures harmony for the Non-believer! This being that reality which actually and constantly governs the world that is all around us and also with that world which exists within us! It is also undoubtedly true that the correct way to understand this natural way of life is to simply support the natural laws that control the "Present Time", which is Godly or Nature controlled for the Non-Believer! For this certainty is the inevitable reality which all our world's major religions and philosophies do target and also preach about! This being our world's growing and ongoing development to which various religions of our world have given many names! For certainly, all religions and philosophies do actually show the way of how to experience "God's Grace", which of course is the experiencing of "Enlightenment"! For certainly, when disciplinary praying or worshipping, the doer can experience "Enlightenment"! This actually being a very personal and individually experiencing of an awareness or a realisation of a condition in which the "obedient" and also the "habitually" disciplined follower, would eventually first experience an awareness which could eventually lead to the experiencing of the realization that they are has one with God's world or the world of Nature for the Non-Believer.

So yes! What actually is "Enlightenment?" This being that target which ALL our worlds' religions and philosophies do target! For certainly it should first be known that when we experience "Self-Awareness" and/or "Self-Realization", we become aware or realize that they are certainly conditions which cannot be normally explained. For it is an experience which may be described has a "blissful" unthinking but also has an all knowing state in which people can genuinely experience the reality of Gods world or the world of Nature for the non-believer. This being awareness or that realization which occurs when one or all of our five senses are stopped from constantly sounding their "I Want for ME" into the mind.

For certainly, it should now be known that this is the only targeted purpose of all our world's "religiously" imposed praying and chanting, for it is this concentration which actually stops the mind-blocking "I Want for ME" animalistic thoughts from taking place, these again being stated are that which is being sounded into the mind by one or all of our animalistic five senses. This now being known to be that truth which stops the Soul from observing through a clear mind the creation that actually exists all around the it – has it does within it! For certainly, actually praying and also an imposed chanting within the mind, does disciplinary replace the "I Want" verbiage which is constantly coming from one or all of your five senses, this being their animalistic "I Want" which is blocking the mind with their past and future "I Want" thoughts! For again it should be said that this mind filling "I Want", this being that which is filling the mind, is coming from one or all of your animalistic five senses. This being a realty which brings a condition that actually blocks the Souls view of the outside world and therefore stops the Soul from seeing the needs of that which exists in the singularity of the "Present Time". For is it not true that "Self" disciplined worshipping via a religious or philosophically imposed praying, does create an unthinking empty mind within the automatically in-canting and disciplined prayer?

This being a praying activity which disciplinary silences the habitual "I Want" that is usually being sounded into the mind by one or all of the five animalistic senses. For it is then, within such a mind silent condition, that a non-thinking "awareness" of the "Present Time" can be fully and unthinkingly experienced to exist! For certainly it is only within the silence that occurs within an empty mind, that the Soul can see and also "experience" 100% of that reality which exists in the "Present Time"! This certainly being a "Self-Aware" enlightening experience which can only occur without any mind-filling "I Want" thoughts that are usually emanating from one or from all of the animalistic five senses!

Therefore, it is truly a "scientific" fact that "Nothing" i.e.; "No Thing", except that reality which can only exist in the "Present Time", can be experienced by the true observer – which is your Soul! For certainly, is not this truth based upon a personal awareness or a reality which can only happen when a person's mind is actually empty and so filled with "Nothing"? This being non-thinking ever-silent condition which does actually allow a person's soul to obtain a clear view, through the empty mind, of that reality which we call the "Present"! So does this not mean that only a person who has an empty mind can actually "experience" that world which we call the "Present"?

Is this not also a historically well-known ancient truth? Is this not a truth? This being a truth which states that all people can be "religiously" self-aware and so Self-Realize that their being aware of the "stillness" of all that exists is a reality which can only be experienced within the "Present-Time"? This being that "Present" which can only exist has God's world or exist has the world of Nature for the Non-Believer? For certainly, is it not true, that the "Present-Time" is an existence which is truly the factual real-world? Also is it not true that it is the only world that can exist in the "Present Time"? For certainly, it is a "Present" that is for all life and also all non-life! Also, is it not true that this is a "Present" which cannot exist in the future or exist in the past, for these times do not exist and never will exist?

So Yes! The "Present Time" must "scientifically" be the only existence which has been given to us by God or been given to us by Nature for the Non-Believer. For indeed, if your understanding is that "All the creation is Nature's Creation" is a more true way of thinking than "All the creation is God's Creation", then factually both "thinkers" will still acknowledge that

"Nature" or the "Creation" will grow only according to a pre-planned development, this being a planned development that cannot be stopped.

Therefore is not true that we should actually and always keep in mind, when reading "Life's Purpose'" and its scientific revelations, that it is only the "Present Time" that exists! For is it not true that it is only the "Present" that a person can be aware of and so actually realise the honour of this Godly gift or a gift from Nature for the Non-Believer! Also, is it not true that "Time" does actually measure the on-going planned development of God's target or the planned target of Nature's Harmony for the non-believer? This being a target which is explained later in Life's Purpose! For that reason can it not now be seen to be true that that harmony, which can exist only in the "Present Time", is there has a life supporting benefit? This benefit being that realism which also exists in the world that is all around people just has it does harmoniously exist within all people! This therefore being the creation of a natural and harmonious world in which there exists in unity not only people but also all known life and also all Non-Life? What's more is it not a well known truth that the only known realities that can destroy this existing and ongoing Harmony, this being that truth which is supporting everything within the creation - is people!

So certainly, does not this "scientific" fact also prove the truth that it can only be people who have the ability to "choose" how to live or how to die, this being within the support that they receive inside this "Present", this being a "Present" which we call "The Creation". Therefore, is it not factually true that this could be the reason why it is only people who have that gift which we call "The Freedom of Choice"! Therefore and truly, is it not a religiously known fact that we should endeavour to support Nature's growing changes, these being changes that we can only support within the "Present"? Also, is this support not a true way in which we can experience God's world or of Natures world for the non-believer? This being a Godly, or Nature gifted awareness for the non-believer, which has been given only to people so that they can be aware of or realise the needed support for that Harmony that is unfolding in the "Present Time"! For certainly is it not a positive truth that it is only people who can genuinely help support the creations or natures for the non-believer, future developments?

But sadly, is it not also a well known negative truth, this being a truth which can be easily identified, that many people's *"I Want for Me"* activities did and still do selfishly change the way of and also the supporting needs of the developing creation, this being that world which in unification exists all around them just has it does within them! For is it not correct that our world's history can actually prove that they were "scientifically" wrong to, in ignorance, break this unification? For certainly now is the time for people to "scientifically" sit still and take note of these oft destroying facts! For "spiritually", which is a word that the Non-Believer also understands, does state a well-known fact! This fact being that it is only people who are the life force that has been given the gift called "The Freedom of choice"! This also being a reality in which they can choose death if this is the chosen action, sadly this being a well-known fact, has in acts of war.

So yes! Indeed, this "Freedom of Choice" is certainly a gift that has been Godly given or Nature given for the non-believer. Therefore, is it not also a known truth that it is only people who can support or not support all the lives that exists within the developing laws of the creations Harmony? This being a harmony which does naturally evolve within the changing laws of nature or which may be a harmony that is endeavouring to evolve within racial Harmony, this being a harmony that can often be in conflict.

For indeed, the first endeavour, for every person, is to actually become "Self-Aware", meaning that they experience, without added thoughts, that they are a part of that creation which exists all around them, just has it exists within them! This being an awareness which can eventually lead to an experience which is called "Self-Realisation"! This experience being when there is no observer for they actually "Realise" that they actually are the whole of that which we call "The Creation"! For certainly, this is also the experience which our ancient wise called "Enlightenment" and which is known to be a "Realization" that can only be attained by "Personal Choice". For certainly it is via this "Freedom of Choice", that a person can actually support, without thought, the developing needs of the creations evolving "Harmony", this being that which is all around them just has it is within them! For certainly, the purpose the life, this being that which rests within all living people, is to actually support that evolving unity which can only develop in that truth which we call the "Present", this being that unified reality to which all life and also all non-life is has only one life.

For is it not true that this unification is that reality which has been constantly stated by our ancient and also our modern wise, i.e.: "I am that I am"! This "I am" being the true "Self" that all people call the "Present", this being that "Present" which exists all around them has well has it exists in unity within them! For is it not true that all people have been given the "Freedom of Choice"? This reality meaning that any person, via their God given or Nature give for the non-believer "Freedom of Choice"; can actually choose not to accept the reality of the emerging "Present Time", but to attack the positively emerging "Present" by negatively inflicting a personal "I Want" for ME – this being against the positive development of this on-going creation.

For is it not true that such an endeavour to gain a personal "I Want" for ME is a sure way to create that troubled world that we call Hell! This being a truth which actually signifies that the attackers animalistic "I Want" can only exist within their own mind. This being a mind in which the Soul cannot see the "Present", this being because it is blocked by past or future "I Want" animalistic thoughts, these being thoughts that are coming from one or more of the animalistic five senses. This being that reality which brings the thinker to live in that place we call "Hell". So, the new question which should be asked now is: *"What performing activity is needed to bring to the observer, the rewards that are stated to be experienced has contentment and bliss?"* This being a question that is usually coming from a person who is living a life which is NOT bringing to them the happiness that is based upon peace, contentment and bliss? For certainly it is an interesting question, for is it not true that an observing answer to this question must be - *"Which person is living in "Heaven" while on this Earth and which person is living in "Hell" whilst upon this Earth?"* For what must be further understood is that the Creations developing Harmony or Nature's developing Harmony for the Non-Believer, is continually seeking and pursuing an enlivening and an on-going harmony which cannot be changed - for it has only one purpose and this purpose is to achieve that God given or Nature give for the non-believer, the target of sustained unity!

Therefore, it should be carefully accepted that it is only within the "Present" that people can endeavour to pursue their need to become has one with the creation, this being a unity in which only people can realise that they are has one "Present"! This being the only target of all religions and philosophies' and which is a target which can be "scientifically" recognized as being has one with an ever still and an ever moving creation – which knows where it is and also where it is going! For this is a unified creation which actually exists all around us just has it does within us and which is actually a creation which is an on-going ever still and ever moving reality, this being that fact which cannot be denied?

For certainly, is it not also true that we has people, can actually recognize that the on-going ever-still and ever-developing "Creation" is actually an exciting and incomplete searching "Present" which is an ever moving ever still development? Therefore, is it not also true that this unified ever-growing "Creation" is actually an on-going "Present Time" force that actually and often peacefully corrects un-wise people's "I Want" thinking! This foolishness being that which often creates "I want what you have" wars! Yet is it not also true that goodness can also emerge which is a "Godness" that actually seeks a peace-keeping pursuit which will constantly bring people repeatedly back to the path of Harmony? Is it not also true that this search for Harmony is an agreed right for all life just has it is for all Non-Life? This truth being that which is recognised to be a reality which is all around them just has it exists within them! So is it not therefore useful to publically look around our world and understand just what it is that is breaking these developing natural laws that are always seeking a peaceful Harmony?

So yes! By such "scientific" understanding, does not the Creation or Nature for the Non-Believer, always actively target a continuation of its ongoing harmonious "Present", this being that unity which usually exists within all the environmental locations in which people are enabled to contentedly exist? For is it not "scientifically" accepted that there is no need to find how people can exist in a non-harmonic reality, this being in those environments where people cannot exist? For is it not clearly accepted that people cannot change God's laws or Nature's laws for the non-believer, these being those natural laws which always and unsurprisingly do pursue Harmony? Yet! Is it not also strangely true, that many people think that they can copy the creating ways of God or the creating ways of Nature for the Non-Believer? Hence many a stable countries massive population expansions, this being that which can only lead to surplus sons fighting wars for land, these being the disputes that regularly occur within the creation or within Nature for the non-believer! These wars' usually being between people with different languages and cultures has surplus sons seek food growing lands which can feed them and their developing families. For is it not true that the tribes of countries which are isolated by language, do actively follow their chosen leaders "I Want" more for ME and my tribe!

So yes! Is it not also true that these simple "I Want" for me and also my family, are early disputes which do not always start between countries or communities, but first occur within individuals and also within existing families? For does not our world's history always show that this state of unrest within expanding families always grows and therefore constantly shows this truth? Is it not also a confirmed truth that the most disastrous breaks in Harmony that do occur upon our planet are imposed by surplus children's personal "I Want"? For is it not true that this growing "I Want land" pressure which came from surplus sons did force tribal leaders into wars for more land? For it is under such conditions that an "I Want" your land for my expanding tribe did become a needed reality which changed older established laws which did previously did contentedly control their tribe? For is it not still a known truth that when the father dies the older son becomes the new owner and all surplus sons and their families have nothing! For usually only one family can live in that which their father owned or traded in. For certainly, such younger sons would need a future which will take care of them and their families – which means land is required and is it not the expected work of the tribal leader to fulfil all tribal needs.

So yes! Eventually in time, such strong needs especially upon the death of fathers would become "I Want land", this being that strong need which is coming from difficult to feed surplus sons and their families, especially pending families! For certainly, this "I Want" is a growing need which does actually create wars for certainly these are wars which target the control of new land for these surplus sons. For is it not true, has history shows that all such "leaders", these being those leaders who do pursue an "I Want" land war, are always supported, unto death, by their tribe. Also is it not sadly true that many leaders did agree to a pillaging war just to remove these surplus sons. For certainly, cannot it now be modernly witnessed that in the "East of our worlds North of the Northern Hemisphere", which was controlled by the USSR, that the control of all foreign speaking countries has just been returned to that country's pre-existing language borders? This meaning that they are again being governed by the will of the majority of people who speak that countries language?

For is it not true that this economic collapse of the governing USSR was caused by a controlling government which pursued a financial policy which banned profit! This being because the "Russian Government" understood that adding profit to a market value was actually a greed based concept that increased the market price of goods, these being that which people needed in order to live! This being a reality so that the owners of companies could make more profit for their own personal use – this ideology of making profit was banned by the USSR government! The reason for this being that this surplus to costs, this being that which is called "profit", was seen to be a greed-based capitalist "I Want" which would increase market prices for the people of a country – which of course is not true. For certainly, it was this concept of not making a profit that actually caused the collapse of the Soviet Union, for it was also applied to wages which were not attached to the work achieved but to the time spent working. Simply put, this meant that a worker could produce only 15% of what they were actually capable of producing and still receive full wages. This certainly being that truth which caused a serious deficit in the required market needs of people who had plenty of money and which then led to the collapse of a Soviet Union!

But is it not also recognized that God, or Nature for the non-believer, does contain a constant search that seems too based upon the love of unity, has if the creation is actually one body! For is it not also true that this constant searching for a togetherness in unity, does always return control of a country to the people who speak the original language of that country? For indeed, can it not also be said that invading foreign leaders are not only the perpetrators of disharmony and the breaking of unity within their own tribe, but also the tribe that they attack, this being in their desire to greedily achieve their own "I Want" for ME! Therefore, the factual question now is, what regenerates i.e.: recovers, the Harmony within these oppressed foreign countries and where does this energy come from that manifests and brings forth these harmony seeking corrections? For certainly, does not our worlds history show that we, this we meaning the people of our world, always "culturally" target a "harmonious" existence? This being that which is allowed to continuously grow all around us, just has it does within us!

So yes! It certainly must now be understood, that at this early stage of these writings within ""Life's Purpose", that "Believers" and "Non-Believers" will find it most useful to be aware of just what is that reality which does factually and constantly rest within the Creation or within Nature for the Non-Believer? For indeed does not our history show that there knowingly exists, within this creation, an entity or a law that always seeks to develop a "Harmony" within that reality which exist within all people! For is it not also true, that that harmony, this being that which is resting within the creation or within Nature for the non-believer, can always be identified has a God based or Nature-based harmony? Is it not also true that this search for harmony ALWAYS corrects the breaking of a peaceful and contented harmony and this reality is always that which only people can achieve?

Indeed, is it not true that there is a Godly given, or Nature given for the non-believer, an existing "Harmony" within the creation? This being that which is all around us has well has it is within us? This also being a growing reality that is continually re-adjusting itself in order to re-balance the harmony of a Creation which actually exists in and also all around us! Is this not also an existing reality which actually contains some people who strangely use the "Freedom of Choice" in an endeavour to steal this

Harmony for themselves by saying, *"I am better and stronger than you, and this harmony which is all around us I know is only to serve me and not you, because I know that I am stronger than you!"* But does not our history show that many of our ancient wise did constantly endeavour to remove from people this inflicting animalistic "I Want" for ME desire, this being within the regions in which they live?

For certainly our wise ancients, who were those Godly people who created our entire world's religions and philosophies, did bring to their followers and non-followers, awareness or a realization that God's Harmony actually existed for all of life and also for the unity of all of Non-Life.This actuality being the experiencing of a "Self-Awareness" in which you actually become "aware" that you are an integral enjoined unified part of all things within the creation, this being that which is all around you, just has it is within you! For certainly, our wise ancients knew that this was an experience which could also lead to a "Self-Realization" experience in which you actually did become everything"! But more about how to achieve this awareness and/or realisation later in "Life's Purpose"! For indeed it is certainly true that our wise ancients gave to their listeners a way to achieve these experiences which cannot be seen but which can be recognised and so named by that reality which in our modern times is called "Enlightenment"!

This anciently named "Self-Awareness" or Self-Realisation" is a known experience that actually occurs when people first become aware that they are has one with the creation that they are observing and experiencing which can lead to the realisation that they are the Creation and that there is no observer. It is then that they truly exist and so realise that they have actually become Gods world or the world of Nature for the Non-Believer.

So yes! This first step towards "Self-Realization" is known to be the experiencing of a "Self-Aware" reality! This simply meaning that you become "aware" of only the "Present Time" and so experience that you are without thoughts and so you experience yourself to be has one with the creation that is exiting all around, you just has you know that you are has one with that creation which is within you! Thus it should also be known that the experiencing of "Self-Awareness" is described in the Christian religion to be to the experiencing of ***"The Peace that surpasses all Understanding"***! Or being religiously described by Christians has being unified has one with the "Holy Spirit" or the "Holy Ghost", which is the name that is used by Christian worshippers who are mainly distributed has Catholics 50%, Protestants 37%, Eastern Orthodox 9.4%, Oriental Orthodox 2.5%, Others 1.1%.

What is further known is that Christians state and believes that there's only one God, and that He created the heavens and the earth and also that this divine Godhead consists of three parts: The first being the father (God himself), the second being son (Jesus Christ) and the third being the Holy Spirit whose seven supporting gifts to followers are wisdom, understanding, counsel, fortitude, knowledge, piety, and fear of breaking the laws of God, or of nature for the non-believer. This certainly being that energy which works in support of the faithful! It is also known that this mainly worshipping of Jesus is divided between an Eastern and Western theology and within these two beliefs there are six branches called Catholicism, Protestantism, Eastern Orthodoxy, Anglicanism, Oriental Orthodoxy, Assyrians and Restorations, which is sometimes considered to be the seventh branch?

Yet, sincerely, "Life's Purpose" acknowledges that this experience of the *"Peace that surpasses all Understanding"* is actually an experience which "Life's Purpose" calls and many others call "Enlightenment"! This being an experience which "Life's Purpose" describes has being a state in which the experiencer of "Enlightenment" would find that within this "Enlightenment" they would actually become "Aware" that they were has one entity with the "Present Time" and that, in truth, everything that existed was really "THEM"! Thus meaning that they experienced themselves to be has one entity with that creation which was all round them just has it is within them! This "Self-Awareness" experience being because your mind, when you are just observing, would be empty and so it existed without any "I Want" mind filling concepts that would be constantly sounding within the mind from the animalistic five senses.

So Yes! What our wise ancients endeavoured to achieve, has all our entire world's religions and philosophies do endeavour to achieve for their listeners', was a silent and ever still mind. This being an aware reality in which no animalistic "I Want" could be heard to be sounding in the mind, this being that verbiage which would be coming from one or all of your animalistic five senses – which is NOT you for you are the "Soul" which is the observer and the listener to these sounds which are entering the mind. For knowingly, was it not the mind silent listening of our "wise ancients" that gave to our ancestors all our worlds culturally-based religions and philosophies! All of which are knowingly based upon a culturally worded belief system that was designed to lead a practicing follower to that experience called "Enlightenment"! This being that "enlightening" experience in which we become has one with the creation that exists all around us, just as we are has one with that creation which exists within us!

So yes! These ancient teachings, which still exist throughout our world, were all based upon known religious and philosophical tradition that constantly sought a "scientifically" based pursuit of a way to achieve "Enlightenment"! This being that "Self-Aware" experiencing of the singularity of the worlds harmony that existed within the creation that exits all around us just has it exists within us! This being a constantly searched for reality which sprang from the preaching words of our wise who did continually show to their followers just how to attain a mind empty reality which led to that unified stillness called "Enlightenment".

For indeed, this reality that we call of "Enlightenment", is a realisation that can only be experienced by those who "disciplinary" bring their mind into the stillness of the "Present", this being that which exists all around them just has it does within them! For certainly it is true that this "Self-Aware" experience cannot exist when a person's Soul cannot see through a mind which is blocked by many past or future selfishly created "I Want" thoughts that are being sounded by the animalistic five senses! This being that false world in which many people animalistic ally live for this is truly an "I WANT" for me world which is certainly animalistic in nature. For certainly, it is a non-existing false world which has undoubtedly been animalistic ally created by a personal "I Want"!

This truly being a scientific fact because the "Present Time" is the only real world and ever more shall be so! For certainly, the "Present Time" is a real world and it is not an imaginary world which is falsely being created by the machinations of an "I Want for ME" thought! This being that "I Want" for me thinking reality which is certainly a mind blocking verbiage which coming from the animalistic five senses! For certainly, is it not true, that these are "I Want" mind filling thoughts do always impose a animalistic "I Want" dream world upon the reality of the "Present Time"?

So yes! The experience of being has one with the creation, is called by our ancients "Enlightenment", which is that gift which only people can experience! It is also a factual reality that the experiencing of "Enlightenment" always ban's and so stops the mind filling request of the animalistic five senses from targeting their never ending "I Want". For certainly it can only be your God given or Nature given for the non-believer, "Freedom of Choice" that can support your transfer into the real world, this being that world which we call the "Present"! This being a "Present" in which you must via your gifted "Freedom of Choice", choose a way that will free your Soul to experience the world that it is in unity within you and all around you! For certainly this Self-Aware" or "Self-Realisation" experience, this being an awareness or a realisation that you are has one with the creation that is all around, you just has it is experienced to be within you! This can certainly be achieved by your "Freedom of Choice" for you can "choose" to stop the "I Want" animalistic activity that is filling and so clouding your mind which blocks the Soul from seeing through that which needs to be an empty mind! For certainly, it is this animalistic "I Want" that is that animalistic reality which creates a mind-filling "I Want" for "ME" animalistic world, a reality which is certainly filling the mind and so blocking the view of the real you – which is the Soul that rests within you!

For certainly, these animalistic ally based "I Want" mind filling and demand creating activities, can again and again destroy the pursuit of Harmony that should be naturally targeted by your friends, also your family, your community, your district, your region, and your country! This being that ongoing reality which achieves wars and it is a realty that is always created by the selfish "animalistic" claiming of an "I WANT" for ME! This being that reality which again should be said to be emanating from one or more our animalistic five senses! For certainly, this "I Want" for me is a way of life which creates an animalistic world which certainly births a world that is usually set against natures ongoing pursuit of harmony, this being that reality which is endeavouring to surround and also care for people.

For indeed, is it not also "scientifically" correct that many people who are chasing their "I Want" for me, are actually stealing or attempting to steal from Nature's ongoing Harmony – thus making them thieves or that which some religions call "Satanists" i.e.: worshippers of the devil. For has stated in the Christian religion and many other religions, it is the devil who rules "Hell", which is the negative of "Heaven", thus it is this reality which makes the devil the known opposite of God! For certainly the Devil does constantly tempt people to sin and so personifies the spirit of evil by his name- which is Satan. For certainly, it is religiously and positively known that God is the friendly all-powerful all-knowing creator of the universe and our God is worshipped as the only God for there can be no other!

Is it not also true that miss led people tend pursue their personal and animalistic "I Want", this being in order to gain something for their animalistic five senses! Is this truth not a reality because such people actually believe that these animalistic five senses are really them? For "scientifically" how can a person be that which they taste, smell, touch, see or listen too? Therefore, cannot this false "animalistic" pursuit be likened to the ignoring of the real world and so creates a world which is being aggravated and pursued by an animalistic "I Want", this being an "I Want" that is coming from one or more of the animalistic five-senses? Therefore, if it is sounded in the mind – it cannot be you – for the real you is the listener! Therefore, can it not be "Honestly" said and also "Scientifically" stated, that this happens because a person's animalistic ally created "I Want", is being sounded in mind by one or more of their animalistic five senses? Is this not true? For certainly, is it not important to remember that you cannot be that to which you listen too, or taste, smell or see and we should add touch? For is it not also true that you can actually touch the body that is carrying your Soul! Also is it not true that upon death those who are present at this event will say "He or She has gone!

So is it not true that a personally claimed "I Want" world is truly that world which is really being created by an animalistic "I Want"? This being an animalistic "I Want" which actually takes a person from the existing "Present" time" and into a non-existing future! This certainly being a future that is an imaginary world which really does not exist! For it is a non-existing "I Want" imaginary thought created world which is a world that "Life's Purpose" says takes you out of the "Present" and into a personally made Hell! Therefore, is it not good to know just what it is that creates this never ending "I Want" mind filling verbiage? This being an excessive personally created verbiage that keeps many people locked in a heavenly world that they have actually made into a real self-punishing "I Want" Hell?

This being a false world which is created to exist within such a self-punishing mind, for truly they live outside the Heaven that truly exists upon our Earth. This being that Godly produced heaven that can only exist within our "Present" time! For really should it not be said again and again that the "thinking" about ways to change the present, in order to create an "I Want only for ME" future, is truly an endeavour to create a false world? These being worlds that in reality are certainly NOT for people who do and can only exist within the "Present" Time! For who are YOU? Are you not the observing energy of the unified creation that exists within you and also all around you? For is it not true that upon seeing a person die, it is knowingly stated by all those present that they have "Gone" – meaning the energy has gone that rested within them – which of course is their Soul! Is it not also true that a woman who is awaiting the birth of a child that she is creating within her, will give a big "ooops" when the soul enters the child that she is carrying within her body, the question now being "Are these two facts not true?" YES or NO!

So yes! What actually is "Enlightenment"? This being that reality which was well described by the wise ancient that we called "Saint Paul"! For Saint Paul was an apostle in the Christian Bible and who actually experienced "Enlightenment" on his way to Damascus. His description about "Enlightenment", which was stated within the Christian bible, was regarding an experience that occurred to him on his journey to Damascus! This journey being to satisfy his personal "I Want" desire which was to persecute and harm Jesus and also to persecute the disciples of Jesus! But it is now well known that he actually became one of the most essential introducers of the teachings of Christianity, but this was after his encounter with Jesus who he met on this road to Damascus. For certainly prior to his meeting with Jesus, he was known to be a dedicated *"I Want my religious beliefs to be followed not yours"*, which created a desire within him to attack and harm Jesus and also His disciples. But it is historically revealed that on this road to Damascus and on his way to seek out and personally attack Jesus, he experienced that which is called "Enlightenment"! This being said to have happened when he actually began to attack Jesus but when Jesus touched him suddenly all thoughts and desirers to persecute and harm Jesus immediately stopped. He then turned and endeavoured to calm his aggressive followers by saying to them, *"Therefore, each of you must put off speaking falsehood and speak truthfully to your neighbour, for we are all members of the one body!"* This being that reality which is religiously called "Enlightenment" a condition in which you actually become one with the creation i.e.: The "Present Time" and there is no separate "Observer"

This being a complete reversal of St. Paul's previous idea which was to attack and harm Jesus for what he actually experienced, when he was touched by Jesus, was that reality which is called "Enlightenment"! This being an "Enlightening" experience which is known to be an experience in which you become has one with the creation that is not only within you but also that creation which also exists all around you. This actually being a known religious experience in which you actually become "Self-Aware" that you are an integral part of the creation which is all around you, just has it is experienced to be within you! Also it is an awareness that can lead to "Self-Realisation", this being a realisation in which you experience that you really are "Everything" that exists within the creations "Present Time". For certainly it is anciently known that this experience of being has one with the creation, is that reality which St Paul did truly experience when he actually met Jesus - on his way to Damascus.

What was therefore shown to St Paul, upon his road to Damascus, was that the cheating and punishing of others was actually the cheating and punishing of the true self, which is YOU! For in the experiencing of the final stage of "Enlightenment", which is called "Self-Realisation", you actually realise that you are everything that exists and that there is no observer! But what is also known, throughout our world's history, is that in your first movement towards "Enlightenment", you become "Self-Aware" that everything you observe is experienced to be "YOU" and so you cannot harm your-self -- which is "Everything"!

For you are certainly has one with everything that we call the Creation or the world of Nature for the Non-Believer! For certainly, within the experiencing of both "Enlightenments" IE: being "Self-aware" or being "Self-Realized", you do really experience the creations unity for become aware or do actually realise that everything that you experience is really "You" and that there is nothing that exists within the "Present" Time that is not YOU! These two experiences are certainly the target of ALL our worlds' religions and philosophies!

So yes! This "Self-Aware" or "Self-Realization", is the experience in which you become "Aware" that you are has one with all that exists within the "Present Time" or you "Realise" that you actually are the "Present Time" and there is no observer! For certainly, it is philosophically and religiously known that this "awareness" or "realisation" is anciently known to be a "physical" experience which is knowingly spoken about by ALL our wise ancients! For certainly, is not this "Self-Realization" or this "Self-Awareness" actually that condition which was written about in our entire world's religious and philosophical writings?

These actually being factual experiences which were being recognized and explained by our ancient ones many thousands of years ago! For certainly the target of "Life's Purpose" to actually use a 2020 language which will convincingly explain that the first experience of "Enlightenment" is actually Realized when a person becomes "Self-Aware" and so experience that they are "Everything"! Thus it is wise to state that you actually become "aware" that you are the observing Soul, this being that reality which experiences that everything you see, touch, hear, smell, or taste you do knowingly become aware that it is "You". For certainly you actually become aware that what you are experiencing is your true "self" – which is everything!

This being a "Self-Aware" experience in which you actually become "aware" that you are that which you hear, taste, smell, see, or touch and this is that awareness which "Life's Purpose" says can lead to "Self-Realization"! This being a well-known "religious" reality in which there is experienced the fact that there is no observer and which is certainly that reality which actually encompassed Jesus and also those many others who also created our world's religions and philosophies. For "Self-Realization" is an experience in which you actually realise that you are "Everything"! Therefore, you do not experience see, touch, hear, smell, or taste for you actually become the "The Creation", meaning that there is "No Observer".

For certainly, it is also a well known fact that in this experiencing of "Self-Realization", which is an experience that conclusively and blissfully engulfs the experiencer, it becomes Realized that there is only one living body and this is that which we call "The Creation"! Therefore and certainly it should again be said, that it is this "realization" which is targeted by all our world's religions and philosophies! For without doubt, it is an important fact that within this experiencing of "Self-Realization" it is Realized that there is no observer for the experiencing of your body falls away and your "Soul", this being that which is the real you, is Realized to be has one with God or with Nature for the non-believer! This being a reality which ensures that you are never born again, for God or Nature for the non-believer enjoys the birth of that Soul, which of course is the target and also the true purpose of the creation which is all around you just has it is unified within you! This being the sole purpose of the creation which is so God or Nature for the non-believer can experience their selves!

Now the ancient story of Gilgamesh certainly explains this target which exists for all people, and this is a story which was birthed nearly 4,500 years ago. For our History conversationally states that God told Gilgamesh to become "Holy", which means to become "whole", i.e., to become a self-Realized person! For indeed, this meant to silence his five senses and so increase his "vibrations" with the "Present Time" and therefore become on the same wavelength has his "Divine Being" and so be enabled to pass through the "gate" and so experience "Enlightenment"! And this quest was pursued 4,500 years ago. For indeed, is it not true that Religions and Philosophies are certainly not crutches to be used to support a person's desires to accomplish their "I Want for ME! For all our world's religions and philosophies' are actually educational systems which state that only people within our world have been actually gifted with a "God" given "Freedom of Choice", whose purpose "Life's Purpose" is constantly explaining!

So now dear reader, what is your choice? Is it to have controlling power over others or a controlling power over your "Self"! This choice being that which even God or Nature for the Non-Believer does not compel or do you freely "choose", via your Godly given or Nature given for the non-believer, "Freedom of Choice"? This choice this being to care for that world which is all around you just has you care for that which is within you? Thus reflecting how God or Nature for the Non-Believer does actually care and support "You". But it should also be known that the experiencing of being "Self-Aware" has described in "Life's Purpose" is that you are experiencing that you are everything that the experience of your silent five senses are bringing to you! Also it is the awareness that you are a truly "silent" observer and that everything that you observe and so experience, is actually the real you! Therefore you are self-aware that your body is also a part of that observation in which total unity is experienced!

For is it not anciently stated, in the early times of Saint Paul's conversion and soon after his becoming "Enlightened", that he added these following words of wisdom which explains the knowledge that one always experiences within a "Self-Aware" condition. These words actually revealing an experience in which you actually KNOW that you are living in a Heaven whilst you currently exist upon this Earth! For indeed there are things that you actually KNOW that you should not, must not and also cannot do! For did not the "Self-Aware" Saint Paul say in Ephesians' 4:26 *"In your anger do not sin. Do not let the sun go down while you are still angry, and do not give the devil a foothold! And Anyone who has been stealing must steal no longer but must work doing something useful with their own hands that they may have something to share with those in need."* Also, *"Do not let unwholesome talk come out of your mouths, but only what helps build others up according to their needs, that it may benefit all who listen".* Then he added, *"And do not grieve the Holy Spirit of God, with whom you were sealed for the day of redemption".* This statement "redemption" meaning to pursue the way of life "sealed" by the experiencing of that which we call "Enlightenment".

So yes! "Enlightenment" truly, exists and can be experienced by those people who have had many lives for certainly people attached to the Christian religion, who have had many lives, describe it has the experiencing of the Holy Spirit or Holy Ghost, this being that which has been previously forbidden to rest within them by the animalistic five senses. The ancient ones within the Islamic teaching, who have also had many lives, describe "Enlightenment" has being bodily filled by the

Angel Gabriel and for truly it is also a fact that many of our world's religions and philosophies that have been created by such ancient ones with many lives, describe it has the experiencing of *"Paradise"*, *"Eden"*, *"Heaven"*, *"Nirvana"*, *"Promised Land"*, *"Moksha"*, *"Shangri-la"*, *"Kenshō"*, *"Svargamu"*, *"Kā bāga"*, *"Vāṭikā"*, *"Kā jagaha"*, *"Sukhabhavana!* These certainly being heavenly names created by our world's many religions and philosophies that do energetically exist throughout our world. All of which show to their own culturally different followers a way to experience and so achieve such "Enlightenment"! For indeed all "anciently-advanced" people, these being people who have had many lives, do inwardly "feel" that their Soul is seeking the freedom to join with the world of which they are existing in unity with! But sadly this "Feeling" is often translated by the early re-births from the animal kingdom to mean that all the world beings to THEM! For certainly and undoubtedly, it is this conscious feeling of an "awareness", this being when a person experiences that they are has one entity with the creation that is not only within them but which is also all around them, which is a very positive but "mysterious" experience! But it is also a known unifying feeling which actually compels such people to become an active part of a local religion or a philosophy. So, they then "choose" a religion or a philosophy to become has one with and so without knowing the real truth has to why they have this strong "I Want" to be with a religious people feeling, thus enabling them to become has one with a self chosen religious group!

    Therefore, "Life's Purpose" now knowingly says that it should be Realized that many of those people who attend religions are really people who are knowingly or unknowingly seeking that reality which is known has "Enlightenment". This also being an "Enlightenment" which the "Life's Purpose" says is, born within a person when they actually encounter a "Self-Aware" experience in which they actually experience that they are "Everything!" This reality being when they fleetingly experience that they are has one with that life force that is not only within them but which is also all around them! Therefore, it should be clearly known that this early "Enlightening" experience is further developed by supportive praying which keeps the thinker in the "Present Time", this being that which stops the animalistic "I Want" from filling the mind. This silencing of the animalistic "I Want" is also stopped from entering the mind by the more scientifically based disciplinary sounding of a single repetitive mantra (i.e.: word) into the mind! This is being that activity which is designed to disciplinary silence the five senses from sounding their animalistic "I Want" into the mind of the observer.

Thus praying and incanting is certainly that practice which religiously stops our five senses from sounding their animalistic "I Want" into the mind of the prayer– which "Life's Purpose" says is like the training of five wild pups to come to the heel of their master, this often being achieved via that single world "Heel", which directs and controls them.

Therefore, and frankly it can be said, that all the people who attend our world's many different religions and or philosophies, do culturally belong in unity to the all the religious and or philosophical people who are actually seeking to become has one with Gods world or the world of Nature for the Non-Believer. For certainly, this seeking of a unified singularity with that "Present" that exists all around them, is because many "seekers" have fleetingly experienced and so inwardly "know", that they are has one with the world that exist around them, which is the most beautiful experience that has ever existed within this "Present", which is our known world.

So Yes! It is now useful to understand that the experiencing of "Enlightenment" is an aware condition that can only be Realized when a person uses their God given or Nature given for the non-believer "Freedom of Choice" to seek this freedom! This being a "Freedom of Choice", which is God's gift or Natures gift for the non-believer! For certainly this "Freedom of Choice" gift is that reality which any person can use to consciously "choose" to silence and so stop within the mind the "I Want" demands that are being sounded there by one or more of the body's animalistic five senses. This being the true and anciently known reason for meditation i.e.; which of course is a praying practice that silences the five animalistic senses and so disciplines them to become "silent" in order for "Soul" to become has one with that which we call the "Present", which of course is your true "Self". For certainly, you are the singularity of the creation, this being that which is not only within you but which also all around you and the target and purpose of our existence is will be explained later in "Life's Purpose"! But for now it is indeed good to know that our life's first disciplinary task is to leave that which we "think" is our individual and alone selves! For certainly it is necessary to "Choose", via our "Freedom of Choice" to silence the "animalistic" mind filling "I Want for ME" thoughts and so, with a silent mind, fully experience the awareness of your Soul which is has one with that which we call "The Present", this being the praying target of ALL our world religions and philosophies. Indeed, this is the Soul that is resting within you and which is an "observing" entity that can only exist in the "Present Time", for certainly, this being that "Present Time" which is God's world or the world of Nature for the Non-Believer.

So yes! Being filled with the Holy Spirit or Holy Ghost is a Christian's way of describing someone who is "Enlightened", which is the living in the Heaven that does genuinely exists in the "Present Time". For certainly, is it not true that all our wise ancients spoke about that which can be explained only by saying that living in the "I Want" world that creates a past or a future, is really the living in personally created "Hell". This being an "I Want" for me world which is yours or another's personally created "Hell"! Therefore, is it not stated that Saint Paul's complete turnaround from living in a Hell to living in a Heaven whilst upon this Earth, is an actual reality which Saint Paul the apostle clearly described. For Saint Paul, who was a Christian apostle that spread the teachings of Jesus in the first century world, did actually experience himself to be has one with the "Present"! For he experienced no separation from the creation that truly existed all around him just has it did within him! For certainly it should be known that this experience of being has one with the "Present" Time is the target of ALL our world's religions and philosophies.

Therefore, it should be known, that our own world's brothers and sisters who practice Hinduism, Buddhism, Jainism, Sikhism, and many other religious teachings, always refer to a state of meditative consciousness which is called "Samadhi"! This being highest religious state that people can achieve when their body becomes has one with the "Present" time. This being a known condition which is said can be attained when a person disciplinary pray's or meditates! It is also interesting to note that "Samadhi" is known to be an ancient Sanskrit word that is actually mentioned often within this ancient Sanskrit language. It is also interesting and educationally important to note that the Sanskrit language is also known to be a very ancient language and it is also a language that is actually considered to be the *"Mother of all Languages"*. So this ancient word "Samadhi" is an ancient word that is "scientifically" translated to mean *"something that cannot be described"!* It should also be known that "Samadhi" is a name that anciently explains a condition known has "Spiritual Enlightenment", which describes something that is "Mystical" and also "Nonphysical", plus Transcendent, Holy, Sacred, Divine, Heavenly, Pious and Devout etc, and this emanates from a language that is known to have been used over 5,000 years ago.

It is also further said, in this ancient 5,000 years old Sanskrit language, that by the practice of "Yoga", which is a meditational practice that is now known to be over 10,000 years old! That such meditational practice will bring to the practitioner the experience of "union" or "unification", (within your mind body and spirit) with all that exists within the "Present" time! This meaning that which is now modernly described has an experience that is called "Enlightenment"! Therefore it is known that your "Self", which is the real "YOU", becomes "Self-Realized", this meaning that you actually become has one with the "Present" time. Thus, actually explaining that such a personal meditation is the final stage in which union with God or with Nature for the Non-Believer can become a blissful reality.

For indeed, it should also be known that this "reality" has a beginning and also an ending! For certainly it is a realty which is first experienced in that condition which "Life's Purpose" explains to be a "Self-Aware" experience! This being a well known religious experience in which you actually become "aware" that that which you're five senses are revealing to you, is the real "YOU", this certainly being that first step towards a physical reality which our ancients called "Self-Realization". For indeed, "Self-Realization" is that which "Life's Purpose" does modern ally explain to be the final stage of a holistic reality in which you "experience" that "YOU" are everything that exists in the physical world and that there is no observer! For again, this is a reality which our wise ancients knew could be genuinely experienced by any person – and of course, it still can?

For certainly, that which is historically known to be true, in the East of our world, is that which was "historically" forgotten by many people in far "The West" of our world! For certainly there were people in the far west of our world who did forget this anciently sought and so well targeted reality! For certainly "The Ancient West" of our world did enter a religious belief system which was and still is called "Maya"! This being a religion which consisted of an ancient group of people who lived in the west of our world and who actually built an ancient civilization that stretched across much of Central America. The Maya civilization reached its peak during the first millennium A.D., and Maya ruins can still be seen across much of Central America and the word Maya loosely means that everything within the Universe does actually exist has a separate entity to that of the observer.

Unquestionably, this is actually a "Maya" belief in which those wise ancients who lived in the East of our world aptly described as being an illusion and therefore could not be reality! This being a distant western illusion within our world which the existing Godly created or Nature created unity for the non-believer, was really "thought" to be a unity which actually consisted of many separate entities. This being a world which ancient eastern religious people described has being the world of "Maya", a world in which people believed in many Gods and also that some of the

Gods were considered to be more important and more powerful than the other Gods.

For certainly the Maya people of the West of our world referred to a powerful God named "Itzamná" plus several other names, including Kukulcan and Itzam Cab Ain, and modern scholars now simply call him God D. It is also interesting that Itzamná's name is derived from the Maya word for "shaman", translated to mean "wise person" and with his full name – being roughly translated to mean "lizard house". Indeed the most important and most powerful Maya God was called "Itzamna" who was also the God of fire and who was actually believed to be that God which created the Earth! It is also known to be certain that Itzamna was amongst the oldest and most important gods in the Mayan religion. He was the son of the creator god Hunab Ku and, he was also associated with the sun god Kinich Ahau as well as the goddess Ix Chel. There are also known to be many stories and myths about Itzamna since he was considered a cultural hero by the Maya.

It is also this many Gods beliefs that actually created within our ancient wise a mind filling condition in which a person's undisciplined consciousness become entangled with an "I Want for Me" for me illusion! This being an illusion in which "Life's Purpose" does modern ally explain to be an ancient animalistic "I Want" mind filling reality which does block the true "Self", this being that which rests within all people, from observing all that truly exists within that which we call the "Present Time".

This reality certainly being a constant mind filling condition in which a person's "animalistic" five senses do create within the mind that false condition which our wise ancients factually called the *"Cosmic Illusion"*. For certainly, our wise ancients did discover the need to become has one with the "Present Time" and so actually and methodologically sought a unity seeking meditation reality (Praying etc). This being an activity which "disciplinary" stops the animalistic "I Want" illusions from entering the mind, a known realty that blocks the soul from seeing the outside world. Thus it was known that this meditational, i.e.; praying reality did actually bring people back to the knowing that all that exists around them is their true "Self", and that there is no separation from that which is known as Gods world or the world of Nature for the Non-Believer, this being that realty which is called "The Present"!.

Therefore and truly, "Life's Purpose" does modernly explain that these mind filling "I Want" illusions are certainly an animalistic based ignoring condition in which a person's mind is being filled continuously with many never ending "I Want for ME" thoughts! This being that world which "Life's Purpose" does factually call a personally created "Hell"! This being a world that is being personally created by many constant on-going "I Want" thoughts that are indeed emanating from the animalistic five senses of the undisciplined thinker! Therefore, is it not factually true that this false world is a personally created world? This being a falsely created world in which "Life's Purpose," says does actually block the Soul of a person from seeing through a clear mind the true existence of the real world? This being that world which is knowingly called the "Present" and which is the true and only world that has been created by God or by Nature for the Non-Believer.

Therefore again, can it not be said to be true that people who personally created this false "I Want" world of Hell, were often told by our wise ancient that they are creating a false world, this being a world which our wise ancients called "Naraka"! Described to be a place where a person's soul was sent has a punishment for committing sins. It is also mentioned primarily in the ancient teaching of Dharmashastras, Itihasas, and the Purina' and it is also described in the Vedic samhitas, the Aranyakas and the famous Upanishads although it is known that some Upanishads speak of 'darkness' instead of hell. These also being in texts that were written in ancient Sanskrit has: नरक, which literally names the false world that is created by people! (i.e.: Human kind!) This also being that world which "Life's Purpose" says is a world in which some people have created a personal world of "Hell", this being a negative world that is further explained in the ancient teachings of Hinduism, Sikhism, Jainism and Buddhism. For certainly this false world of "Naraka" is known by our wise to be a place of torment which "Life's Purpose" explains is simply created by the "I Want" thoughts of newly birthed people with many being re-born from the animal kingdom! These being people whose thoughts are continually and habitually emanating from their previous animalistic life, a life in which they previously existed upon our world and so they can be, without doubt, that reality which ignorantly believes that they are living "Hell".

Therefore, "Life's Purpose" positively states that these mind blocking "I Want" thoughts are always based upon a personal animalistic "I Want" that is being generated by one or many of the animalistic five senses! For certainly, should it not be a now known truth that this "I Want For ME" is a mind blocking thought that always generates a mind-filling cloud which always stops the inner Soul from viewing, through the mind that which can only exist in the "Present" time? For certainly, "Life's Purpose" constantly endeavors' to explain that it is only in the "Present" time that Gods world or the world of Nature for the Non-Believer, can actually be experienced! Also is it not true that many of our world's religions have previously described such a "non-thinking" experience as a "mystical marriage", this being that term used by St Teresa and St John of the Cross to designate their mystical union with God. This being that which is stated to be the most exalted condition attainable by the Soul in any person's current life! It was also called by our ancients a "transforming union" and a "consummate union" plus serious adoration for it was a reality which did actually create a sense of unity with the entirety of the creation. For certainly it not also true that most of our world's religions and philosophies actually state that the Soul can actually merge and therefore be has one with Gods world or the world of Nature for the Non-Believer!

For certainly, is it not historically stated to be true, this truth being stated by many of our ancient wise, that via mediation and praying, we can actually become has one with God, or become has one with Nature for the Non-believer? Therefore, must it not be true that all personal actions being created within this "Self-Aware" experience must be Godly targeted, just has is targeted the nature that is all around us and also within us? For indeed is it not also realized to be true that mantra-based meditation, which is designed to silence the five senses, will eventually remove the illusion of being separate from the creation that exists within us and also that which exists all around us? For certainly, it is true that mantra meditation silences the animalistic "I Want" that is constantly coming from one or more of the five senses. This being that activity which fills the mind so that the Soul cannot become has one with the creation that exist all around it just has it exists within it!

For is not this mind empty reality that which brings people to become aware or even realize that all that exists around them is their true "Self" and that there is no separation from that which is known as Gods world or the world of Nature for the Non-Believer. For certainly, this historical way of praying is known to be that which brings to the prayer an awareness or even a realization that that which is known has the totality of the creation is certainly "THEM"! For without doubt it is a known truth that such praying or the repetitive sounding of a mantra, is an ancient way to achieve this reality of being has one with the creation and it is certainly a way that is still being used by ALL our world's religions and philosophies! For certainly, this "Enlightening" experience, this being that which brings an awareness or a unified reality that occurs when the mind becomes empty and without any "I Want" thoughts that are being sounded by one or by all of the animalistic five senses, which of course are animalistic in nature!

For certainly "Enlightenment" is a religious and/or a philosophically sought experience in which the worshipping practitioner does actually become has one with the creation which is all around them just has it is within them? Therefore, can it not now be knowledgeably explained that the praying worshipper and especially meditation can actually bring to the doer a state of "Enlightening" awareness of only the "Present Time"; this also being anciently described as the experiencing of *a "Peace that Surpasses all Understanding"*! This experience is certainly a one-pointed mind condition that is also anciently explained as being in a *"state of perfect equanimity and awareness"* and in the oldest texts of Buddhism mantra meditation is explained has an exercise that is used in the training of the mind which is called "Bhavana", which means to develop or cultivate and so produce the existence of unity, this unity being a singularity with that entity which we call "The Creation"! This activity, which is normally achieved by meditation, was stated to be a praying activity that was needed to withdraw the mind from the automatic "I Want" responses coming from our animalistic five senses! These really being mind filling "I Want" animalistic soundings and so the task is to refuse these mind filling defilements that are coming from the "I Want" of the animalistic five senses – likened to be like five untrained pups. For certainly the Sanskrit word: भावना, or bhāvanā, literally means "development" or "cultivating" or "producing" or in a sense the "calling into existence" a silent mind! This being that which is an important reality not only in Buddhist practices for it is also the target of ALL our world's religions and philosophies!

For certainly in Buddhism, has in all our religions and philosophies, through their acts of "religiously" seeking equanimity via prayer and singing in chorus, you understand that you are has one with the creation that is all around you just has it is within you. For truly, our world's religions and philosophies actually target a state of mental control and even mind silencing awareness in which you are inclined to do a particular thing or act in a particular way! For certainly, it is one of the Four Brahma-viharas, that when religiously pursued become potent forces through which the worshipper cares not only for themselves but also for others who they associate to be has themselves.

For definitely, it is known that these are our worlds' religious targets which are certainly used for resolving all conflicts including the promoting of healing, and certainly for creating a social harmony, which is the true purpose of all our world's religions and philosophies. Therefore it is always wise to practice the seeking of equanimity with your Soul! For certainly your personal outcome and your way of life depends upon your own actions and not upon your wishes or upon the wishes of others. For no matter how you might wish things to be otherwise, things are as the creation or nature for the non-believer pursues them to be! For truly our religious leaders do and should pursue only what is the best for the creation that is all around them has it is within them, but your happiness and unhappiness depends upon your own actions or non-actions and not upon any religious or philosophical words of truth, for is it not a truth that many wars are created by surplus sons who are animalistic ally seeking land or the wealth that belongs to others?

For certainly, it should now be known that there is no past and there is no future, for in truth they do not exist. For the certain truth, which can be experienced, is that there is only one life and it is the unified "YOU" dear reader! For you have a life that can only live in the "Present", which all our religions and philosophies call the place of "Enlightenment"! For certainly this is that clarification which can exists only within the "Present" and it is also that experience which the Christian religions explain has being filled with the Holy Spirit or the Holy Ghost and the Muslim faith explain has being with the Angel Gabriel. For without doubt, because of this known religious and/or philosophical "enlightening" experience, which is truly experienced when the body is without thought, thus ensuring that they actually becomes has one body with the "Present" time! For certainly, it can be said, that it was this self-awareness that the biblical St. Paul did actually oppose foe he then condemned the many non-religiously separating "I Want" for me factors that he once actually believed in.

This change in the biblical St. Paul was because he now began to truly understand that his past beliefs were actually created by animalistic "I WANT" thinking! This being because his animalistic thoughts created an imagination which was based upon a false *"I want for me"* greed, this actually being an "I Want" for me animalistic way of thinking which cannot be a reality in God's world or the world of "Enlightenment" for the non-believer! For within the experiencing of "Enlightenment" you actually become aware and so realise that you are "Everything", this being a unified world which can only exist in the "Present" time! For indeed it is certainly true that the experiencing of "Enlightenment" is a reality which cannot be Realized by a person's thoughts of the past or by their thoughts regarding the future. For the "Past" and the "Future" are truly unreal non-existing worlds which are a being animalistic ally created by an "I Want" for me dreamed illusion.

For certainly, is it not also true that the Christian St. Paul, who had obtained letters from the high priest authorizing him to arrest any followers of Jesus in the city of Damascus, then gave a good religious "Enlightening" advice to his listeners by saying the following words: *"Get rid of bitterness, rage, anger, brawling and slander, along with every form of personal malice!"* Thus, St Paul was actually describing how to move away from the "I WANT for ME" world, this being that world which he had personally just left! It was also at this repentance that he actually added a description of the new world in which his "Enlightening" experience had presented to him by saying: *"Be kind and compassionate to one another; forgive each other, just as Jesus Christ forgave you!"* For certainly the new St Paul would know that other people were not separate from him. For it is written that St. Paul knew that Jesus had actually forgiven him, this being when he was actually on his way to Damascus in order to destroy Him! Was it not also this forgiveness from Jesus that did actually create the feeling of "Enlightenment" within St. Paul? This being the enlightening experience of a oneness that arose within him when He became Self-Aware or Self-Realized that all the people that he spoke to plus the creation that existed all around him, was actually a unified part of his "Him-Self"!

For certainly is it not a known truth that St Paul had actually "Self-Realized" that all that existed within the creation was a singularity which Jesus had called the only child of God, this being that totality of everything that totally existed within the "Present"! For certainly Jesus gave a needed answer to the world by saying, *'I tell you the truth, no one can enter the kingdom of God (The "Present") unless he is born of water and the Spirit. Flesh gives birth to flesh, but the Spirit gives birth to spirit. You should not be surprised at my saying, "You must be born again"* (John 3:3–7). For certainly, is it not true that the Kingdom of God physically exits in the "Present" time and water is that which gives life to "Everything"! For is it not also true that if you take water from anything, it ceases to exist in its current form! For certainly is it not clear that no matter what culture the words of the incarnate Jesus are read, the reader can become FULLY aware or even realise the oneness of the "Present" time, this being that reality which exists within them just has it exists all around them! For certainly, by fully listening to the answers that Jesus revealed to his listeners such has: "*I tell you the truth, the child (The creation) can do nothing by itself; it can do only what it sees its Father doing, because whatever the Father does the child also does.*" Now it is good and well to understand, that this quote is actually the father of the creation speaking directly to YOU dear reader for there is no other to listen to the fathers words! For certainly, our Godly Fathers laws manufactured all that rests within that which we call "The Present". For certainly, it is our Godly "fathers" laws that are silently and constantly informing us that the laws governing His "Present", this being that world in which His only child exists, cannot be broken! For is it not said in Matt 5:18, this being within the Christian Bible, "*I tell you the truth, until heaven and earth pass away not the smallest letter or stroke of a letter will pass from the law* (Gods law) *until everything takes place"*.

So yes! The above truth is always endeavouring to be explained in our modern worlds religious teachings for certainly "Life's Purpose" is also endeavouring to reveal that Jesus was actually speaking has the totality i.e.; the oneness of the Creation; For certainly, Jesus' words in the Christian bible can now be understood to mean: **"*I tell you the truth, this being that people can do nothing by themselves; people can only do what their Fathers Creation obediently allows them to do***! Of course the Father mentioned is God or Nature for the non-believer. This statement therefore means that we have to be obedient to whatever the unified life of our Father's Creation targets, which of course is same has our own bodies obediently supporting our Soul – which we should now know to be has one with that which exists all around us just has it does within us. Therefore, should we not be "Self-Aware" or even actually "Self-Realise" that our entire world's religions and philosophies do preach and so target the experiencing of this singularity with the creation that is all around us just has it is within us? Therefore, is it not now useful to truly acknowledge that the "Creation", this being that which is all around us and also within us, is that supporting reality which can only exist within the "Present"? Is this not because the Past and the Future are imaginary worlds which do not and also cannot exist?

For certainly, is it not known that 2,382 billion Christians, representing around 33% of the global population, believe there's only one God, and that it was "He" that created the heavens! This heaven being a negative reality in which it is said that all people are enabled to be re-incarnate from! Also is it not a fully accepted truth that it was God that created the physical universe, this being a positive world in which exist our planet Earth. Also all our worlds Christians believe that our divine God consists of three parts: these being the father (God himself), the son (Jesus Christ) and the Holy Spirit, this being that energy which "Life's Purpose" calls the "Mother of the Creation". For is it not true that a Mother is the needed life supporting energy which can only exist in God's given "Present" time! For without doubt these words of truth, which are spoken by Jesus, are pursued by people of the Christian faith, for Jesus was knowingly well beyond that unifying experience that we call "Enlightenment" - this being because Jesus was indeed "Self-Realized", meaning that Jesus of the Christian Faith was has one body with the Creation, which of course is the only child of God or of Nature for our non-believers.

Of course there are many other religions and philosophies' within our world which are all based upon the language and culture of the originating country such has our Earths Muslims who have 1.6 billion followers (23.2%) and whose main belief is that there is only one God and that the "Self-Realized" Muhammad was also a Messenger of God, this being a central teaching within the Islamic religion.

Also our Earths Hindus, with a stated one billion followers (15.0%) believe in the doctrines of Samsara, this belief being in the continuous cycle of life then death then reincarnation plus karma (the universal law of cause and effect). One of the key beliefs of Hinduism is "atman," or the belief in an undying soul. This philosophy holds that all people have a soul, and that they are all part of the supreme soul and that their Soul is influenced by a person's actions, these being that which have been performed within their current life.

Our Earths Buddhist religion with 500 million (7.1%) followers did originate 2,500 years ago in India. It is also a certain truth that Buddhists believe that the human life can be one of suffering, and that meditation, spiritual and physical God supporting endeavours combined with good behaviour are the ways to achieve enlightenment, or nirvana meaning to become has one with God or with Nature for the none-believer.

Also our Earths Indigenous religions with around 400 million (5.9%) followers believes in a native or home grown indigenous spirituality as a "way of life" and also "way of knowing" which was all centred on a relationship with the Creator of the land and also "all our relations. This usually included all other beings and forms of life, including what are commonly perceived as inanimate objects. It is also stated that there are around 58 million people pursuing other religions (0.8%)

Non-religious people around —1.1 billion (15.0%)

Therefore, it is always good to remember that Jesus of the Christian faith was not a "Wise Man" nor was He a "Saint" but that He WAS certainly the unified totality of the Creation. This totality being a reality in which Jesus knew that he was the only child of God and that Jesus He was everything and therefore He certainly knew that what he was saying to the world was a truth that could not be broken. Therefore it is good to understand that "Self-Realization", in which you become has one with the creations, is not an experience in which you know that you are an "observer" of everything, including your own body! For in a "Self-Realization" experience there is no observer! For the experience of being has one with the creation is that which "Life's Purpose" calls a "Self-Aware" that you are everything experience, which is the first step towards "Self-Realization".

For indeed, it is also anciently known that within the experiencing of "Self-Realization", a person is no longer an observer of the creation, thus meaning that they have become has one with that which we call the "Present"! For the "Present" is experienced to be a unified singularity which exists in unity with that which is within them and also that which is all round them! This being the experiencing of a "Present Time" reality in which a person does knowingly experience themselves to be in total unification with all that exists within the "Present Time"! This being a truth in which a person does truly "Self-Realize" that there is no observer but what does actually exist is the singleness of God's world or the world of Nature for the Non-Believer – and there is no other!

So yes! Jesus of the Christian faith "Self-Realized", probably in childhood, that he "WAS" the unification of the Creation and therefore certainly knew that He was the only Child of God! For certainly did Jesus not wisely say too many "I Want" non-believers: ***"By myself, I can do nothing; I judge as I hear, and my judgment is just, for I seek not to please myself but Him who sent me".*** Thus stating has the personification of the creation that all people should obey God's Harmony which exists within the laws of the ever-developing creation. For is it not true that these developing natural laws must be contained within God's on-going plan – or within Nature's on-going plan for the Non-Believer.

Therefore, is it not also known to be true that Jesus, who knowingly was the singularity of the creation, did simply explain this revelation by saying, ***"The eye is the lamp of the body? If your eyes are good, your whole body will be full of light."*** These words explaining the reality of being an "Enlightened" one, which is a condition in which a person's Soul is enabled to see the developing "Present Time", but only through an empty non-thinking mind! This certainly being an empty mind condition in which a person, who is without any mind-filling "I Want for ME", actually becomes "Self-Aware" of a reality which will enable them to "Self-Realise" that only the "Present" time" truly exists. This being the only time in which a person will actually experience that they live in the "Heaven" that truly exists in Gods world or the world of Nature world for the non-believer: this being that realty which can only exist in the "Present" time.

For indeed a mind that is filled with many animalistic "I Want" for me thoughts, this being a mind that is filled by past or future "I Want" images, does unknowingly live in a self-created animalistic Hell! For there is certainly no need to take the minds energy to "think" about what to do for the Soul automatically knows what heavenly supporting activity is needed to be done – but only in the "Present Time"! These being the heavenly world that can only exist in the "Present" and it is certainly not the Hell which is created by animalistic mind filling "I Want for ME" pursuits and demands! These pursuits and demands are actually animalistic "I Want" for "ME" mind filling thoughts that are emanating from one or from all of the animalistic five senses. This being that truth which stops the Soul from seeing through the "I Want" cloud filled mind and so makes it unable to evaluate the needs of the Creation, these being needs that can only exist in the "Present Time". For is it not true that Jesus of the Christian Faith said *"But if your eyes are bad,* (Unable to see the world around you) *your whole body will be full of darkness* (a mind blocked by "I Want" words). *If then the light within you is darkness, how great is that darkness!"* Thus it was indeed that Jesus did actually describe the darkness of those who lived in an "I Want" for me Hell, this being whilst they currently upon this Earth! For indeed, is it not true that the soul cannot see through a mind which is blocked by "I Want" thoughts?

So is it not also truly stated that Jesus then gave a clear description of that which He was speaking about when He said: *"**No one can serve two masters**". **Either he will hate the one or love the other, or he will be devoted to the one and despise the other**.* For it is certainly a truth that you cannot serve both Gods developing nature and also I want more "Money" and/or power over others! For is it not true that God or Nature for the non-Believer, is the actual "Creator" of all the laws that exist within the Creation, and that it is only people who create and evaluate money. Therefore is it not true that worshipping money is likened to be an "I Want" for "me" thought? For certainly is it not therefore true that these are mind-filling animalistic "I Want" for ME, desires? These being ongoing desires which do actually keep a person's mind chained to a non-existing

"I Wanted" past or to a non-existing "I Want" future – is this not true?

For certainly these "I Want" for ME claims will continue to exist within the "I Want" thinking that "animalistic ally" fills a person's mind! For again it should be said that these "I Want" greed based claims are usually coming from one or several of the body's animalistic five senses. Yet truly it should be known that all people have been given the security and freedom to enjoy and experience a mind empty and very personal "Enlightenment", this being that realty which can only be experienced in the "Present Time". This also being an enlightenment in which everything that you experience is the real YOU for you are "Everything".

Yet many people do not know of this simple truth and so worship a false "I Want" world that can only exist in an animalistic mind that is filled by thoughts which are usually seeking an animalistic greed-based past or a future "I Want". For certainly and for sure, this animalistic thinking is that mind filling condition which constantly stops the inner Soul from seeing through the empty mind and so becoming aware or realising that they are actually has one with the existing creation – this being that which is all around them has it is within them. For without doubt, an animalistic ally based mind, this being that which is mind-fully claiming many an "I Want" for ME', will never experience the fruits of "Enlightenment". For truly, the experiencing of "Enlightenment" is that reality which can only be experienced when the mind silently rest without any mind filling "I Want"! For certainly, it is only then, with an empty mind – that the true you, which is your inner observing Soul, can, because your five animalistic senses have been silenced, experience its oneness with that reality which is called "The Creation" - although a taste of this truth may have previously occurred during the pauses within your bodies animalistic "thinking".

So yes! In a free world, which is a world in which all people can rightfully seek "Enlightenment" and so establish an awareness or even a physical realization that they are has one body with not only that which exists within them but also with that which exits with-out them! Yet! Is it not sadly true that many people are fleeing from countries that exist within our world which are not free, meaning a freedom which is designed to treat others only has you would like yourself to be treated? For truly, are there not also many people within our world who are fleeing from countries where a non-harming "Freedom of Choice", especially regarding religions and philosophies - is forbidden? Is it not also true that some people, even with their children, do try to leave such a punishing country? These being their birthing countries in which they are sadly being subjected to a punishment which creates hunger, unemployment, oppression, violence, plus torture and the persecution and the killing of their loved ones? Is this not that condition which makes them want to flee their homes of birth? This being in an endeavour to across borders in their search to live in a non- inviting country that is prosperous, peaceful, and rich in opportunity! But is it not also true that in such fleeing many do actually close their eyes to that countries law, this being a law that actually forbids their entry? For is it not a certain truth that they are "legally" and "enforcedly" forbidden by the law of such countries to pursue such in-habiting ventures!

But certainly, if they are not financially viable, should not the countries from which they are fleeing, be "legally" charged with the cost of their maintenance? This being so that the countries that are being abandoned will endeavour to correct the reason has to why these people are fleeing their country!

So yes! A "Free World", this being a world which is controlled by the will of the people, is also a world that can mobilise people to achieve the good things in life! For certainly such a world supports the search for "Enlightenment", which is the path of wisdom for the non-religious or a Godly supporting path for the religious. It is also a path towards wisdom which should be religiously or economically made available to ALL people, for certainly it is an experience in which a person will "realise" that they are the totality of everything that exists in the "Present Time", this being a "Present" in which does actually rest a truth that cannot be explained.

Therefore and truly, all people should know that the "Present" is the time in which people should know that they have been created in order to support the Harmony that is emerging or endeavouring to emerge, all around them. Therefore our world's clear and understandably religious or philosophical truth is to endeavour to serve the needs of the factual "Present", this being that which cannot exist in any past or future thought.

For certainly is it not also true that all thoughts can only create a future or a past "I Want". For again, and certainly, the above described world shows that the target of all our wise ancients, these being those people who have lived in the many countries of our world, was to bring to their people "Enlightenment", thus enabling them to live in the "Heaven" that can only exist in the "Present Time", which is Gods world or the world of Nature for the non-religious!

This "Present Time" certainly being a world where you do not belong only for your-self! For you certainly belong to and so are truly a part of, all that exists in the "Present Time".

So Yes! Your religious target must be to live a life that is in accordance to this "I am everything" reality and therefore actually experience that upon your own worlds "Present" there resides the reality and/or wellbeing of "Enlightenment"! The question now being if you are actually seeking to experience this "Enlightenment" and so actually becoming the Creation and so certainly seeking a way to not be controlled by the animalism of the five senses and there preoccupation with physical rather than spiritual needs - then read on:-

6. HOW THE CREATION PURSUES GOD'S OR NATURES HARMONY FOR THE UNBELIEVER

So yes! It is only people, within this creation, who are the only life form to have a freedom seeking soul; therefore it is only people who can "choose" to obey or not to obey Gods developing creation. This creation certainly being a Godly quest in which only people have been given the "Freedom of Choice"! Thus it should be Realized that it is only people who are not Godly controlled like are all life and all non-life forms that automatically obey their needs within the "Present Time". For certainly, this is a "Present" in which there exists for all people a "Freedom of Choice" which enables them to live a life that supports developing "Nature" or to live an "I Want" for me life that does not support the world that exists all around them. For again, is it not true that it is only people who can be "Self-Aware" or be enabled to "Self-Realise" that the "Present" time is the only world that personally exists not only within them but also all around them? Also does not this factual "Freedom of Choice", this being that which exists only within people, not be that reality which has been actually designed to support the creations developing harmony? For is this not a harmony that can only exist in the "Present Time"!

So yes! Is it not also very true that the world of Nature can only exist in the "Present Time?" For that reason is not the "Present Time" the only reality in which people can support the needs of their families and also their friends' families, plus their communities, their districts and also their country? For certainly, if you "scientifically" and or "religiously" believe that the "Creations" pursuit of harmony is essential and also that you personally acknowledge that it is a dominant factor for your own personal well-being? Then you will also acknowledge the truth that you will "personally" need to support the Creations targeted purpose, or that target which can be called Nature's objective for the Non-Believer!

So yes! This Godly supporting of the "Present", which we call the "Present Time", is the target of all our world's religions and philosophies and it is a target in which "Life's Purpose" explains, is the becoming has one with God or the becoming has one with Nature for the non-believer! This certainty is a known and also a fundamental truth which was seriously pursued by our wise ancients and it has been religiously sought in many variable ways by all our Earths on-going religious and philosophical belief systems. Sadly, it is now Realized these ancient words that were preached by our ancient wise, have become difficult and challenging to understand in our modernized and culturally developed newly developed world?

Therefore is it not now true that there are many good modern explanations being birthed within all our world's religions and philosophies? These explanations being about the need to pursue only harmony seeking energies which will continually remove disharmony from the Creation and so replace it with a purposeful seeking unity! Yet is it not a scientific truth that within some religions there must be some people in existence who are early rebirths from the animal kingdom? These being people who have just been reborn from the animal kingdom and so still believe that the needs of their herd or their pack should not be shared with other animalistic pacts! Is this not true? For certainly if this reality is not personally believed, then look around your existing life and acknowledge its circumstances and also realise the harmony that protects you or the disharmony that disturbs you!

So is it not a truth to understand i.e.: to stand under Gods laws or the laws of Nature for the non-believer and so acknowledge that these personal attacks to change the emerging creation must be wrong! Especially if you are destroying that Godly or Natural harmony that exists or is emerging to exist all around you just has it does within you! For is it not a truth that if Nature is emerging and constantly growing then it must have a purpose? So is not the question that we should now ask being *"What is it that controls and monitors this reality that we call "Nature"?* This being energy whose only purpose is to pursue a growth that rest not only within ourselves but also our ever growing creation! This growth being controlled by an energy which can go by many names but may it now be said that the name "Life's Purpose" has "scientifically" chosen for this reality, this being that reality which actually cares for our creations growth is the name *"Mother of the Creation"!* For is it not true that it is the Mother which is actually the personification of a family's growing needs? Also is it not a well known fact that it is the Mother who "cares" for the growing child, this child being that which "Life's Purpose" calls "The

Creation!" For is it not also true that it is the Mother who is the family "carer", and also the family "activator" for all caring work that has to be done! Is it not also true that it is the "Mother" that is the seeker and supplier of the needed harmony that is required to be distributed safely around her children? Therefore is it not also a natural truth that it is the "Mother" who is the natural supporter of all those emerging and growing lives that exist throughout our natural world, for certainly all life knows that it is certainly the mother who cares for all the life that she gave birth to!

Therefore, is it not also true that a story of God's or of Nature's Creation for the Non-Believer, can be likened to the law that controls an agreeable public dance meeting? This being a dance in which the dance manager fixes everything that needs correcting prior to the birth of the dancing! Such corrections actually being the position of existing tables, chairs, drinks, glasses, bar, lights, walls, floors, people, and all that physically exists within the confines of that public place.Therefore, can it not be reasonably said that our world, in which we live, can be likened to that world which actually exists within this dance situation? This being an organising activity in which the five senses do factiously experience all the life and also all the non-life that exists within this controlled area of the dance site! Therefore, is it not also true that at the dance each person does "naturally" endeavour to obey the interpretation of the rules that do habitually control this dance area? Also to truly and habitually obey the rules of the chosen type of dance in which they are pursuing! In addition are there not also known to be outer imposed controlling rules of movement within each dance, this being has it is within our own lives, which have also been fixed in a certain way - by God's laws? For certainly, is it not also known to be true that all the attending dancers are being blissfully controlled by the rules of the dance, these being those people who are actually taking part in this "Self" creating dance meeting"! Also is it not true that they accept this dances "Present Time" reality and so "choose" to joyfully pursue the established laws that govern its existence!

The questions now being: *"What are the natural "Dance" rules of the Creation that is all around us and also within us?"* Also *"What are the rules that support its growth?"* Plus *"Why do all attending people within the dance i.e.: The Creation", have the "Freedom of Choice" to either pursue or not to pursue its laws?"* For indeed all people know that any dance laws can be broken just has God's laws or Nature's laws for the Non-Believer can be broken! This being accidentally or deliberately by people or even by the growing development of God's laws or Nature's laws for the Non-Believer! For certainly these laws can collide and so change that which did lawfully exist, this being in order to support the development of some changes that are needed in the "Present Time"!

For certainly is it not also true that this can happen in our personally created dance rooms and or our collective parties? These changes being when tables are knocked over or drinks are spilt and also when dancers bump and collide with each other etc! Therefore is it not a known fact that we can actually witness when harmony is being destroyed, this usually being when developing movements collide within themselves! Therefore, is it not also seen to be true that, has time moves forward, all people can witness that the only activity that can remove or change the currently developing ongoing harmony of the creation, this being likened to that which is within us and also all around us, is a personal "I Want for ME" dance movement! For certainly such a personal "I Want for ME" will certainly disturb the unified creation that obediently exists within the "Harmony-Obeying" dancers - this being has they all endeavour is to move rightfully and harmoniously within this "being has one" existence.

For certainly some accidents can occur within these rightfully dancing movements in which our lives exist. This being that reality which can also create a "disharmony" within the life that exists around us and truly, this is that which "Mother of the Creation" is continuously correcting. For certainly it should be known that God or Nature for the non-believer, will never change His "purposefully" created laws, these being natural laws which are continually unfolding within the "Present Time".

For without doubt, it is in the "Present Time", which is the time that their only Child, this being that totality which we call "The Creation", does seriously need the freedom to continue its Growth. For certainly, a person should be aware or realize that within this child, this being that which we call "The Creation", there actually exists a "growing-up" law, this being that which supports all life and also all non-life! For without doubt, this Godly or Nature born law for the non-believer, is certainly an existing reality which is similar to the laws of dancing, for they are also the controlling rules that bind any dancing event together.

For certainly God or Nature for the Non-Believer, does actually know just what the "Present Time" needs" This being in order for all life and also all that, which we call non-life, do need in order to grow with good health! For Certainly, God or Nature for the Non-Believer, does certainly know that His laws will certainly achieve their ultimate purpose and also that the "Mother of the Creation" will always be able to "legally" maintain the harmony of the Creations "dance", this being that reality which can only exist in the "Present Time".

So what we must now clearly understand is that this is the purposeful reason why God or Nature for the Non-Believer, did give to all people "The Freedom Choice!" For just has in our make-believe dance it is the "Mother of the Creation" who cares for and actually supports Her only child, who is the totality of the creation! Therefore, the certain and logical truth is that the "Mother of the Creation" really needs people in order to support Her harmony pursuing activities, just like the needs of all mothers! For certainly, the supporting activity of many people can likened to them picking up fallen tables and broken chairs and glasses at the previously mentioned ever-evolving ongoing "dance" of the creation, which is an activity which can only take place in the "Present Time"!

This being that reality in which all people should be aware or realise that it is only people who can put these disorders back in a way that will support the harmony that exists all around them, this being an activity which is always supported by the "Freedom of Choice"! This being a "Present Time" supporting activity which should never be taken from people, for is it not true that it is only people that have the "Freedom of Choice"? This being a personal "Freedom of Choice" in which they can even choose to die, has in wars if they feel the need to do so.

For certainly it is not easy to be disciplinary aware or even to realise that this freedom of choice has only been given to people upon our Earth! For is it not true that it is only people who have been birthed with the ability to negatively do nothing or to positively do something in order to positively support or to positively not support a way of life which obeys the laws of this constantly emerging world, this world being the creation that we call "Earth". For truly it is religiously known by many people that this creation can actually, via an inner awareness or an inner realisation, to be experienced has a singularity! This being that singularity which exists all around people just has it exists within them. For undoubtedly it should be known that there is only one life form that exists within this physical world which is called "The Creation", this being that creation in which all people truly exist – but what for and for what purpose?

For unquestionably is it not true that all people have the "Freedom of Choice" to choose what dance to do or what dance not to do, this being has they participate in that unified world which growingly exists all around them just has it does within them! For certainly it is known that because of this "Freedom of choice" any person can "choose" to dance with themselves or with others has they "create" a world which is based upon their personal skills to achieve loving twirls! This being a personally created world which, because of their "Freedom of Choice" any person can choose or not choose to pursue. For certainly it is a known fact that any person can choose or not choose to develop, via inner thoughts, a few unknown dance steps in which they would create and so develop a new world in which other people could to dance to! This "New World", which is first created by thought, would usually be a world that desires to establish new group laws that do not obey current laws and so there occurs "Revolution", this being when one type of dancing endeavours to destroy a the current way of dancing.

So Yes! It is therefore good to allow all people, within a group environment, to "democratically" take an active part in establishing and so creating new rules that will endeavour to control their communities' way of life. For, has "Life's Purpose" says, dancing can be compared to a politically created way of living, for it too is based upon group law which allows people to perform an activity that supports their sought way of life. For certainly is it not true that an elected government, like a band of musicians', must produce the music which is agreed by the majority of its voters, i.e.: dancers. This being the music in which people do happily enjoy the "harmony" that is created within them and also within their participating group. For certainly, is it not also true that within the comparative world of dancing, that if you actually created a new music which also sought a new way of dancing, then this could be seen has an aggressive action by the majority of dancers i.e.; worshippers! For this newly introduced music and its new way of dancing would undoubtedly create a new harmony. This "New Harmony" being within the new dancer's ever developing on-going search for a new unity with others. Therefore, could not this newly accepted music i.e.: new religion, actually create a harmony that could physically, mentally and culturally "enlighten" its participators', making them has happy has all other dancing "religions"? For certainly and a modern example of this group searching realty being the introduction of new music (religion) and way of dancing (worshipping), this being that which the world called "Rock and Roll", of which I was an active participant. For is it not true that all our world's religions and philosophies' do target the unification of ALL its followers who do "religiously" dance the dance that unifies them to be has one entity?

So Yes! Is it not true that it is only people who are enabled to pursue a "Freedom of Choice", even unto death if so required! For certainly it is true that it is only people who can, with this "Freedom of Choice", positively plan **'To do or not to do'** or **'to be or not to be'**, these quotations being words which were famously stated in the works of Shakespeare, who was obviously an "Enlightened" person. It is also a "speech" that brings forward the question: *"Why do only people have the freedom of choice"?* For indeed without people all life and especially all "Non-Life" would live a life that is controlled by the natural laws that exist in the world that is emerging all around them! This being a harmony seeking reality which is controlled by God's laws or by the laws of Nature for the Non-Believer!

For certainly, is it not well known that these are the creations laws which have been produced in order to support all life and also to support all the non-life that also exists within Earths "Present"? These being that truth which "Life's Purpose" says are the laws that "Mother of the Creation" does harmoniously endeavour maintain! For certainly is it not also a known truth, has "Life's Purpose" explains, that it is usually the mother who looks after the "Present Time", whilst the fathers mind is always occupied by thoughts that target the future – such has in hunting and the planting of food for consumption at a "Future Time"! Therefore it is because of this planned way of living that people have been created with the "Freedom of Choice", this being an ability to do or not to do to be or not to be! For undoubtedly, this "Freedom of Choice" is also needed in order to support the Godly needs or the growing needs of Nature for the non-believer. For is it not also said to be true, has "Scientifically" and also "Culturally" stated, that people have been gifted with the "Freedom of Choice"? This "Freedom of Choice" being to choose or not to choose their own actions, even if their chosen action actually creates their own death or the death of others has in war! For certainly these are actions that have been personally chosen, via their freedom of choice", to support or not support the natural world that is emerging all around them just has it is constantly emerging within them!

Therefore, does this "Freedom of Choice" reality mean that there is a Godly or a Nature based reason for the non-believer, has to why all people have been birthed with a "Freedom of Choice"? Could this reason be that God and the "Mother of the Creation" who "Life's Purpose" calls "Nature, are actually seeking to be "loved" by that which they have created? For is it not a usual truth that all parents like to be loved by their children, these being children who have been birthed via a parental "Freedom of Choice". Indeed, is not also true that within our lives we accept and also acknowledge that personal love must be "freely" given to another, for is it not true that "love" for another cannot be enforced?

So unquestionably, cannot this "Freedom of Choice", in which we choose to love our parents or others, be said to be a choice that is based upon "Natural Law"? For is it not true that "Love" is an experience in which God or Nature for the Non-Believer, did purposely create this feeling of oneness with another - and this being for all life to blissfully experience? For is it not also true that we can be aware or even realise that God's laws or Natures laws for the Non-Believer, are perfect for all the creation and so should be supported or even enlarged if possible - is this not also true? So does this fact mean that when a non-supporting person "selfishly" destroys God's harmony by "choosing" to personally create for themselves a harmony destroying "I Want" only for Me activity, that they cannot be punished - this certainly cannot be true! For what must be true is that there will be no "Sugar in the Water" for their current ongoing life, and certainly, without repentance, their next re-birth would be in a remarkably interesting place of correction.

So yes! The "Mother of the Creation" is the name that "Life's Purpose" offers to the "Believer" and also the "Non-Believer"! For without doubt, there must be, according to natural law, a mother to inwardly grow this only child that we call "The Creation"! This being a child who will live and grow within their Godly fathers created "Present" or Natures created present for the Non-Believer! For certainly is this not the only way to understand that there must "Scientifically" be a male father to seed within a pending mother the growing of this child that now exist has that which we call "The Creation" or that which is called the "Universe" by the Non-Believer! For is it not true that a female mother who "Life's Purpose" explains to be "Nature", is needed to give birth to this only child that we call "The Creation"! Furthermore is it not also a known fact that it is the mother who awareingly, via a realisation, knowingly supports the harmonious development of Her growing child, this being a child which "Life's Purpose" does knowingly call the "Present", meaning that this child is actually everything that exists within this unified has one "Present"! For certainly, all that exists in this Godly given "Present" or this "Nature" given "Present" for the non-believer, is that reality which does constantly confirms, via a conscious inner awareness, that all life and non-life do actually exist in unity with this singularity that we call "The Present"! This being that reality which is all around us just has it exists has one unified entity within us! For truly there is only one child and if dear reader, you would like to experience this fact, just stop what you are doing and without thought just look around you! But also it is good to acknowledge, that if an animalistic thought appears just say "Not This" and return to experience the "Present" which is all around you just has it is within you! With practice you will eventually experience that everything that exists within this creation, this being that, which is all around you, is really "You"! Of course this is the target of ALL our Earths religions and philosophies' and it is the reason has to why they pursue disciplinary controlled hymn singing and imposed praying – this being to silence the "I Want" that can be constantly sounded by one or all of the animalistic five senses!

So yes! The "Mother of the Creation", who is certainly a supporter of those natural laws which the non-believer understands are supported by "Nature", is truly also a motherly supporter of that which is needed by Her created children! These being people who have been purposely created to support the ongoing development of all life and also of all of Non-Life and in particular to live by the natural laws that bind in goodness their fathers' creation! For indeed, it is "She", known has the "Mother of the Creation", who brings the harmony and also the comforting aid to those children who help Her to support Her and Gods only child – which is that which we call "The Creation"! This "Present Time" teaching being that we actually exist has an entity within the creations unified harmony, this being that truth which our Earths wise truly explain in many variable ways within our world's major and minor religions and also all our worlds philosophical teachings.

But sadly, is it not also a true reality that many people have become too attached to personal belongings? Thus committing them to not fully understanding these ancient teachings and practices, a fact that has certainly led to their personal neglect? For certainly, is it not further interesting to factually and via non-thinking, to freely become aware and so realise that this is the reason why "Life's Purpose" uses a modern "scientific" explanations, this being in order to explain the target of ALL our world's religions and also our non-religious philosophical concepts?

For certainly, these modern explanations being needed in order to describe the root seeds that actually brought into existence the teachings of all our world's religions and philosophies! For certainly our worlds many religions are constantly pursuing a personal practice that can be used by a worshipper in order to experience their personal and unique all encompassing "Soul", this being that reality which can only be experienced in the non-thinking stillness of that which we call "The Present"! For certainly this book target is to "Enlighten" the reader! For "Life's Purpose" is written to be likened to a modern business plan! This being a business plan which will produce a way to experience this remarkable reality which will enabling the Soul of the reader to experience that which we call "The Present"! This being that which our entire world's religions and philosophies seek and certainly it is accomplished without changing or replacing any current religious or philosophical teaching, which also includes the mentioning of the "Mother of the Creation"!

For truly the "Mother of the Creation" was mentioned by Joshua, the son of Sirach, who translated a book that his father had written in 132 BC; this being around 2155 years before our current time and about thirty years after his father had completed his book. This ancient translation was also used has an introduction to the Christians "Old Testament", in which the word "Mother" arises and which "Life's Purpose" clarifies to mean to be the "Mother of the Creation" who "Life's Purpose" also explains to be the controller of Her only child, this being that creation which we call "The Present". For certainly, it was the Son of Sirach who did translate the following statements, which are numbered accordingly, and so revealed to the entire world his father's knowledge of just who controlled the "Present"! These selected statements being:-

5. The root of wisdom – to whom has it been shown to Her who knows them? *(For certainly the Mother of the creation was at the beginning of this child that we call the "Present", has are all mothers!)*

7. The Lord himself created wisdom; he saw Her and apportioned Her. He poured Her out upon all his works. *(Meaning that the Mother of the creation is within the child and that She controls this only child!)*

8. She dwells with all flesh according to His gift and He supplied Her to those who love him. *(Explaining that "She" is the mother of everything that exists within the "Present Time", whilst God is the father of the "Creation" which is their only child!)*

12. To fear God is the beginning of wisdom; she is created with the faithful in the womb. *(For certainly it is true that it is correct to only acknowledge the natural laws that control this only child that we call "The Creation", this truly being an only child! i.e. So it is good not to break the laws of God' or upset the Mother of the Creation who is the carer of this only child, this being that which is called "Nature" by the non-believer).*

13. She made a lasting foundation among men, and among their descendants She will be trusted. *(So yes, She, the mother of the creation or nature for the unbeliever, will be trusted by the wise who always live has one unit with all life and also all non-life!)*

14. To fear the Lord is wisdom's full measure; she satisfies men with her fruits. *(So yes, to non-fearfully exist in unity with the creation also means to acknowledge having only one body, meaning to be the totality of* *the creation, which brings forward all the fruits that are born by Nature.)*

15. She fills their whole house with desirable goods and their storehouses with her produce. *(*So yes, the mother of the creation provides all that is necessary for the life of those who live within the Present Time!

17. He saw Her and apportioned Her; He rained down knowledge and discerning comprehension and He exalted the glory of those who held Her fast. (So yes, God or Nature for the non-believer constantly supports the work that the Mother of the creation constantly pursues.)

18. To fear the Lord is the root of wisdom and Her branches are long life.

So yes, all life and non-life is seeded by God whilst the Mother of the creation cares for this ongoing growth. For certainly, the above is an excellent "ancient" description of the "Mother of the Creation", but it seems that those long-ago male creators of many of our world's religions "culturally" moved away from the sayings of our wise ancients and their religious teachings. This move being to create a "mans" only chauvinistic world, thereby denying the fundamental truth that only a male and a female, when together, are the only caring unit that can "Create" and so control and care for a growing child, this being a child which can only grow within the "Present Time"! For neither a male nor a female can create such a loved one on their own nor teach their child a wise way of life! For certainly, is it not true that a man's mind lives mainly in the future whilst a woman's mind lives mainly in the Present!

Maybe the reason why such male chauvinism developed was during the 1,200 years of darkness that was named to be "The Kali Yuga", this being that which was stated to be the age of vice and misery and also the age of quarrel and hypocrisy. For certainly it is known that a complete description of "Kali Yuga" can be found in the Mahabharata and also in the "Vishnu Smriti", which is an ancient Hindu text that is attributed to the God Vishnu, who is one of the major deities in the Hindu pantheon, which is a temple dedicated to all deities. These all being writing in which God is considered collectively and it is also one of the eighteen traditional Hindu law books (Dharmasutras), for it is primarily concerned with the laws and customs of Hindu society.

For certainly, it is known that the religion called Hinduism believes that humanity was in its darkest age. This current period in time being known as Kaliyuga which is an age that is stated to be full of sin, plus corruption, misery and all around each person there is evil.

Again is it not also said that this Kaliyuga age lasted from the year 500 AD to the year 1700 AD and it was said to be "the age of Kali" (the demon) also "the age of darkness" and "the age of vice and misery", or "the age of quarrel and hypocrisy". For certainly, it was also said that people's consciousness was limited to accept only gross matter and so people became attached has one to the physical animalistic world and not the spiritual one. It was also noted that during this "Dark Age", that most people lost their spiritual abilities plus their mental clarity and their normal understanding became animalistic in nature.

For certainly, this age was characterized by the belief that all matter was fixed and unchangeable, i.e. could not be changed. It was further stated by the later wise, that this was the reason why people were trapped in a physical animalistic "I Want for ME" world and so became attached to a ghostly feeling that they can only do what they their religious managers told to do, usually these being richly appointed managers who actually treated their worshippers has slaves. For example, during this period, many religiously written truths, that were really "I Want" demands coming from such richly appointed "religious" managers, were accepted as unconditional definitions or even dogmas that should be firmly believed and also pursued – but this was not the way to achieve "Enlightenment" in which the worshipper eventually experiences that they are truly the creation and that there is no observer, which of course is the only target of ALL our world's religions and philosophies'!

So it was that eventually and factual their arose unbreakable scientific evidence that presented the entirety of the universe to be a static but ever growing reality which contained divine laws that were believed to be "Godly" birthed or Nature created for the non-believer. For certainly, it was also noted that these ever evolving ever growing "Godly" birthed or Nature created laws for the non-believer, were truly unbreakable plus unchangeable and therefore could not be altered but which could actually be blended together in order to unify that which we call life. This being a life in which "Life's Purpose" states that it is only people who can become "Self-Aware" and thus become aware that they are has one with that which exists all around them just has it does within them! But it should also be noted that "Self-Awareness" can lead to "Self-Realisation"! This being that reality in which there is no observer for the soul or consciousness for the non-believer - becomes has one with the creation or with nature for the non-believer and there is no observer – which of course is the target of all religions and philosophies.

For certainly, it should now be known that it is because of our "Freedom of Choice" that scientific facts cannot obliterate "Religion"! For is it not true that it is this reality of an "I Want" which can actually create our religions and also their proposed "I Want" targets? For is it not also interesting to know that the people of our ancient times, such as farmers, herdsmen, artisans, soldiers, and slaves, were all mainly involved in physical labour, this being in order to achieve their bodily needs! For without doubt, in our past ancient times, were not all people's activities directed towards obtaining physically needed ends, such as food and clothing? Is it not also true that this way of life also made the social order of most people become static? For certainly, is it not also true that at this ancient time religious events took the form of rituals which were fed by "habitual" offerings to the instigators of such "worshipping" events. These being events which often created other painful sacrifices which were also supported by an "I Want" for Me prayer! For certainly, it is now well known that during this ancient period most people were ignorant of the true reality that existed all around them and so became afraid of any changes to their way of life! This ignorance also being created in such endeavors' which attempted to destroy all prior knowledge of philosophies and religions, such an example being the third-century destruction of the ancient Egyptian texts at Alexandria! But also is it now known that this ignorance and its enjoining fear all ended in the year 1700, this being the beginning of our current "Present Time"! For certainly, it was at this time that the Indian Sanskrit pursuing Hindu people, the most developed of our worlds people, began to actively disprove of the "Kali Yuga". For it was now seen to be an age of darkness and of vice and misery, which certainly created life of subordination and of misery for the majority of people! For without doubt, it is anciently and knowingly stated that this was after the "Kali Yuga", this being the third of the four "Yugas" (Ages) which ended 5,122 years ago.

So it is a known reality that it was actually 5,122 years ago that we entered the age known has the *"Dwapara Yuga"*, which when translated means "the age of two"! For certainly this is that condition which "Life's Purpose" modernly translates to mean when the observer becomes "Self-Aware" that they are that which they are also observing! This being that awareness which can lead to that second experience which is called "Self-Realization", this being that reality in which there is no observer for the experiencer actually becomes "Everything" and so is not born again – the reason why will be explained later in "Life's Purpose"!

These two experiences are of course are still the target of all our world's religions and philosophies' and it was certainly explained by the people of that time to be the age of *"Two Ahead"*, this being that reality in which a person actually experienced themselves to be everything that currently existed within "The Creation". It was also explained in those ancient times that this new age would be based upon "compassion" and "truthfulness", with "compassion", being described has meaning empathy, sympathy, concern, consideration, care, kind-heartedness, and benevolence! These also being the attributes that were seriously attached to the female of our species! For certainly, this new age was also called "Two Ahead", which "Life's Purpose" explains to be the unification of love and belonging has one which without doubt lovingly occurs between man and woman but only when it reflects the "Present Time"!

For certainly such a unification should contain truthfulness and honesty plus frankness, openness, reliability, correctness, faithfulness, accuracy, straightforwardness and certainly these attributes should emanate from the stronger male, for both are a recognized unity which was "religiously" named by our ancients to be the "Two Ahead"! This "Two Ahead" certainly being that unified two which can only exist in that reality which we call "The Present"! For certainly, there must be a constant search for unity with that which we call the "Present", for this is the only truth that does currently exists in this age of the *"Dwapara"* - which is wisely explained to be the third age of the four Yugas which are periods of people's who have had many lives upon our Earth – for remember it is a scientific fact that energy cannot die and so it must always be reborn somewhere else.

For without doubt, this modern age that we call the *"Dwapara"*, was also an age in which it was actually stated "Scientifically", that there was a shared unity that actually existed between the Man and Woman! For this religiously stated "Two Ahead" was explained by our wise ancients to be the "Created Man", who silently experiences, within himself, all the future needs that are required to feed the "Present Time" and also the "Created Woman", who silently experiences, within herself, all the needs that are required to satisfy the "Present Time"! For again it should be known that it was the "Created Woman" who was birthed to control that reality which we call the "Present", this being the actual "Present Time" which must contain the unity of that which can only exist between man and his worshipped and worshipping woman.

Still, it is a known fact that this "Golden age" did begin 5,122 years ago. For it was at that time some of our wise ancients said we actually moved out of the "Kali Yuga"! This was the age that we, now in our current time, recognized it to be the age of conflict, strife, discord and friction! This age, which was called the "Kali Yuga", was certainly an age in which there existed a very quarrelsome way of life which was being created by a selfish animalistic "I Want for ME"! For it is historically known that our wise ancients forecasted that the end of this brutal and personal "I Want" Kali Yuga would be in the year 2025, which in the west of our world is named to be the Common Era. For certainly it has been said, by our ancient wise, that this year 2025 will see the start of a "Glorious" age and an age when our world will return once again to be the joy and happiness of all our Earths people. For indeed, this coming "Golden Age" is anciently said to be an age in which we will see the arrival of peace plus prosperity and a happiness that will start in the year 2025. (UK time)

Indeed, it has been said in the past that that during this "Golden Age" period Darwin's theories will be proved to be very wrong, this being since the opposite of his theories have since been proved to be correct! For certainly this new age of goodness (Godness) is forecasted to begin in 2025 CE and it was actually showing a developing start in 2022! This beginning of the "New Age" goodness began has many people started to show unrest at the commercial distribution of market produced wealth! There is also appearing in our modern time, an even a greater unrest at those rebirths that are newly emanating from the animal kingdom and who are now being engaged to protect the wealth of others'.

For certainly in the beginning of the "Golden Age" our ancients' did state that the rich will not be against the poor and neither will the poor be against the rich and also age will not be against youth or education against illiteracy. For in the Golden age, it is said that the past colonization based "I Want" for me wars and its imposed laws will cease to exist! This also being the ceasing of the animalistic desire to hoard wealth! For certainly it will be known that in this new era all life and also all non-life will actually recognized to be a part of that which is actually observing of this unified creation! For indeed, it will be known that man will also continue with his desire to create children, this being because of his natural desire to provide "Future" needs and the woman will always teach her growing children to take care of the "Present Time", this being that "Present" which is all around them just has it is within them!

So yes! The good news, which will be Realized by most people, is that the Devil and its evil attacks do not exist! Also what will be known by most people at the start of this "Golden Age", is that the animalistic "I Want" demands which are always occurring within a person's mind, are the uncontrolled "voices" of their animalistic five senses, this being that reality which in the past people did genuinely believe to be the real them.

But in truth, although we have previously permitted our five senses i.e., these being Taste, Smell, Sight, Listening and Touch, to act as if they are "US", we now know that they are NOT us, for the real "us" is that which all our senses report too, which is the real you! This being that which religious people call the soul and non-religious people call the energy that rests with in you – for certainly, neither of these realties can die and so the fact remains that this energy will seek another reality in which it will be born again. For certainly, this inner energy, which many religious people call "The Soul", cannot be that reality which requests from you, who is the observer and the listener, an ever demanding "I Want"! This being because this inner energy, which is the real you, is has one with everything and so now we should understand that it is our animalistic five senses that always cries or barks for that which is all around it or even existing within it. For certainly, it is well known that the demands of our animalistic five senses can actually make a person do things that many say are caused by the Devil that is within them and therefore they cannot be held responsible for their actions. But the truth, regarding people's creation of an inner devil, is simply used as an excuse to avoid disciplining our real selves. For certainly it should be said, that the real truth is that we are probably and also falsely, pursuing an animalistic "I Want" that is coming from one or all of our five "animalistic" senses and of course this can be stopped, just has any pup can be trained to be obedient to its master.

For certainly, after the reading of "Life's Purpose" a person will know that the real truth is that they are allowing their own "animalistic" five senses to sound a mind-filling and very animalistic ally demanding "I Want". This being that condition which is "animalistic ally" allowing into the mind the many tempting "I Want" thoughts which are certainly coming from one or all of their animalistic five senses – this being that reality which is certainly affecting their "Present", for has a person they are now able to live in a life in which they can become "Everything"!

For surely we now know that these animalistic "I Want" thoughts do always lead to the destruction of the harmony that is constantly trying to exist or are endeavouring to exist all around you, just as they do within you! For is it not true that many people's animalistic five senses are always endeavouring to steal from this harmony and so they enforce their own animalistic "I Want" by claiming secretly or by knowingly stating "This is mine"!

So yes! It should now be known that it is this animalistic "I Want for ME", is that which creates the selfish acts that do "illegally" and "immorally" break Gods developing laws or Nature developing laws for the non-believers! These being developing laws which provide a direction that targets the creation of a heavenly unity for all that which exists in the "Present Time"! For indeed, it should now be known, that it is only without an "I Want" thought that a person can truly be aware of or even realise just what actions are needed to fulfil the needs of the developing "Present Time"! For is it not true, that it is only people that can, with a silent mind, become "enlightened", meaning that they can become aware of or even realise, that they can stop these animalistic "I Want" thoughts from constantly sounding into their mind. This being because these mind filling thoughts can only be animalistic "I Want" thoughts which are being sounded into the mind by one or maybe all of the body's animalistic five senses? For we should now know that these mind filling thoughts are usually animalistic memories of the past or are mind filling thoughts that are targeting what they want in the future, this being that world which our animalistic five senses are constantly tempting our body to pursue?

For is it not now known by all people to be true, that these animalistic mind filling thoughts, these being that which are coming from our animalistic five senses, can sometimes hurt another person's life? This being the pursuit of an animalistic ally created way of life which can only be pursuing an animalistic "I Want" for ME! This being that reality which should now be known to be a mind-filling "animalistic" chatter which is arising from one or from all of our animalistic five senses! For certainly, it should now be known that that which is being sounded into the mind are thoughts which are coming from one or from all of your animalistic five senses and it should now also be known that these thoughts are usually targeted by the words "I Want". But indeed, how can you be that which you are listening too? For is it not true that you can only be the listener?

For certainly, is it not also true that you cannot be anything that you smell, taste, observe, touch or listen too, for you are truly that which is experiencing these realties. For is not the real you that which is enabled to realize or be aware of this mind filling chatter and also its clamouring of many animalistic mind-filling "I Want" desires that are being "allowed" to constantly fill the mind? This being a mind filling certainty in which our animalistic five senses are constantly endeavouring to target and so obtain their own "I Want"! For indeed, should it now again be said that the words and thoughts that are being sounded in the mind are certainly coming from an animalistic "I Want"! This being that which is being sounded into your mind by one or by all of your five animalistic senses! This certainly being a mistaken situation in which our animalistic five senses are seeking their own "personal" "I Want" pleasures!

For certainly, and again it is good to remember, that you cannot be that which you observe, or listen too or taste, see, or smell, these being those five senses which are animalistic ally preoccupied with physical rather than spiritual needs! For certainly, it is known that their animalistic mind-filling "I Want" requests always takes the silent "listener", which is the real you, into a mind filled animalistic "I Want" past or an "I Want" present or an "I Want" future, all three being worlds that do not exist but should really be known has that world which we call "Hell", this being stated in our modern-day terminology. For it should now be a known truth, that this non-existing negative world that we call "Hell", is a world that is being personally and physically created by our animalistic "I Want" for me thoughts, these being thoughts which are coming from one or from all of our animalistic five senses! For truly is not this falsely created imaginary world being animalistic ally produced only in your mind? For certainly, can it not be easily confirmed that these mind filling "I Want for me" thoughts are certainly emanating from one or from all of your animalistic five senses?

So indeed, is it not now easy to understand that these mind blocking "I Wants", which are actually coming from your animalistic five senses, are actually that reality which is stopping your Soul from seeing through your mind that which we call "The Present"! For certainly, it is a known fact, that any of your animalistic five senses can verbally create an "I Want" within your mind, thus creating an animalistic "I Want" world that falsely exists has a mind blocking thought! For truly, is it not factual that all the thoughts which are filling your mind, are being created by one or all of your animalistic five senses? For indeed this is truly that world which we call Hell and therefore it is a world that is being created to exist within that reality which we call "The Present"! Therefore it should now be acknowledged that the true you, which are your Soul, are unable to see "The Present" through a mind that is filled by thoughts!

For is it not now a known fact that this negative and falsely created "I Want" for me world is that world which we call Hell? This "Hell" being that unreal world which is being falsely birthed by the animalistic "I WANT" mind filling words that are coming from one or all of a person's animalistic five senses. For certainly and truly, this unreal world is that false world which we knowingly call "Hell" and it is a world that is accepted to be a place of misery, torment, agony and suffering!

But truly, is it not more knowledgeable to understand that this unreal imaginary world that we call "Hell" is only enabled to be lived in by people because of their gifted "Freedom of Choice"! Therefore, and so in ignorance they choose to live in a world in which they are controlled by animalistic "I Want" demands that are coming from one or from several of their animalistic five senses! For certainly, it is this "I Want" life that is constantly bringing woe to them who choose live it, this reliving also being when their body dies and their Soul returns to their creator, this being before being born again – for certainly, the Soul cannot die.

For is it not true that energy cannot die and that God or Nature for the Non-Believer can only exist in the "Present", this being that which exist for all life and non-life and is that which is known by all life to be the "Present Time". For certainly it is really a "Present" that God or Nature for the Non-Believer did actually create for all life and all non-life to rewardingly use – but more about this later in "Life's Purpose"!

So yes! What is quite amazing to understand is that truth, which all readers should now be aware of and so by reading "Life's Purpose" may soon be enabled to realise, is that it is these thoughts, which are clouding into an undisciplined mind, are being sounded into the mind by one or all of your animalistic five senses! For certainly, they are not coming from the "REAL" you, who is the observing Soul, this being that entity whose dutiful view of the creators "Present", or Natures Present for the non-believer, is being blocked by these animalistic mind filling "I Want" creations.

So Yes! Now it is good to be enabled to understand i.e.: "Stand Under", the actual knowledge that those thinking "words" and "pictures", which are being sounded into the mind, are really "I Want" for "ME" claims that are being sounded into the mind by one or all of your undisciplined unruly five senses. For certainly, has the "Life's Purpose" truly states, you are not that "animalistic" entity which is sounding words and pictures into your mind, this is definitely a mistaken misunderstanding! For without doubt, this is a misunderstanding which actually allows your animalistic five senses to entice you to do acts that will make you take the values that nature says belongs to others. For undoubtedly, is not the stealing of that which belongs to or is the responsibility of others an animalistic "I Want" for me activity? Meaning that that which belongs to others has not been "naturally" earned and so nature will see that happiness and contentment will constantly elude such thieves – is this not true?

Therefore is it not true that the actual and noisy mind-filling "I Want" for me thoughts are without doubt that reality which can be constantly clouding a person's mind! This being that certainty which ensures that many people are being driven by animalistic "I Want" appetites rather than by spiritual needs, a condition that is constantly blocking the Soul from seeing through the mind the "Present" time! For definitely this animalistic "I WANT" that is filling the mind is definitely being sounded into the mind by one or several of your animalistic five senses! Therefore, it is without doubt that any of the five animalistic senses can be verbally sounding words into your mind that are saying that you should pursue their animalistic "I want"!

So yes! Is it not now "Realized" to be true that such a claiming "I Want", this being that which is now known to be coming from one or from all of your animalistic five senses, can be an "I Want" that is actually blocking your Souls view through the mind of that which we call "The Present"! Therefore, should we not now be aware and so realise that this is a certain truth? For certainly, cannot this mind-blocking reality of words and pictures be now knowingly witnessed to be constantly happening within your own mind? This certainly being that mind-blocking activity which stops your Souls ability to see i.e.: be "aware" or even to "realise" the factually truth of that which is actually happening the "Present" time! For certainly and again it should be said, that this "silent" observer within you is your Soul, this being that which knows that it is an integral and unified part of everything that exists within that which we call "The Creation"!

For certainly what else can it be that is observing these inner-mind sounds and pictures, these being that which are being created by one of or by all of your animalistic five senses? All of these being sounds and pictures that are certainly requesting an animalistic "I want" for "ME", but who is it that is listening to those words which the five animalistic senses are sounding into the mind? For certainly, this can only be the "Soul" which exists within the bodies of all people! This being that entity which knows itself to be has one with that reality which we call "The Creation"!

For definitely is it not true that the creation exists has one unified realty? This also being that reality which continues to exist within you just has it exists all around! For the Soul must be in total unity with the creation, this being that which "Life's Purpose" names to be the totality of the true "You"! Therefore, within the knowledge of this truth, how can your Soul be that which you witness? For certainly, is it not true that the

Soul, this being that energy which rests within you and all around you, cannot be that which you listen to, or see, taste, smell or touch? For certainly the totality of that unification which we call "The Creation", is actually that reality in which your undying Soul does actually experiences to be "ITSELF" – remember these words in the Christian bible – "I AM THE I AM"! This being that which "Life's Purpose" states to mean that you are "Everything"!

So yes! This wholesome truth that you are "Everything" is proven by your Souls God-given or Nature Given for the non-believer, "Freedom of Choice"! For certainly, it is this truth that you are "everything" that proves that these "I Want" words that are being sounded in your mind are not coming from the true "You!" For certainly, it is now well to know that this animalistic ally pursued "I Want" cannot be for that which your Soul, which is the true you, does seek! Nor can it be for anything that you listen to, or smell, taste or touch. For certainly, this mind filling "I Want" world that can dominate your life, is being created by one or all of your bodies animalistic five senses! This truth being because you are allowing their animalistic "I Want" demands to fill and so cloud into your mind! For certainly, this living has an animal which has no soul, can be that reality which you can "choose" to believe is the real you; but this is not the real you! For has a person, you are really the observing Soul! This being that which is the witness to the reality of the entire world that is all around you and also that world which is within you! But frankly, this "misunderstanding", particularly within those people who have just emerged from the animal kingdom and so do have a strong belief that the animalistic five senses are the real them, is a belief which certainly takes a person away from the knowing of their true self. For without doubt this is a sad misunderstanding because the real you, which is your Soul - is unable to see the creation through a mind that is blocked by many animalistic "I want" thoughts!

For certainly it should be known and so should be often stated, that your Soul, which is the real you, cannot observe the creations "Present Time" through an animalistic mind that is filled by "I Want" thoughts! This being because the mind is blocked by animalistic greed based "I Wants" that are being sounded into the mind by the uncontrolled animalistic five senses! This, and again it should be said, that this "I Want" reality which can be constantly clouding the mind, is not the real "You", for you are truly your Soul and it is this, which is the real you, that cannot see the creation that exists all around it! For certainly, there is only one Soul per person, but wisely it should also be recognized that your Soul is known to be has one with all other Souls.

So yes! The real reason for the Soul and the existence of only peoples "Freedom of Choice" is so that the Soul can use the body and its five senses to be enabled to freely "choose" and so pursue any task that is required to harmonize that which has been placed in front of it by the "Mother of the Creation". It should also be known that is essential to be able to do this task without any interfering "I Want for ME", this being that which can be blocking and so clouding the mind! For certainly, this often being an "I Want for Me" which, by clouding the mind, does actually stop a person's Soul from seeing through the mind that which is needed to support the "harmony" that the "Mother of the Creation" is carefully placing in front of it. For certainly, when an "I Want", this being an animalistic "I Want" which is coming from one or from all of a person's animalistic five senses, then such a person has personally become like an untrained dog which does "bark" and "snarl" into the face of any food needing listener, meaning that such a person is beings driven by physical appetites rather than spiritual needs.

For without doubt, many people may also feel the need to ask for "scientific" proof that will actually support the above statements! These truthful statements' being that we are not the five senses and that our five senses are just instruments for our use! For certainly, what now can be wisely explained, has is stated by most of our worlds ancient wise, is that each person's Soul, apart from being a guiding companion, is not just an observer that can be experienced to be in unity with the creation that exists all around it, but the Soul is also a much needed creative observing servant of how to "Support the Creation" that is unfolding before it! This being an observer that is in unity and so is has one with the creation that exists all around it! This final bit being that reality which can only exists within people and not within the rest of our world's animal kingdom!

Therefore, the "scientific" fact is that it is only people who can experience a unity with that which was previously being observed, or more scientifically and more simply put, *"An observer, with a still mind, will become "Self-Aware" that they are has one with the world that their Soul is observing! It is only when a person actually becomes "everything" i.e.: a creation in which there is no observer, that they will become "Self-Realized", this being when their Soul becomes has one with the creation and there is no observer.* This of course being that realty which our ancients called "Self-Realization", meaning of course that you realise that there is no "observer"! This being when the experiencer actually becomes the unified totality of all the "Creation", which is a stage above the experiencing of a "Self-Aware" condition, but both conditions, are certainly a reality which can only be experienced in the "Present Time"! But more about this later in "Life's Purpose"!

So yes! It is certainly known that many religious people often state that they are deeply religious and so they give much importance to their many requesting prayers, these usually being prayers that are seeking a personal benefit. For certainly it is known that many people who exist within our worlds many different religions and philosophies, do actually attach themselves to a severe "self-punishment" or some such task, this being has they seek to experience a unity with their God! For certainly this can also be a personal attempt to achieve a private "I Want", a reality which is attached to a belief that God will love them more for punishing themselves! Their belief being *"I want a religious loving gift from God"* this being why they religiously pursue this self-inflicted "religious" punishment for they believe it will bring to them better Life's tyle! For certainly it should be known that this is actually a sought life-style which is simply targeting personal "I Want"!

For certainly it is also known that some religious people believe that to receive "Enlightenment" from God, what is required is a self-hurting penance which does inflict pain upon themselves and concerns others!

But it should be known that it is certainly not wise to do this! For self-punishment is a self-inflicted pain that is artificially placed upon yourself or upon others and it is certainly not necessary to suffer in order to become "Self-Aware" of that which you truly are! Thus to become wise, a person must unthinkingly become "Self-Aware" of the creations unity, meaning a singularity in which there is no other! This being that reality in which a person can experience the freely given contentment and also the happiness that actually abounds in God's harmony or in the world of Nature for the Non-believer! This actually being the experiencing of that unified ever moving ever still reality which is all around you just has it is within you!

For without doubt, this will be a "Self" experience that can only be Realized to exist in the unity of the "Present Time", this being that "Present" which is legally and carefully governed by the "Mother of the Creation" who is constantly endeavouring to replace disharmony with harmony. This of course is being in support of God the fathers' commitment that all people should be given the "Freedom of Choice", this being to either choose to want nothing but to live has a supporting life force in His world and so, upon death become has one with Him, or to constantly pursue, via many lives, an animalistic "I Want for ME"! Forgetting that the unity which exists within the creation is really "them"!

But more about this later in "Life's Purpose"!

For again and certainly, it should also be known by all people, that no penance is required in order to achieve a peaceful and contented balance within your current life or, if necessary in your next life to come. For certainly you can and smilingly said, "Painfully" stop the overeating of food and drink, or in the pursuing of other "I Want" for ME - overindulgences! For now it should be known that personal fasting is excellent tools that will disciplinary prevent the constant demands of the animalistic five senses from commanding you to seek their "I Want"! For when these animalistic five senses are not controlled, they can be "observed" to scream into your mind like five wild dogs that seek to taste, smell, touch and all this "I Want" being at the sight of food!

So yes! The real purpose for fasting, which is well known in all our worlds' religions, is to learn how to control and so stop this greed that is emanating from one or all of our animalistic five senses! But now it would also be wise to know, that in our ancient days and prior to the beginning of most of our world's religions, it would be impossible to establish such a way of thinking. For indeed in those ancient times it was a known truth that a saying such has: *"You are the Observer', and so you cannot be that which you observe in the mind".* This statement would certainly not be fully understood by the people of our distant past. Yet in truth, the personal experience of being "Self-Aware", this being an awareness that you are has one unit with the creation, can also develop into to becoming "Self-Realized"! This being a "Self-Realisation" in which you "realise" that you are actually "Everything" that exists within the creation and that there is no observer! For certainly it should also be now known that these two realities are the targets of "ALL" our world's religions and philosophies, for it means, that via prayer and other incantations', that you actually experience that you have become has one with Gods world, or has one with the world of Nature for the Non-Believer!

Therefore truly, it must now be known that our modern age should be called the age of forgetting, for certainly forgetting is our worst enemy! For is it not known that in our current age the body's five senses have become that which mainly controls a person's "I Want" activities! It is also interesting that in some ancient religions, this demanding "I Want" of the five senses was alleged to be coming from unseen bandits which did actually enter the body – but more about this later in "Life's Purpose".

However, is it not also true that many religions and philosophies state quite clearly to their followers the words *"Thine will be Done",* this truly meaning, of course, the harmonising "will" of God and not the "I Want" "will" of our animalistic five senses. These clearly being that inner life forces which are always fighting for personal claims, these being "I Want" claims that do truly and wrongfully steal from God's Creation or the world of Nature for the Non-Believers.

Therefore, should it not be wrong to force this animalistic ally created "I Want for ME" upon others but correct to force it upon our animalistic five senses! For certainly, when the five senses are subdued and quiet and so are not factually sounding animalistic "I Wants" into the mind, then this silence will allow your Soul to "observe", through your empty mind, ninety to one hundred per cent of the "Creation" that is existing all around you, this being that which we call "The Present"! This first condition, which "Life's Purpose" calls "Self-Awareness", is an experience in which a person becomes fully aware of God's creation, or of Natures creation for the Non-Believer. This being an experience in which exist no accompanying thoughts for it is certainly an awareness which can only be experiencing the silent unity of the "Present".

For certainly, this "Self-Aware" experience is that realty in which a person becomes "unthinkingly" aware that they are has one with the creation that constantly exists all around them just has it also exists within them! Therefore and truly, it should now be known that a silent mind does allow the Soul to see through the mind and so experience itself to be has one with the "Present". This being a "Self-Awareness" that actually brings forth an awakening in which a person's soul can, by seeing through the empty mind, "Self-Realise" itself to be has one with that "Present" which we call "The Creation"!

Yet, is it not also true and without doubt, that in ignorance seventy to ninety per cent of a person's mind can be clouded by many an "I Want", this being that which is constantly arising from a their animalistic five senses? This fact actually being a reality which does constantly create many mind blocking thoughts which creates a personal "I Want" non-existing dream world! This being a false non-existing dream world which is created in the mind by the "I Want" of the oft arguing and uncontrolled five senses, this being that reality which is actively true in all our worlds animal life forms! But is it not true that this is also an animalistic "I Want" mind-filling reality in which people actually believe is coming from their true self! But truly, this that is being sounded into your mind is NOT coming from the real YOU! For truly they cannot be you, this truth being because you cannot be that which you observe or that which you listen too, for the real you is truly the observer and also the listener!

For again and certainly, this false belief that the real you is personally sounding these "I Want" words or pictures into your mind, just cannot be true! For these words or pictures that you experience to be entering your mind are an animalistic ally created "I Want" which is coming from one of your animalistic five senses! This being because they are selfishly-claiming a world in which they are using your body to provide for "THEM!" For certainly this is that reality which can actually be called "animalism", for it is without doubt one or more of your animalistic five senses which are constantly shouting into the mind their greed based "I Want" for ME! For certainly a true awareness should now be Realized that you are truly the observer of this animalistic mind-filling reality, this being that which does constantly and verbally pursue an animalistic "I Want" for ME!

For certainly and truly, you should now know that you cannot be that which you see, taste, touch, smell or listen too! For you is truly the experiencer of all these realties. But now it should be known that controlling these animalistic five senses, which always rest under your observation, is not as easy as it seems. The reason being for this dilemma is that this behaviour, in which people are habitually driven by animalistic desires rather than spiritual needs, may have been in control of you for an exceptionally long time! For is it not true that many people do actually "think" that the animalistic five senses is really "them", but they cannot be you! For again it must be truly said that you are the experiencer and the observer of that which these animalistic senses bring to you!

So yes! It should now be known that within this false lived truth, in which you believe that your bodies animalistic five senses are the real you, they will actually and "very" noisily put up many mind-filling arguments so has to defend themselves – and this is a truth no matter how strange it may seem! For, after all, for many years you have actually believed that these five senses are the real you and so you will acknowledge that the words that are being sounded into your mind are "common sense". But truthfully, should we not be aware and so realise that this "talking" in your head is truly that which is being listened to by the real "YOU", this real you being that which we historically call "The Soul"! Yet sadly are they not mind filling words which are being sounded into your mind by one of your animalistic five senses? This being that reality which in childhood you "Chose", via your Godly gifted or Nature gifted for the non-believer, "Freedom of Choice", to believe that the five animalistic senses were the real YOU! Therefore is it not for this reason that you, the real you', which is your Soul, has actually permitted them to freely sound within your mind because you "chose" it to be so, this being because you believed that the five sense were the true YOU! For now is it not known to true, that your untrained animalistic five senses will constantly contradict and also argue amongst themselves? Also is it not true that they can do this in a loud mind-filling voice, this being that certainty which actually stops the Soul from seeing through the mind that which we call "The Creation?

For certainly, the truth now is that you, dear reader, should always remember that you now truly know that your five senses are not you, just as you know that a dog is not you that you hear barking for your attention. For indeed the stillness and silence of that reality which is "observing" or "listening" to all these sounds that are entering your mind, is certainly the real you! For you are truly the observer or listener to these sounds that are entering the mind and this is a truth that shall always be so! But "Life's Purpose" also states that there will now come that time, in which you will silently ask, "Who is the observer?" The answer to this question is that which "Life's Purpose" does scientifically prove! This being that the observer and listener is truly "The Soul", this being that which rests within ALL people – and only in people!

So yes! Again it should be said, that the Soul of all people, this being said to be that independent energy which rests only within people, cannot observe the outer world through a mind that is blocked by thoughts! These usually being mind filling thoughts which are usually animalistic "I Want" for ME thoughts! For certainly and it is truly again stated that these animalistic "I Want" for ME thoughts are coming from the clamouring five senses! This being that "animalism" which we now know does actually block the Soul's view, through the mind, of the outer world, a viewing reality which can only happen through the silent mind of the observer.

Thus factually, this "I Want, which is coming from one or from all of the animalistic five senses, does actually make the observer think that are seeking a "personal" gratification! But certainly, this is a desire which is actually emanating from one or all of the "animalistic" five senses. These also being personal "I Want" thoughts that are usually based upon past or future concepts, and they are always animalistic ally targeting and arguing to obtain a personal "I Want". For certainly, this is an enforced "I Want" for ME world which always leads to great arguments within people and also within a person's the mind.

It is also interesting that people can always make for themselves and for others, very good "I Want" or "I Need" excuses! This being so that in this animalism they can continue to do bad things even when their "I Want" is painfully inflicted upon others! For certainly, some people in this ancient animalistic forgetfulness, do constantly endeavour to seek and so achieve their "I Want" for ME - thoughts! These certainly being animalistic thought based conversations which can also unite similar "I Want" groups of likeminded people and even whole countries.

So yes! One of the first things to understand and also to continually ask your self is the question, *"How can I be that which I observe?* Or even more clearly and also better to be known is the need to know just what it is this energy that is keeping these activities moving forward and also going onwards? These being the body's activities that you know are within you and yet are also without your control? The answer to this question is to understand that truly and really you are your Soul! This being that life forces which wants nothing and which also actually needs nothing! The reason for this being that you're Soul already has everything for it is actually unified with everything! For certainly, this reality which we call the Soul, is genuinely the real YOU! Meaning, of course, that the Soul of each person is not a solitary isolated individual but actually is the authentic "Self" of all that exists! This "all that exists" reality being that which we call "The Creation"! For is it not true that our wise ancients often called the Soul "The Self of All"! For certainly, it is true that our wise ancients believed that the individual Soul is an energy that is attached in unity not only to ALL Souls but to also everything that exists within that which we call our Creation!

For indeed, in the real world, the "truth of reality" is that the Soul is joined, i.e.: is has one with the actual "Self of All", meaning that is attached has one to all life and also all non-life! For certainly, it is also anciently stated that a person's Soul is not only in unity with the "Self of All" i.e. the totality of the creation, but it is also anciently stated to be in has one with a *"Peace That Surpasses All Understanding".* This being that reality which can be said to attract football spectators and also all our worlds other sports spectator or attendees to be has one, not only with the team that they are attracted too, but also with all other worshippers of that team! For is it not also true that this group mind that is without thought, engages only with the singleness of the "Present" time"! A singleness in which they experience a unity with everything that is occurring all around them just has it is within them. For certainly, this experience is that which can only be "self-Realized" in the "Present" time".

Therefore is it not true that sport spectators do also actually experience a desire to belong in unity to the creation that is all around them, just has exists that unity that rests within them! Thus, for that reason do we not say that they are likeminded people? These being people who, when watching their favourite sport, do actually seek to experience a unity of togetherness not only with the players but to be has one with all other worshipping spectators! This being a happening in which ALL that is being observed in front and around them is also experienced to be in unity with that life that is within them, which means that they are experiencing everything to actually be their true selves! Thus, is this not the reason has to why watching that ongoing activity which we call "sport", is one of our world's greatest attractions'?

For truly "Life's Purpose" says that this is because the spectators and also the players, do actually experience a being has one with God or with Nature for the Non-Religious – meaning that they experience that they are "Everything" and so nothing exists accept "Them", which of course is the truth for certainly the whole creation is only one life form! Therefore, can it not now seen as "scientifically" correct, that it is only people who, unconditionally and also genuinely, do seek, within all our worlds religions and philosophies, to actually experience their being has one with the "Creation", this being that which is all around them, just has it is within them!

For certainly, is not true that all our world's religions and philosophies do truly endeavour to teach to their followers just how to experience a reality in which they can fully experience the unity of their Soul to that which we call "The Creation"? This being so that their followers can peacefully exist has a unified part of "Everything"! For truly are we not always told, by our world's ancient wise, that all people are of the one body! This being the one body that we call "The Creation"! For certainly, is it not also true, that our past and also our present ancient wise, all realized that those people whose earlier lives had been has an animal in the animal kingdom do have great difficulty in seeking unity with the creation in which they are now birthed has people! These being people, who after many lives, began to feel a need to belong to a world in which they are has one and so, with this "Enlightenment", they would eventually experience no animalistic "I Want only for ME"! For certainly just how to "Scientifically" achieve this ever-calling ever-wanting target of becoming has one with that which exists all around you, just has it knowingly exists within you - will be truly explained later in "Life's Purpose".

So now, has an example of this unity with the creation that has been previously stated, this being that it is wise to know that the word "Woman" is a shortened version of the name "Worshipped Man"! For is it not true that "historically" and in our "Present Time", a man will go onto his knees when asking a Woman to become has one with him in marriage? Also is it not a known historical reality that, when in public or private places, a man will stand when a "woman" enters the room he is in? Is it not also well known or should be well know, that the stated reason for this male standing when a woman enters the room, is that a man's Soul does actually rise in honour of the woman's entry – this being that which compels the man's body to follow it! Is this not a well known truth? For truly, it is very compelling for the man to stay has one with his Soul, this being that which rests within him and which can also rest without him. For certainly it is truly a well known fact, that a man will instinctively become aware that their Soul will leave them if they do not stand at the woman's entry into their "Present" time. Of course, is it not true that God or the Natural law for the Non-Believer, has designed man and woman to actually be has one unified entity? For the woman's given "Nature" is to understand how to control the "Present", while the man's given Nature is to understand how to control all their "Future" needs. This is that fact which does ensure that the two needs to become has one creating and supporting entity, and the only difference being that the man always needs to create children to support future needs, whilst the woman eventually sees no need for this - but honours the man. This reality being until the man gets older, and then he too then recognizes that he is unable to provide more children – but life goes on!

7 FALSE BELIEF SYSTEMS

Is it not also true that one of the most robust belief systems in the world is the belief in the value of money? For certainly, is it not true that if you actually believe that money has a true value, then you must also know that "anything" you want to feel is truly of real value, is very important. But is it not also true that if you lived alone on the proverbial dessert island, what value will your money have? Therefore, can it not be true that certain of your stated beliefs are not always correct – so is this belief about the value of money, not also an incorrect viewpoint? For is this viewpoint about money not just has false has the viewpoint in which you actually believe that your five senses are the only real you, when in truth the real you is the observer of their messages! Therefore is it not true that money has no real value and the truth is that paper money is only coloured paper?

For example, if you were actually air-dropped £20,000,000 in variable UK notes, or Euro or USA currency notes, or several other countries paper money, and this money was air-dropped to you when you were living with an Amazon tribe deep inside the Amazon jungle and who had never been in contact with our modern world! What value would this money be to you?

For is it not true that in the beginning of this Amazon tribe receiving this dropped £20,000,000 in paper money, they would probably be very annoyed, but then would pleased to discover that this paper was very beneficial for the starting of their fires?

Now, what would happen if you dropped the same bundle of money over the centre of London or any of our world's cities? Is it not true that this "I Want from "ME" belief, this being that which was emanating from one or from all of the animalistic five senses, would bring chaos and maybe the loss of life? For certainly this animalistic ally created belief, this being that which would be aroused by many people in these cities, would be very different from the created "I Want" belief of the Amazon people, but it would certainly be an imposed animalistic "I WANT FOR ME!

But truly are not these vastly different "I Want for Me" ways of thinking, actually being created by different animalistic-ally enforced "values" - these being very different values which are being imposed upon the same amount of money? For is it not a correct truth that this printed paper, which we call money, does actually have no practical value, except to start a fire? Therefore, is it not true that this mystical belief, that paper money has a good value, does actually fool the majority of people who live in that which we call "The Civilised World"?

For can it not now be truly said, that that reality which we call the civilised world has another falsely accepted truth? This truth being that which can be likened to the belief that the animalistic five senses, these being that which are constantly chattering their "I Want" into many people's minds, are animalistic ally thought to be the real them, but of course they cannot be you! For you are truly and certainly the observer and listener of these animalistic "I Want" messages that are being constantly sounded within your mind! For is it not true that you can only be that entity which is observing, tasting, seeing, touching and smelling the world that is exists all around you! This entity being that which is religiously and knowingly called "The Soul"!

So again and truly, you are certainly that reality which is actually listening to or observing these words that are being constantly and "animalistic ally" sounded within your mind! This certainly being that mind-filling realty which blocks the Soul from seeing the world that we do actually call the "Present"! Therefore is it not a certain truth that these thoughts, which are arising in your mind, are all being silently witnessed by your observing Soul? For certainly, is it not also true that these mind filling thoughts are being created by one or by all of our five animalistic senses, this being that animalism which is known to be always creating a selfish animalistic "I Want for ME" world? This being a world in which our five senses are allowed, in ignorance, to create a mind-filling "I Want for ME" thought! This certainly being an animalistic "I Want" thought which is constantly and selfishly endeavouring to claim and also take something from the unified-creation – but only to benefit its animalistic itself!

Therefore is it not true that such "I Want for Me" thoughts can only be an animalistic way of thinking? This being because they are observed thoughts so they cannot be coming from the real "YOU", who is truly the observer of these thoughts! For has "Life's Purpose" does constantly state, these thoughts are actually coming from the "uncontrolled" animalistic five senses, this being that which is not the real you for you cannot be that which you observe, touch, taste, smell or listen too, for you are the experiencer of these reporting realties! For certainly, you are that which is called the Soul, this being that reality which is has one with that which we call "Present"! For can it not be proved to be true, that the real you is that observing reality which is named to be the Soul or the silent five animalistic senses for the non-believer?

This being that which can only observe the world thru a silent mind, for in reality it is an observer which can actually experience, without added thoughts, the singularity or the oneness of all that is being observed, tasted, heard, smelled and also listened too? This being that reality which is knowingly experienced to be the totality of that which we call "The Creation", which can only exist in the "Present-Time"! For certainly it should be acknowledged that the "Creation" is a growing totality which actually survives has a singularity of that which exists all around you, just has it also exists in unity with all that exists within you! Therefore, is should now be accepted to be true, that these "I Want" thoughts, these being that which you sound into your mind, can only be coming from your undisciplined animalistic five senses?

So again, can it not now be said to be true, that all our world's religions and philosophies do constantly endeavour, via imposed and disciplined praying and also obligatory incantations, to bring to their followers the "enlightening" experience that they are actually has one body with that reality which we call "The Creation", this being that which can only exist in the "Present" Time! This certainly being that which "Life's Purpose" calls a blissful "Self-Aware" experience and which "Life's Purpose" names to be a reality in which the experiencer becomes aware that they are has one with the Creation! This being an experience which all our worlds' religions and philosophies' do target for their followers to achieve! For without doubt, this "Self-Aware" experience is an awakening in which the prayer becomes has one with the creation that is all around them, just has it is silently experienced to be that totality which is within them!

For certainly and again is should be said, that this anciently known "Self-Aware" experience is that reality in which the experiencer knowingly becomes aware that they are has one with the creation that is all around them, just has that creation which also resides in a supporting unification within them! Thus such a "Self-Aware" experiencer knowingly understands themselves to be enjoined has one with the creation that is within them and also all around them and so they do fully understand i.e. Stand under those words "I am that I am!"

This certainly being that realty which can lead to "Self-Realization", which is the targeted purpose of all our world's religions and philosophies', but more about this later in "Life's Purpose"! But for now it can be said, and without any doubt it should also be known, that all our world's animalistic life forms, this being those life forms which are not people, can only be controlled by their physical appetites which are created by their five senses, rather than by any spiritual needs! Thus, they unavoidably live in an animalistic "I Want" for me world, which should be avoided by people. Yet is it not known to be true that some people do organize individually or by ganging up together, to animalistic ally pursue an "I Want" this world for ME – but why is it that they pursue this animalism?

For certainly, is it not a known truth that all animals are driven by their animalistic appetites rather than by spiritual needs? Thus, and it should be said repeatedly, that pursuing such an animalistic way of life does actually create a private "I Want for ME" world which is threateningly supported by many animalistic "I Want" for me thoughts! Therefore it is certainly true that this animalistic "I Want for ME" pursuit is actually being created by a person's animalistic five senses! Therefore, it should now be "unthinkingly" accepted to be true, that such "I Want for ME" animalistic thinking is a reality which does actually create for a person a false imaginary world? This being an "I Want for ME" world which can only exist in animals because they cannot experience that they are actually the creation that is within them which is has one with the creation that is all around them! For certainly it is only people who are without thought, that can actually "Self- Realise" that they are "Everything", meaning that they truly experience that they are the totality of the creation!

Now, and again it should be said, that all mind-filling thoughts can only be animalistic "I Want" for me thoughts! For certainly, this is because they are created by one or several of your animalistic five senses for it is your

Soul or your inner energy (Consciousness') that is observing such thoughts! Therefore, and again it should be said, that these thoughts that are clouding the mind are really coming from your animalistic five senses which are, seeing, smelling, taste, touch and hearing! For indeed, is it not certainly true that these mind filling thoughts actually do stop our Soul or the energy that rests within us for the non-believer, from experiencing the real world in which we truly live? This being a world that can only exist in the "Present", which is our gift from God or from Nature for the non-believer!!

For certainly, is it not also true that this personal "Present", this being that which is within us and also all around us, is the only reality in which we can disciplinary and physically practice a religiously acknowledged belief system or a philosophically acknowledged belief system for the non-religious? This mind silencing practice being in an effort to become has one and to actually stay has one with a creation that exists all around us, just has it exists within us! For truly is not our body, this being that creation which exists within us and all around us, a unified creation that only "People" can experience – but only when they exist in an unthinking "Present" Time! This being an unthinking present time which can be experienced via disciplinary imposed praying! Therefore, and unquestionably, is not this "Present" which we exist in, a present that should be acknowledged to be far more valuable than the belief that exists regarding the universal value of money? Therefore is it not true, just has our worlds history shows, that many people do knowingly experience this awareness of unity with the creation that is all around them just has it is within them! Is it not also true, has our history shows, that the creators of many of our world's religions and philosophies did actually become has one with the "Present", this being a realisation which can only be experienced in the now time?

Therefore and truly, is not this unifying experiencing, which is the becoming has one with that which we call the creation, an experience which all our worlds' religious leaders constantly spoke about? Also, is it not true that our worlds' religious leaders produced sermons and advice which sounded too many "I Want" for me animalistic listeners, to be irritatingly tedious and very over bearing? This being because of the animalism that existed with their uncontrolled five senses and thus they animalistic ally pursued an "I Want" for me world!

Therefore, is it not a truth that many such "animalistic" listeners, which "Life's Purpose" explains to be people who are early re-births from the animal kingdom, find it very difficult to accept the living has one life within the world that exists all around them, just has it exists within them! Yet their growing through many lives has people they will eventually desire to realise the purpose of their existence, which is to becoming has one with God or with Nature for the non-believer! Also, is this not the reason why many people, via religion, endeavour to more fully understand the truth regarding the purpose of their existence?

This being a truth which strengthens their search for a creation which they can realise! This "Self-Realization" actually being an experience in which they become has one body with all that exists within the "Present" time and that there is no other! For truly this is that "Self-Realization" which is experienced when a person removes all "I Want for ME" thoughts plus the pursuing of any "I Want" for me thoughts! For what is it that a person can want when they experience that they are truly "everything"! This certainly being an experience which is based upon an affectionate feeling for the singularity of a creations unity which is fully harmonised! This being the experiencing that you actually are a single entity, which is the experiencing that the creation exists has "only one" unthinking all knowing existing reality that has been created by God or by Nature for the non-believer! This certainly being that all-knowing wisdom which you experience when you "Self-Realise" that you are a unified one with all life and all non-life which is that reality which does naturally rest outside of the animalistic "I Want" for me world?

For indeed, is it not an absolute truth, that the majority of people do actually experience that their personal life is of a much higher value than that of their accumulated "I Want" wealth? For certainly, is it not also true that there rests within many people an internal non-thinking consensus that their real "work" is to add supporting value to the activities of God's developing Creation or the creation of Nature for the non-believer? Is it not also reasonable to remember that this support does not mean that people must glibly give their wealth away or target to live in poverty or in need? For certainly, is it not true that the owners of such wealth have been placed into a position of great responsibility. For certainly, Godly chosen owners of such wealth have an all encompassing Soul that will wisely inform them just what the creation, this being that which is unified all around them, needs in support from their assets? For again is it not true to say that such knowledge, this being an "unthinking" experience which automatically occurs when you "religiously" and mind-silently allow the Soul to observe that which God, or Nature for the non-believer, has created or allowed, via the "Freedom of Choice" to be created, within the "Present" that is within you and also all around you!

Therefore, and is it not true to say, that within our world any person can culturally "choose" to partake in and also "choose" to personally contribute to, any religious and or philosophical belief system that they choose to? This being a personal "Self-Chosen" religious or philosophical system which does knowingly appear to exist in unification with that entire world which is all around them, just has it exists in unity within them? For is not this creation, this being that reality which is experienced to be within us and also all around us, a God or a Nature given reality for the Non-Believer! This also being a known reality within which all people do exist with a "Freedom of Choice", this being to do or not to do, to be or not to be and even to choose die or choose not to die, has in war etc!

Consequently is it not true, that it is only people that can "choose" to either live in a selfish "I Want" for me Hell, or "choose" to live in unselfish unity with that reality which we call "Heaven", this being that which can only exist in the "Present" time! This being a "Heaven" in which it is only people that can, via a non-thinking awareness, actually experience that they are a unified "Everything"! For certainly, it is only people that can, with a mind that is free from any "I Want", become "unthinkingly" aware that they are in unity with that which is observed to be all around them just has it is within them! Or even "unthinkingly" realise that they actually are the unified "Heaven" and that there is no observer!

For certainly it should now be known to be true, that it is the laws of "Heaven" or the laws of "Nature" for the non-believer, that constantly endeavour to reveal to all people that it is truly "Heaven" that exist all around them just has it exists in unity within them. Therefore, it should now be known to be true that it is only people who are allowed to experience these two ways of living, meaning to be separate from the creation or be has one with the creation? For is it not also true that both ways of living are allowed or are created to be allowed by the God given or Nature given for the non-believer, "Freedom of Choice"?

For without doubt, is not this "Freedom of Choice" a reality that can only be Realized by people? For is it not true that it is only people who can "choose" to either live in the **"peace that surpasses all understanding"**, this being that world which we call "Heaven", or they can, via their God given or Nature given for the Non-Believer "Freedom of Choice", choose to live in a confusing and very punishing animalistic Hell!

For certainly is it not a truth that the life of people upon this Earth is based upon every individuals "Freedom of Choice"! This freedom being a reality in which you can deliberately kill yourself or animalistic ally create a personal "I Want" which can develop into a gang or district or even a country pursued "I Want"! This being a country based "I Want" which can lead to very damaging wars! Yet and sadly, are not these conflicting *"I want what you have"* wars a reality in which a group based "I Want" for me, can never obtain satisfaction.

So in reality, is it not true that you should "always" personally ask yourself this question! *"What kind of world do I want to live in?"* Do I want to live in a world in which I "animalistic ally" want more and more for myself, or a world in which I know that **"I am that I am"**, which means that I experience that I am truly "everything" and there is no other! This certainly being that awareness which is targeted by all our world's religions and philosophies, for it is certainly known that this experiencing of "Enlightenment" can be truly Realized!

For without doubt it is also known that such "Enlightenment" is certainly achieved via praying, these being mind filling incantations that do disciplinary silence the "I want for ME" wording that entering the mind via the animalistic five senses! It is then, due to this disciplined silence between the praying, that you're Soul, which is the real you, is enabled to see through your empty mind that which exists in the stillness of the creation, this being that which exists all around you, just has it exists has one entity within you! For beyond doubt, via such disciplinary praying, you will actually experience that your body has become likened to an open door through which the unified creation, this being that which is all around you just has it exists within you, can be seen and experienced, but only via a silent mind! Thus ensuring that you know that you are has one in Gods world or Nature world for the unbeliever, this meaning that you knowingly exist in an unthinking "Present" time! For truly, it is also an experience in which you will also know that the energy which is resting within you cannot die, this being because it becomes has one with the energy that is truly resting all around you!

It is then that you will fully and truly understand the following ancient statements, these being statements which are found in the Gospel of John which are: *"You are the bread of life"*. *"You are the light of the world"*, *"You are the door"*, *"You are the good shepherd"*, *"You are the way the truth and the life"*, *"You are the true vine"*. Therefore, is it not now seen to be factually true, that to understand the world in which we live, we have to "understand" i.e.: stand under, that we are really and scientifically, living in a God created world or a Nature created world for the non-believer, in which all life and all non-life is but one entity! But is it not also true that this world is controlled neither by God nor by Nature for the non-believer, but by the majority of people's "I Want" or by a group of rich pr powerful people who want to increase their wealth or power over others!

These certainly being "Just-is" worlds for they are certainly not worlds that are created by "Justice"! For they are worlds that are sadly lived in by the majority of that countries people! These workers certainly being "animalistic ally" controlled people who are unable to install their own life-controlling natural laws, these being natural laws which remove the imposed "I Want" only for me' that is demanded by such leaders!

For is it not true that some countries leaders can and do impose their "I Want" for ME upon those people who they do physically and legally control? This being an imposed way of life which does actually exist in many countries because their laws are meant to support a way of living that is actually chosen by those countries leaders to be the only true way of life. For certainly it is a known truth that marketable goods can be produced for either the majority of people or for a minority of people- but in the real world there is only one life so that when you are looking at another person – you are really looking at yourself! For truly there is only one body and one reality, this being that which we call "The Creation"! But more about this later in "Life's Purpose"!

Therefore and certainly, is it not also very true, that to change the creating laws of a person or a countries marketing system, this is a reality that can only be achieved within that that which we call the "Present" time? This being a "Present" in which a leading person can actually introduce a way of life that can lead to the establishing of an immediate "Present" for themselves or for all others. This actually being achieved by the controlling of all the "Present" and also all the pending future events! These all being supported unifying events that are being targeted to occur in a future time"! For certainly, it is known, that this is a marketing activity which is empowered by its "Integrity" or it is actually empowered by a created inner feeling of "Fairness", for after all there is only one unified life upon this planet – which of course is the entirety of the planet Earth! This being likened to an Earthly existence which does constantly acknowledge that it is only that life force which is known has people who have been given the "Freedom of Choice"! This being that reality which is clearly explained by William Shakespeare in his quote from the play called Hamlet, ***"To be, or not to be? That is the question—whether 'tis nobler in the mind to suffer the slings and arrows of outrageous fortune, or to take*** *arms against a sea of troubles, And, by opposing, end them?* The idea of whether is it better to live in supporting unity with the creation or to live by wanting it for yourself, is certainly an ongoing question!

For without doubt, is it not true that that reality which created this creation did constantly endeavour to provide all that is needed to exist within that which we call "The Present", a world which knowingly includes the "Freedom of Choice" for all people? Also is it not a certain and natural truth, that Gods laws or Nature laws for the Non-Believer, do automatically "correct" the forces that are miss-directing or actually harming this growing unity that we call "The Creation"? This certainly being the only child of God or of Nature for the Non-Believer!

The questions that "Life's Purpose" now raises are, *"How is it possible for God or Nature for the Non-believer, to create and birth plan that does not develop according to the plans of the Creator that created it?"* Also is it not certainly true, that within our Creation, a male and a female are the two needed life forms that are needed to create a third life form? Therefore, should it not be "Scientifically," stated to be accurate, that God first mated with our mother, this being that which we call "Space"! This being that reality which is all around us just has it is within us. Therefore, is it not true that "Space" can be likened to be the creations Mother, this being that only reality in which "God" could lovingly implant a "Male" seed?

So is it not an enlightened truth that "Space" is the only place in which an only child, this being that which we are calling the creation, could born? This birth also being knowingly dated to be at the time which our scientist's call "The Big Bang"! For certainly, is not this "Big Bang" scientifically known to be the birth time of that only child which is called "The Creation"? Therefore, is it not an undeniable truth, that this birthed child, this being that child whom we call "The Creation", is actually the only child of these two realities? These being that father which we call God and that mother that we call "Space"! For certainly, is it not a scientific and historical fact, that these two realties are that power which created the birth of this only child which we call "The Creation"!

So yes! Is it not also a confirmed truth, that this only Childs Mother, who "Life's Purpose" calls "Space", is also being naturally copied by all our Earths mothers? This being a truth which shows the copying of the "Mother of the Creations" constant endeavour to harmonize and secure the life that exists within and around Her only child – which is the "Creation"!

For certainly, like all mothers', the Mother of the Creation must and does, willingly care for the wellbeing of this only Child! For truly She is actually that reality which people call "Space" in which was born Her only child – this being that which we call "The Creation"! For is it not experienced to be true, that this knowable truth not only exist within us but also all around us? For certainly again, is it not true, that this only child, which we call the creation, can be experienced to be a reality which contains within it the harmony, the wisdom, and the perfect balance of all life and also all non-life? This certainly being a creation which "Life's Purpose" states should be truly known to have been created by God the father and birthed within "Space", which is the mother of the creation! This being a creation which is the only child of the father that we call God and of the mother whom "Life's Purpose" calls "Space"! For certainly again, is not this only child that reality which exists all around us, just has it silently exists in unity within us?

Now within this "scientific" fact, it is good to understand that that which we call the Creation is an only child who's "Mother" does willingly care for! For is it not true that the "Mother of the Creation" i.e.: space, will actually ensure that Her only child will have room to continually grow and also to care for the harmony which exists within the unification of Gods growing plan - or the growing plan of Nature for the Non-believer! For certainly is it not a certain truth, that it is the "Mother of the Creation", or "Mother Nature" for the non-believer, that does constantly and practically show this only child, which is "The Creation", just how to support this only child's growing unity? This being that child, who is all around us, just has it rests within us. For certainly are we not aware or even enabled to realise, that it was only recently, when compared to our Earths history, that people were created in order to assist in finalising the growing target of Gods plan? Also is it not undeniable, that Gods main supporter, which can be called "Nature" but in truth is named by "Life's Purpose" to be the "Mother of the Creation", is truly here to ensure that this only child does continue to wisely grow? A reality which can be achieved only by supporting and applying the natural laws of God's created and always growing harmony?

So yes! "She", who is the mother of all life and also all non-life, is all-powerful and can be rightfully called the *"Mother of the Creation",* for certainly "She" loves this only Child which we call "The Creation". Therefore and we can confirm this, that "She" is also a Mother who like all mothers, does continuously work in supporting the "Present Time"! This being in order to support the developing needs of all life and also all Non-Life and in particular the needs of Her birthed sons and daughters, who are all recognised to have a love and a care for God or a love and care of Nature for the Non-Believer!

For is it not true that humankind is the only life force upon our planet which has been given a valid "Freedom of Choice"? This being a "Freedom of Choice" which can be to support or not support any actions or activities that are taking place in the "Present" time! Even a "Freedom of Choice" to continue with life or a choice that pursues a personal death? Frankly and certainly, this of course is not the "Godly" reason why the *"Mother of the Creation"* never interferes with any person's life, nor will the *"Mother of the Creation"* deliberately punish anyone for inharmonious deeds? For certainly it is true that the laws of God or the natural laws of Nature for the Non-Believers, do actually allow this "Freedom of Choice" only to people? For unquestionably, is it not true that this "Freedom of Choice" is a Godly gift that also ensures that a person will not be "Godly" punished for their actions, but of course they are punished if they brake the laws made by the people within whom they live!

Therefore it is certainly true, that a person, who actually lives in a personal "I Want for ME" life, can be living in a life that destroys the "spiritual" harmony that endeavours to exist within them - or within the world around them! Such people will truly be ignored by the Mother of the Creation! But those people who endeavour to silently support the harmonizing efforts of the *"Mother of the Creation";* they will certainly taste the life supporting "Sugar in the Water"! This being when the environment around them "mysteriously" seems to support their ongoing activities! This being a fact which can be likened to a car driver, who upon approaching traffic lights finds that they always turn to a green "Keep going", this being whenever they are approached!

So Yes! It is certainly true that this harmonizing work of the *"Mother of the Creation"* can only be achieved in the "Present Time", for to the *"Mother of the Creation"* the Past and the Future do not exist! This reality being because there is no such thing has "Space" in the "Mother of the Creations" world! For certainly, the reason for this is that there is no "Past" or "Future" within this world, this being that world which we call the "Present"! For certainly, it should now be known to be true that the *"Mother of the Creation",* like all mothers, actually supports the "Present", this being the name of God the fathers child or Natures child for the Non-Believer! For is it not true that within this harmony that exists within the creation that is all around us, just has it exists in unity within us, it is the woman who lives and cares for this only child that we call "The Present"!

Also is it not true that it is the man who lives and creates a future that will support this "Present", this being that supporting world which this only child can live in? For certainly, is it not a fact that this ever-ongoing ever-still reality can only exist in this "Present" that we call time! For it is only in the "Present Time", this being that world which "Life's Purpose" calls "Heaven", simply because is it not a factual truth that energy cannot die, even when it leaves the body in order to find another body to enter! For certainly, you can also ask any pending mother just when it was that this energy, which "Life's Purpose" calls the "Soul", entered the child she was carrying within her!

So again it should be said, that the actions of "Space", which is the *"Mother of the Creation"*, are always deeds that bring sweetness to the life of Her only child which we call "The Creation"! For certainly, is not true that which we call "The Creation" is the only reality to which our lives and our Earth belongs? Is it not also a "scientifically" confirmed truth, that this only child, which we call the "Creation", is a living entity? Also is it not true that within this creation there truly exists a living and growing body that we call Earth? Also is it not a truth that upon this entity that we call Earth, there lives a life special form that we call "people"? Is it not also "Scientifically" true that people are this Earths only advanced life-form which has been given the "Freedom of Choice"? This being a "Freedom of Choice" which allows only people to choose to create some-thing or choose to create nothing?

Therefore, can it not be "scientifically" confirmed, that the purpose of this gift, this being that gift which we can call the "Freedom of Choice", is an option in which it is only people who can "choose" to assist in the developing work of the *"Mother of the Creation"!* Or with this same "freedom of Choice", people can physically choose not to support the activities needed by our ever-developing and ever-growing creation! This certainly being the supporting of a harmony which is being created for all life and also all the Non-Life that exists upon our world! For certainly, this non-supporting fact also means that people, because of their "Freedom of Choice", can act negatively against the "Mother of the Creation" caring work, but now, if you believe that this negative pursuit should not be supported - - Read on.

So yes! It is now important to remember, that within the entirety of the creation, it was only people who were God given or Nature given for the non-believer, that which we call the "Freedom of Choice"! This being a gift which enabled people to support the "Mother of the Creations" unifying work! Therefore, should it not be known that the main work of people is to maintain Gods developing and ever emerging harmony, this being that world which is always active within that which we call "The Creation"! But is it not now a well known historical truth, that our God-given "Freedom of Choice", can also make it possible for a group based religious belief system to be selfishly changed! This change being in order to support a separating groups "I Want to believe in God my way and not in your way"! This change emanating from an inner desire which believes that God will therefore serve only me and not you! Thus believing that their self created God will serve only them because of their own and very personal "I Want" way of worship!

But now it should not be known, via personal experience, that this is a selfish pursuit? This being because it is a religiously named pursuit that is not attached nor can be attached to any of God's or of Natures for the non-believers, developing world. For is it not therefore a known identifiable truth, that some people create their own self-made "I Want" God to be like this? This being a God who they inwardly and personally worship in order to choose an animalistic "I Want for Me" life, this being that "I Want" for me life that they tend to always pray for! Therefore, is not this way of worshipping really an endeavour to require their personal "I Want" for ME! This being an "I Want" which is actually an animalistic "I Want" which is being targeted by one or by all of their animalistic five senses and not there Soul, which is that reality which observes "Everything"! For truly, this in the mind sounding "I Want", is certainly an animalistic "I Want" weakness in which such people are simply behaving like animals, for certainly this greed based "I Want" is coming from one or from all of their animalistic five senses! Therefore, is it not a certain truth, that they have "animalistic ally" created" for themselves a false god? This being a personal or gang created god who is being used to threaten "others" in an effort to gain tributes from them! These "others" being punished has non-worshipping people who are not performing the individual or financial acts that they are being told they should ritually accomplish in honour of their religions chosen God? Also is it not sadly true, that many of these false "religious" leaders do actually command their followers to "Kill" or "Destroy" those who believe in other religions! This being has they seek a possessing power over others!

So sadly is it not also a known truth that some religious leaders often command their followers to claim their imposed religious way of worship should only be for themselves? Also and sadly, are they not also commanded that they should "Punish" or "Ignore" plus isolate people of other religions because they say that such people do falsely worship an untrue God? For certainly, the simple reason for this is because those who attack another religion do always state that their own way of worship is true and others are not! But sadly is it not true that they are simply seeking their own animalistic "I Want"? This being a privately made "I Want" which actually does separate them from the creation which is all around them just has it is in unity within them! For certainly, such religious or philosophical "animalistic" attacks is certainly coming from a personal or an animalistic "I Want for ME" gang created world! This certainly being world which has nothing to do with Gods laws nor with the *"Mother of the Creations"* endeavours to care for Her only child nor Her need to maintain Harmony within Her family, this being that which we call "The Creation"!

So yes! We should always understand the need to support our worlds worthy leaders, but it is always good to remember that the best leader is your Soul or your consciousness for the Non-Believer. For certainly this ongoing privately created "I Want for ME" way of life has nothing to do with Gods world or the world of Nature for non-believer! For it is a certain truth that you are an only child, this child being that which we call "The Creation"!

So yes and again it should be stated, that some "I Want" for me, false religious leaders or "I Want" for me false philosophical leaders, are simply people who are claiming for themselves the values being created in God's world! For is it not true that they preach that the creation is a world that punishes people who sin against it? But is it not a certain truth, that God would never inflict punishment upon His only child? For what father could endeavour to destroy or harm their only child? For certainly, it should be further known, that no harm can come from God who is that reality which created the "Heaven" that certainly rests upon this Earth!

For certainly, is it not an undeniable truth that there is not one "Incarnate" nor are there any of our world's wise or holy ancients that actually desired to punish another person? For has, God said, or Nature for the non-believer, this being when speaking through the Incarnate Jesus, ***"If anyone has ears to hear, let them listen!*** For is it not strange, has our history shows, that many of our worlds religious belief systems did sometimes develop leaders who stated that if you do not follow "their" spoken creeds, these being that which they state was personally given to them by God – then God would punish you – through them!

So sadly, was it not this fact that enabled these "I Want" thinkers to pursue their "I Want" has a "Godly" given right to physically punish those who did not believe them? For does not our world's history show that such "I Want" religious leaders did actually burn to death thousands of people who they named to be "witches"? Definitely, was not this painfully inflicted death upon thousands of innocent people actually in order to reinforce via the use of fear, their "I Want" that they claimed from other people? This being in there leadership of a society in which they freely lived but also a society in which they sought to control the lives of others?

Also, did not this type of persecution seriously happen within our worlds newly emerging "Civilisations"? Also, and sadly, is it not strange that some of our exiting world's belief systems still worship these falsely imposed gods whose purpose is to support their "I Want"! But is it not also true, that such worshipping of false Gods did not continue to be recognized? This being when these false religious leaders actually told their believing worshippers' to inflict themselves with some painful penance and to also to do these self-punishing acts that were not only painful to themselves but also to their loved ones?

So yes, why was this religiously pursued "I Want" self-punishing behaviour, so painfully practised by some people but not by others? The reason being, and again it should be truly said, that it is only people, via their God given or Nature given for the non-believer "Freedom of Choice", that can "privately" support or not support any worshipping pursuit that claims their personal "I Want"! This should be a religiously sought "I Want" in which the "I Want" is to become has one life with the creation that is all around them just has it is has one unified life within them! This being that religiously sought "Has One" reality in which the worshipper does experience that they are truly all life and also all none life! For certainly, is it a known truth, that it is only people who can "privately" choose to pursue a negative greed based animalistic "I Want" activity. This brings an activity in which that can "Choose" to experience that they are separate from all life and also all non-life or actually "Choose" to be has one life with the world that exists all around them, just has it exists within them! These being two different existences in which people can, via their "Freedom of Choice", become "Self-Aware" that they are has one with the creation that is within them and also all around them, or they may choose to become "Self-Realized" and so experience that they are the creation and that there is no observer! For certainly is this not a religious truth that is given to only people by God or by Nature for the Non-Believer?

So yes! This greed based animalistic "I Want only for Me" can undoubtedly be identified to be animalistic because it does not support or pursue any of Gods or of Natures developing laws, these being laws which people have been created to support. But it is certainly good to be "Self-Aware" that some people have had many lives and so seemingly understand that the "Godness" of Nature, this being that which is genuinely existing and emerging all around life, has undoubtedly been created for ALL life to enjoy. Yet it must be further understood that some people have just been re-birthed from the non-human animal that they were in their previous life! Therefore and so truly, they do not fully understand that within their current life their personal need is to care for all life and also all the non-life which exists all around them just has exists in unity within them! Therefore, such newly emerging people can be like untrained pups and so they need to be kindly trained and so supported into a way of life where they do honour the laws that are made by our world's wise people! These being the world's wise-people who do constantly endeavour to support the emerging creation, for certainly is this not truly a "scientifically" accurate statement?

For is it not true that the "Mother of the Creation", who is the Mother of this only child, cannot deliberately hurt or punish Her only child? Also is it not true that that within many a person's "I Want" claimed desires, these being desires which are said to be coming from the one God, are falsely leading people into breaking the Harmony that Gods Laws or Natures Laws for the non-believer, do always target! For certainly, are that which is known has people, not purposely targeting these harmful acts because they are pursuing a bullying leaders "I Want" for ME instructions?

So yes! Can it not be said to be true that some leaders of a countries people have created false "I Want" gods for their followers to worship and so they create a greed-based belief system which pursues their own personal "I Want"! This certainly being an "I Want" what you have, and so is it not true that such leaders create a world which harms others and which certainly does not themselves or their followers! For certainly, should it not be fully understood that the person responsible for these "I want for me" claims, will automatically be acting outside of God's laws or of Natures harmony seeking laws for the Non-believer! These being the creations existing and also the creations newly emerging laws which have been created all around them just has are the harmonious laws that have been created to exist within them. For is it not sadly true that such "I Want" for me people, do not support the unity of that which exists within one of the "Mother of the Creations" only child, this being that which we call the "Earth"! For knowingly, is it not also true that those people, who religiously or greedily punish others, cannot enjoy a harmony-based contented life? For certainly, is it not a known fact and also a deemed truth, that such people will create and therefore live in this false world which we call a negative "Hell"! This being a false creation which will completely stop any possibility of such creators from actually achieving or enjoying any of their personally sought "I Want" for ME! For in Gods unified world, which is governed by the Mother of the Creation, you cannot greedily kill or punish others in order to steal their wealth and then say it is your faith in your religion that allows you to do so!

For unquestionably is it not true that this personally and greedily created "I Want for Me" world, is not honouring the laws that have been created by our creator? For is it not "scientifically" true that all activities can only take place within the "Present", this being that which can only exist in God's created world or the world created by Nature for the non-believer? For again is this truth not based upon the scientific fact that in the beginning, before the "BIG Bang" which our scientists say was the birth of our universe, there existed "No-Thing"! But is it not also scientifically stated that from this "No-Thing" there suddenly occurred a "Big Bang"? This being an explosion from which our scientists say eventually developed all life and also all non-life, this being a growing and developing life which "Life's Purpose" emphasizes that we call this still developing big bang creation "The Present"! Therefore can it not now be said to be true, this being a truth for those who have ears to hear! That those people who impose harmfully claiming "I Want for ME" activities, these being claims in which some people want more of the "Present", are claims that can only imbalance the "Present", but such selfish people would be simply ignored by God, or by Nature for the Non-Believer! For certainly it should now be known that any personally created "I Want only for Me, will "naturally" damage its creator! For is it not a well known truth, that as soon as you genuinely perform an activity that supports the love of the unified harmony that is emerging all around you just has it is emerging within you, these being acts that are being silently created within the Present Time, you will be supported by the *"Mother of the Creations", s*ugar in the water! This being a gift of sweetness that only the Mother of the creation can give to you! For certainly it is then, after your act of unifying the Godly emerging "Present", then it is known that all your "I Want" confusions and frustrations will end when you become has one with that which exists all around you just has it exists within you and there is no such thing has time!

But sadly, is it not also a known fact, that in our ancient religious belief systems they also explained this above stated fact, but added that if you do not follow "their" own imposed personal doctrines, then you will go to Hell when you die! Thus stating that you will exist in pain forever and ever! For was it not anciently said within some of our world's religions, that if you, their attending worshipper, did obey their personally written creeds, then when you die you will go to an eternal Heaven! This being a heathen called a paradise, in which you will exist with your loved ones and also your ancient ancestors forever and ever. Is it not also true, that some ancient "owners" of various religious belief systems, even promised that if their worshipper gave them money or inflicted for them disciplinary acts upon others, then they will ensure that such supporters would go immediately to Heaven when they died?

How sad this was! For death is certainly not the end of your being! For truly, there is actually no need to worry about spending an eternity in Hell or be happily contented about spending an eternity with your ancestors in Heaven! For certainly it is better to understand that God and also the *"Mother of the Creation"* have better things to do with their caringly planned time than to create a world to which a person's soul, or that which can be called energy by the non-believer, will go that which goes to exist in either a happy heathen or a punishing Hell – this being forever and forever!

For certainly, this cannot be true! For is it not a true fact that love and its supporting freedom of choice, is the actual basis of Gods and also the *"Mother of the Creations"* world? For is it known to be true that God and the *"Mother of the Creation"* must both care greatly for the children that they have created, has certainly the majority of all mothers and fathers! Therefore, is it not a certain truth, that you're Soul, which is the energy that is the real "YOU", cannot die and so will be born again and again and again etc! For certainly, is it not a scientifically known truth, that energy cannot die! So it must be true, that your Soul is an energy which keeps creating "YOU"!

8 ALL IS UNDER THE LAW OF HARMONY

Is it not always interesting to think about our pending death? Is it not also true that some of our world's religions state that after our current life's good or bad behaviour, we will either go to exist forever and ever in a glorious Heathen or in an ever painful Hell - and this existence being for the rest of eternity! But is this lengthy existence in a painful Hell; has some religions state, not make it difficult to believe that the "Mother of the Creation" could ever allow such a painful and eternal punishment after Her Childs death? This being the religious hurting of Her child in a so-called Hell! For would not this "Hell" be a Godly created terrible place in which many trillions of their children, who had been Godly given the "Freedom of Choice", would be condemned to exist and also be punished for the rest of eternity? Or would God not be responsible for creating an opposite law! This being a law which would continually re-birth a Childs embodied soul and so, with a continued "Freedom of Choice", wait for that Child to knowingly become has one with the creation? This being a life which

contains only one existence, this being that which can only exist in the "Present", for there is no other and so is this not the true purpose of life? This being so that God can experience "Him-Self"!
    So yes! This is the purpose of life, for it has always been the task of people who were known to have a minimal life span when compared to the creations eternity! This also being a person's life span which was known in the "Bronze Age" to be around twenty-six years and in our current modern age, which is recognised within the Christian world to be the year 2022, is known to be around 73 years! This is certainly being a personal life time which is known to be has nothing when compared to the estimated twenty-two billion years which is the "Scientifically" estimated time for the ending of our universe. It may also be a reality that well before the end of the universe, people may become different entities from that which they are now – that is, if they still exist! For this could be an end time in which we will probably have been long gone and to where - no one knows!

    So Yes! Is it not a more logical truth to think that there is, in our reality, a unified perfection! This being the perfection of an on-going ever-developing harmony that is based upon an energy that cannot die! For certainly, is it not true that this energy that is all around us is also unified with that energy which is also within us? For is it not true that all energy is a reality that exists in its own unified perfection and forever more shall do so? Also does not this unified energy explanation also clearly describe that which is called "Three in One"! This oneness being God, the "Mother of the Creation" and their only child, which is that reality which we call "The Creation"! Is it not also true that a part of this unified creations energy does now currently exist within that reality which we call Earth! This being that unified has one concept which all our wise spoke about within all our ancient religions and philosophies!
    Also, cannot this reality be likened to being a "Three in one"! With the first reality being God, and the second being the "Holy Spirit", which is explained in "Life's Purpose" has being the Mother of our entire universe! This being energy based and also a unified creation in which God or Nature for the Non-Believer implanted the only seed that could produce that which we call "The Creation"! This also being that only child which the "Mother of the Creation" birthed and which continues to grow within a life that will eventually end!
    For certainly, do we not already know a truth that within all life exists a paired reality that can, when together, knowingly "Create" a life? This being a paired way of life which occurs when male and female become has

one, this being that reality which produces for them a third life? For certainly, we also know that it is "scientifically" correct to state, that it is the male who, has a father, is needed to give his seed to the female, who will be the mother of their created child! For certainly, it is only the mother who can contain everything that is needed to grow this seed that evolves "magically" to birth a unified third, this being their child. Therefore, it is "scientifically" confirmed that the implanting male is the first of the three that exists before a third can be created!

For again and certainly, the seed must be capable of being produced by a grown man before such planting can take place, this being a constant truth that Nature does clearly state. Also is it not a confirmed truth that it is only an adult woman who can contain the controlling harmony that is needed to create a third, this being a child who is created by that evolving unknown magic that can only rest within a pending mother. For is it not also true that the child is naturally planted within the mother by a small seed that can only be created by a potential father? This being a seed which is almost "No-Thing", but which is a seed that actually grows within the pending mother into "Some-Thing"! This being that reality which is usually in perfect balance when it becomes a unified whole! Indeed, it can be asked, "what is this "Magical" energy that naturally completes this amazingly unified growth?" This being an ever expanding growth that truly comes from a small unrelated seed that is planted within the female mother by a pending male father! This being a very small seed which amazingly grows until birthed has a complete person?

For certainly, is it not also true that the responsible male "father" must be his child's protector has well has the families future needs, whilst the Mother cares for the families "Present Time" needs? Therefore, should we not "knowingly" and "habitually" plus "lovingly" respect our father who is the future provider and also the creator of this only child that we call "The Creation", this being the creation which exists within us and also all around us? Is it not also true that we named our "Creator" to be called "God" - or named to be called Nature" by the non-believer! God being the name that is always use to identify that which all religions call the "Father of the Creation – is this not a well known truth?

Consequently and also factually plus scientifically, this reality that we call God or called Nature by the non-believer, can only be likened to be the first of the "Three in One"! For truly is not the second of the three in one named "Mother" or acknowledged to be called "Nature" by the non-believer! For certainly, God or "No-Thing" for the non believer, must have knowingly placed His seed into that reality which must contain "everything" that is needed to create a third, this third being that child which we call "The Creation"?

For certainly, is it not also a known truth that a child can only be created within an existing entity, this child creating entity being that reality which can only be called "Mother"! This being because it can only be within a "Mother" that a new creation can be seeded by a potential father! For certainly it is only within the Mother that a pending child can be fully created from a dormant male seed – is this not true? Also is it not true that when all bodily parts have been fully created or sometimes not fully created within the mother, the child is compulsory birthed into an already existing "Present"? This birth only being into the "Present" when the creations laws or natures laws for the non-believer, have decided that the Soul is fully formed and so enabled to grow or even not fully formed and so not enabled to grow within that which we call "The Present"!

So what is this "everything" that is needed to support this timed incubation and also fruitfully support the creating of the many parts that do exist in unity within this growing and only child that we call "The Creation"? This being a creation which was knowingly birthed has an ongoing and ever aging "Present" and which like all births will eventfully grow to its full maturity – but more about this maturity later in "Life's Purpose"?

But for now, is it not a known truth that this "everything" this being that which births a third, this third being that which "Life's Purpose" calls the creation, is normally known to be a caring "Mother"? For is it not also known to be true that a mother is naturally needed in order to give birth to a third? So certainly, this is the logical reason why "Life's Purpose" states that it was the "Mother of the Creation" or Nature for the non-believer, that gave birth to that entity which we call "The Creation"! Therefore, is it not also true that this child's birth is what our scientists call the "The Big Bang" and also is it not true that this Childs name is known to be "The Creation" or the world of "Nature" for the Non-believer?

Therefore certainly, it must be true, that this individual and unified child that we call "The Creation" was physically birthed by that higher life force that "Life's Purpose" calls the "Mother of the Creation"? For is it not naturally true, that the birth of life require a mother to have accepted a planted seed that was produced by the Father! This also being a "Mother of the Creation" which the "Life's Purpose" has now identified has being "space"! For certainly is not space the only reality into which this birth that we call "The Creation", could have taken place? Therefore, without any doubt "Space", must certainly the "Mother of the Creation" who was certainly that reality which gave birth to Her and Gods only Child, this being that which we call "The Creation"!

For again and certainly, is it not true that according to all the known laws regarding the creation, or all the known laws regarding Nature for the Non-believer, it must be accepted that there was a "Mother" who accepted a seed from a father which then grew into the birth of this third life-force that we call "The Creation"! For certainly and factually, the Mother of this only child which we call the "Creation", can only be that reality which we call "Space"! For is it not true, has our worlds scientists say, that the creation was actually formed and then birthed within that reality which we call "Space"! For certainly, is it not therefore knowingly explained that it must be "Space" which formed and then birthed this only child that we call the Creation, or that which is called Nature by the non-believer!

So yes! Is it not true that no one can deny this natural and solitary birth which took place at the beginning of that which we call "Time"! Also can anyone deny that reality which in the Christian bible is knowingly called "The Three in one"! This being described within the Christian doctrine has the unity of Father, Son, and the Holy Spirit, with the Holy Spirit being that which "Life's Purpose" scientifically calls "Space", this being that in which this only child grew and was so formed! For what else can we call the creator of everything that is necessary to form this only child that we call "The Creation", but the name "Mother"?

Also, is it not true that "Nature", this being that reality which is all around us and also within us, does indeed accurately inform us that a natural mother must be the "creator" of any life which is to be born? Therefore, is it not a factual reality that there must be a "Mother" of the creation? This being a reality which did create a life which grew from a seed that was installed by the father that we knowingly call "God"! A seed that grew until it was eventually born as the child whom we call "The Creation" or called "Nature" by the Non-believer?

So Yes! What indeed is this "space" that "Life's Purpose" calls the "Mother of the Creation"? This being an inner and also a surrounding energy which is experienced by all believers and also all Non-believers! For certainly, is it not true that it is only people who can understand these energy based beliefs! These being beliefs which state that "Nature" which "Life's Purpose" calls the "Mother of the Creation", can only be that reality which we call space, this space being that into which God's seed was able to be planted!

For truly, can it not now be said that the birth of their only Child, this being that only child which we call "The Creation", must therefore be birthed within the same laws of harmony that exist within both parents! Is this not true? For certainly, is it not true that within our body is a harmony seeking reality which came from our parents, this being a unity of behaviour which also exists within the bodies of all life forms?

But Yes! Is it not also true that only people have been birthed with the purpose of supporting and also guiding all life forms to always grow together within a unified harmony? This being a unified supporting "togetherness" which constantly occurs within the singularity of the "one" body! This one body actually being the totality of the unified creation in which we live and also in which we do "knowingly" and "growingly" do endeavour to support. Therefore, can it not be true that the *"Mother of the Creation"* must have originally been that empty space which is stated by our scientists to have existed prior to the "Big Bang", this being the birth of that which we call "The Creation", this being that which "Life's Purpose" calls the only child of God. For is it not true that the *"Mother of the Creation"* could only have been that space that must have willingly accepted a God given seed which silently grew into a unified life that was then born! This being a birth which was called the "Big Bang" by our scientists or religiously named to be the "The Creation" by our religious ones!

Therefore, is it not "scientifically" correct that this single birth, that we call "The Creation", does contain within it the "energetic" existence of all life and also all non-life? This life being within this child which was birthed via this seed that our Father, who we call "GOD", did place within our mother, who "Life's Purpose" calls "Space", because space is the only all encompassing reality in which this child could be born! Is this not true?

Therefore, and certainly, is it not also truly known by our scientist that this developing independent life force that we call "The Creation", could only have come into existence via the "Father of the Creation", who is called God by our believers. For certainly, it must have been God who, has the father of the creation, did lovingly transfer the seed of this pending child to be finalised by the "Mother of the Creation", who could only be space according to "Life's Purpose". This being until this child that we call "The Creation" did birth, via a "Big Bang", into being that only child which we call "The Creation"! For is it not true that if you ask any mother about the birthing of her child, she will say that when her child was born, it was like an "explosion", indeed, is it not true that the birth of our creation is even described by our scientists has the "Big Bang?" For truly, even Non-believers must accept the fact that there is needed to be a male and a female in order to create a physical third and also that their created child will actually contain a part of its mother and its father, this being within the body of its new life.

So yes! Is not this male and female togetherness, this being that which is needed to begin parenthood, not a truth that can be fully accepted by all people? Also, is this need for parenthood not a truth that is actually the foundation of all "Scientific" understandings? This being an understanding regarding all the life that exists has people and also all that animalistic life which exists all around people – is this not true? For certainly, does not Nature, this being that reality which exists all-around and within people, truly state, that there must be two to create an animalistic third? For is it not truly said again and again that this reality that we call "The Creation" is the child of God who is the father and that it must be "Nature", the mother that birthed this only child that we call "The Creation"!

For is it not a truth that it is only within "Nature" that all things can and do "Naturally" grow? Is it not also true that within these many births of new life that occur inside our communities, these being births that develop within the mothers of many families! Is it not the "Mother" who actually teaches, protects and cares for her growing children? These being children who are always attached has one to the happenings of the creation that is within them and also all around them!

Therefore can it not be simply put, that that which cares for everything in the universe must "naturally" be the mother who did actually birth this only child that we call "The Creation? This being a mother whom "Life's Purpose" does physically identify has being "Space", because "Space" is the only life-force i.e.: energy, which is all around us, just has it also exist everywhere within us!

For certainly, the physical world, this being that world which we call "The Creation", can only be a child that was Godly "Fatherly" created to grow within the "Mother of the Creation", who can only be "Space" according to the scientific knowledge of "Life's Purpose"! For is it not true that this only child that we call "The Creation" or called the Physical world by a non-believer, is actually living inside that which our worlds scientists call "Space", this being that which the universe does knowingly exist, which of course is the only child of God or of Nature for the non-believers!

Therefore, is it not also true that it can only be within this space that a person can become "Self-Aware", meaning that they feel that they are a enjoined has a unified part of everything that exists within this space? This being a "Self-Awareness" experience, which is historically known, can lead to experiencing that which is called "Self-Realization"! This being a "reality" in which a person will actually experience that they are "everything", and that there is no observer! This being when they become has one with Gods creation or with Nature creation for the Non-Believer! For certainly, it is the creations mother, which "Life's Purpose" calls "Space", that is that reality which was actually seeded by the child's father, who all religions call God or is that which is called "No-Thing" (Nothing) by the Non-believer.

Now for the simple truth, which even Non-believers will agree to! This being that according to the unified world of Nature, which naturally exists all around and within people; it is acknowledged that it is the Mother of the family who controls the growing child within that which we call "The Present" time, whilst it is the father who provides the food for the family. For is it not true that this is why the mind of the Mother lives only in the "Present" time has she serves her family, whilst the mind of the Father lives only in a "Future" time, this being that hunting and growing world in which he is constantly living in order to feed his family!

For certainly Nature is the "Mother" of all that was created to exists within our world and it is also "She" who certainly does care for this only "child", that we call "The Creation". Also, just like the Earth's moon, the Mother will never turn her face away from the needs of Her only Child, which is that totality which we call "The Creation", this being that home in which all Her children growingly live! This being a life in which people have been given the "Freedom of Choice" by their father so that they can support the work of the *"Mother of the Creation"*.

But is it not also true, that that part of this only child, which is called people, can mistakenly think that they are individuals and so are separate from the creation that is all around them? This being an isolation belief in which they can, via their God given "Freedom of Choice", turn their "consciousness" away from supporting the caring work of Nature, which "Life's Purpose" calls the "Mother of the Creation"? These misplaced activities being in order, via their "Freedom of Choice", to choose to pursue their own and personal "I want for ME! Thus, living a life in which they do nothing to positively support the creations needs, but do negatively steal the creations providing needs that are being created for the unified family to which they belong – a belonging in which there is only one created life and that this one created life is "You"! Therefore, you truly are "Everything"! For, has our scientific wise do state, it is a truth that prior to "Big Bang", which was the beginning of this single child that we call "The Creation" or the Universe by the non-believer, there was "scientifically" named to be "Nothing", or "No-Thing" for the ears of the believer! Therefore, it must be true that has a result it must be scientifically noted that the creations father must be that which our non-believers call "Nothing", but which all our earths religions actually call "God", who of course exists has "No-Thing"!

Therefore is it not a scientific fact, that that which was first created by God or Nature by the non-believer, must have been that entity which our scientists call "space", this being that reality which "Life's Purpose" calls the "Mother of the Creation"! For is it not true that a new life must always be grown by a mother and is it not also naturally true that this growth comes from a seed that is planted by the father –this being that reality from which all life is born! For certainly can it not now known that the "Mother of the Creation" is not just a meaningless empty "space"! But is actually a truthful and believable concept for those who seek the truth of that reality which knowingly exists within them and also all around them – this being that child we call "The Creation" which in it unified totality is truly THEM! For certainly there is no other!

For that reason, is it not therefore true that it was actually within the "Mother of the Creation" or within "Space" for the Non-believer, that this only "child", which we call the creation or Nature for the Non-believer, was actually created? This seeding being produced by the male and female coming together in such a way that the male could fully transfer in safety a seed to the female! This seed being a reality which actually contains and an embryo that will grow to become a new life form which is similar to themselves and in flowering plants the seed is enclosed within the fruit.

But is it not also true that this seeding must have originated from that reality which we call God or called Nature by the non-believer! This God, or Nature for the non-believer, must certainly have been a lonely male like entity who did create "Space", this word "Space" being that which "Life's Purpose" scientifically calls the "Mother of the Creation"! For certainly, cannot it also be "scientifically" understood, that within this child, that we call the creation, there must be a part of father? For is it not a known truth that all children contain a part of their father has well has a part of their Mother? Also can it not be factually understood that this child of God, which we call "The Creation", was actually created because God was lonely? This being an unpleasant condition and it is a condition which most people can actually experience and also fear! For certainly, is it not a known scientific truth, that this physical child, this being that which we call the Creation or the Universe for the Non-believer, was actually fathered by God, or by "No-thing" for the non-believer!

Therefore, what is being presented within "Life's Purpose" is the right understanding of that which many Christian people call the "Three in One"; this meaning that there are only three lives within our one creation! But for now and for certain, it should be known that this is a purposeful and a meaningful creation and it is also a creation which has actually been given many names by our world's many religions and philosophies. For that reason "Life's Purpose" clearly states that there truly exists the ***"The Three in One"***, which is a unification of that which is called God the Father, God has the Son and God has the Holy Spirit, this being that life-force which rests within all people who are truly all just one essence! For certainly, is it not true dear reader, that this unification with "God the Father" also means that "You" dear reader, are really that which you look at, what you taste, what you touch or smell and what you listen too! For you are certainly you are that child which can knowingly experience all knowledge, meaning that you can experience that you are "Everything"!

So Yes! The above revelations are explanations of the actual truth that knowingly exists within that which we call "The Creation"! For certainly, this truth is for those who do experience that there is a power greater than their individual selves! For certainly the teachings of all our world's religions and philosophies' are activated in order to explain the experience which arises when a worshipper experiences that they themselves have become unified with "everything"! This being when they unthinkingly become "Self-Aware" that they are really everything that they observe, this being an awareness which leads to that reality which is called "Self-Realization"! This being a "Realisation" in which the experiencer realizes that they are "Everything" and there is no observer. For certainly, this is that condition which all our worlds' religions and philosophies' seek by their praying and hymn singing but experience from the East does show that "mantra praying", this being when only one world is repeated, does conclusively and certainly "disciplinary" stop the animalistic five senses from sounding into the mind their "I Want!"

For it is certainly a known religious and philosophical truth, that an automatically recited prayer and certainly the meditational mantra prayer, will physically and mentally become aware that they belong, has if in unification, to everything that their silent five senses reveal to them! For certainly, they will eventually experience, that they are not observing but experiencing that they have become has one with all that exists within creation that is within them and all around them!

Thus meaning that that which is all around you is experienced to be has one with that which is within you, thus this "awareness" is what our ancients called a "Self-Aware" condition in which they experience that they are a part of a creation which really does care for them! For certainly, via mantra praying they would eventually experience a "Self-Aware" condition in which they would become "Self-Aware" that they are the world that exists around them just as they experience that world which exists in unity within them! But also and very knowingly, they will also become "Self-Aware" that someone or "Some-thing" was caring for them and also caring for the creation that was knowingly all around them! But now it should be known that this caring awareness is coming from that reality which "Life's Purpose" calls the "Mother of the Creation" or Nature for the non-believer! This being the "Mother of the Creation" who caringly teaches Her children by constantly presenting to them a unifying encounter which the "Mother of the Creation" knows that they need to experience!

For certainly "She" is also "The Mother" who does, via her nature, endeavour to protect her children by supporting them as they move through the evolving and constantly growing laws of harmony which the father, who all our world's religions call "GOD", has installed! But certainly, is it not also a known truth that the "Mother of the Creation" does carefully support all life and also all non-life, this being particularly so when the "I Want" of the powerful and animalistic ally controlled people endeavour to punishingly control the weak that lives amongst them! So it is useful now to understand, i.e. "Stand Under", the knowledge that within our entire world's many different languages and cultures there has also been knowingly created many "culturally" different religions and philosophies!

For is it not true that the people of many lands did seek to personally create their own countries worshipping and philosophical systems of worship? This being that reality which did culturally create our worlds many ways of religious and philosophical worship! For certainly, these variable ways of religious worship must have been created in accordance to the seeking culture of the people that did dominate the land upon which these many religions were birthed! For is it not a certain truth that our entire world's religions and philosophies do tend to "culturally" worship only one God, although it is certainly known that these different religions do culturally worship in many different ways! But all claim a devotion which conforms to the worshipping of only one God! For is it not true that all our worlds many ways of worship do factually and culturally pursue a religious way of worshipping which consists of only one God? This being a fact which is accepted by all our worlds' culturally different religions!

Yet and sadly, is it not also true that within our expanding world, that these culturally different ways of worship can be misunderstood by some people within this growing world! This being a reality which could be caused by the truth that the ancient foundations of our worlds many various religions and philosophies', have actually been created by different languages and different cultures? For is it not now a known truth, that some competing religious creeds can lead to a sever misunderstandings by people who have been re-birthed and so now live in our modern age? For is it not a truth, that different ways of worshipping God can make some people, who are attached to other religious ways of worship, actually experience anger? This being when anger develops in a worshipper who states, *"I want my way of worship to be the only true way of worship!"* But is it not a verifiable fact that some worshippers, who can be likened to having just been re-born from the animal kingdom, do endeavour to change the worshipping ways of different religious cultures? For is it not true that this attacking reality is based upon the fact that some "religious" complainers do fearfully attack people who are not of their herd or of their creed beliefs?

For certainly, it can be said that the purpose of "Life's Purpose" is to state an undeniable truth that will reveal a "Religious" and also a "Philosophical" way for all people to be enabled to understand, i.e.: "Stand-Under", their being has one body within "God's world" or the world of Nature for the Non-Believers. For is it not a goodly (Godly) truth, that the peace seeking followers of our worlds various religious and or philosophical faiths, do actually begin to become truly aware of their strongly aroused feelings of oneness with everything that exists within the creation that is within them and also all around them? This awareness being a reality which "Life's Purpose" explains does actually commit them to support the ever developing and ever unifying work of the "Mother of the Creation"! This support being based upon an awareness that the creation is but one life and it is an awareness that will energise people in their endeavour to support their "Mother" in Her caring for Her and Gods world, this being that only child which we call "The Creation"! For certainly, it is also an only child that is constantly growing within the ever developing "Present", this being that "Present" which is certainly the home of their only child which we call "The Creation"!

But sadly, and again it should be said, that it is certainly a known truth, that some people, especially those whose soul has recently been born from the animal kingdom, do constantly pursue an animalistic "I Want" only for ME", this being there chosen way of living, is this not true? For certainly, this truth is unquestionably based upon an animalistic ally dominating "I Want for ME", way of living. This being a way of living which will create a negative "I Want for ME" life and so is not the positive unified reality that is constantly being shown by that ever growing unified child that we call "The Creation"! Therefore the question now should be *"Why do some people constantly destroy the unity of that which is caringly and religiously emerging all around them?"* This being instead of allowing this unity to be treated just the same has that supporting unity which is constantly being experienced within them"?

So yes! Is this purposeful destruction of a life not just another strange truth? These being that some people do constantly pursue a tribal or maybe a religiously pursuing *"I Want for ME and my religions"* claim? This also being an "I Want" for me pursuit in which they also seek to gain appreciation from the followers within their community or their religion! Therefore and again can it not be said, that such people are pursuing a false "I Want" animalism? For certainly, is this not a false "I Want" concept?

This being a personal or religious concept in which they believe that their religious creed is the only truth that should be worshipped? Is this not true? For has it not been stated by some people within our world's religions, that all other religions worship false Gods? Indeed is it not true that many religious wars within our past, future and even in our "Present" time are being pursued because of this personal "I Want" concept? This being that thought pattern which actually created many of our world's past, present and of course pending future religious wars – is this not true? For certainly such an aggressive tribal belief system is based upon a personal "I Want" for ME, which sadly and also without doubt, must be birthed and powered by a gang based "I Want" for Me! For certainly such a belief must be based upon tribal thinking individuals who are "animalistic ally" seeking an "I Want" for Me!

This being an "I Want" pursuing activity which forgets that the "Mother of the Creation" or that which is named Nature by the Non-Believer, does like all Mothers, constantly and without doubt supports an harmony that is provided for Her family, which is ALL life and also all non-life! For is it not "scientifically" true, that the only child that is knowingly alive is called "The Creation"! Therefore, should it not be said again and again, that that which we call "The Creation", can only be the solitary Child of God and the "Mother of the Creation", which of course both are Nature for the Non-Believer! Is this not a very certain and a very undeniable truth? Therefore can it not now be explained that the only reason why a person does constantly claim their own "I Want", must be because their soul has just been re-birthed from the animal kingdom – is this not an acceptable truth? This being a re-birth that came from an animalistic death that occurred within the ever-developing animal kingdom, for certainly the Soul does grow and it certainly matures within its many lives!

So yes! Now is the time to experience a very quiet non-thinking "meditational" moment and without thought – endeavour to become has one with the creation that is all around you just has it knowingly exists within you – for in truth the totality of the creation is really YOU! This being what is anciently known to be a "Self-Aware" enlightening experience which is different from that experience called "Self-Realisation"!

For "Self-Realisation" is a reality in which there in is no observer! This being because you do religiously or philosophically for the non-believer, experience yourself to be a unified one with that which not only exists within you but also with that which knowingly exists all around you, this totality of everything being that which we call "The Present"! For certainly this is a "Self-Realization" which you will actually experience yourself to be the totality of all that which exists in the "Present Time", this being that reality which we call "The Creation"! It is also very true that within this "Self-Realisation" experience you will also fully understand those religious words which state *"I AM THAT I AM!"*

The difference being that in the beginning of "Enlightenment" you will encounter a "Self-Aware" experience in which you will actually feel the love of harmony that is coming from your unthinking unity with that which we call "The Present"! For certainly, it is well known that in the experiencing of a "Self-Awareness" you do actually become aware that everything that you observe and experience, is really your true "Self"! For certainly it is also known, by our wise, that within a "Self-Realization" experience you actually become has one with the creation which means that there is no observer!

These are certainly those constantly targeted conditions which all our world's religions and philosophies do pursue, but the "I Want" makes it very difficult to achieve! This especially being so when many a mind blocking "I Want for ME" is being sounded by one or from all of your animalistic five senses! For certainly, it should be known that "The Soul" has no voice has it rests in unity with that which we call "The Creation"!

Therefore it is without doubt, that it is certainly this animalistic "I Want" mind-filling condition which is stopping your Soul from seeing through your silenced mind the unified truth of the creation that is resting in front of you – but only in the "Present" time! For certainly, this disciplined mind praying condition is that fact which stops the animalistic

"I Want" from being sounded into your mind by one of your animalistic five senses! This truth being the reason for our worlds religious praying "exercises" which is to silence the five senses so that our inner Soul can become has one with the creation that is all around it just has it is within it! For truly, it is then that you will "religiously" experience the blissful unity with a creation that is not only within you but also all around you - which of course is the target of all our world's religions and philosophies! For certainly God is the father of that which we call the creation and the only Mother is that which is called "Nature" by our non-believers! But certainty it should now be known that it is an animalistic mind-filling "I want" which actually stops a person's Soul from seeing through the mind and so becoming has one with that which we call "The Creation"!

Therefore, dear reader, to experience this blissful truth you should begin, via a disciplined mind silencing meditation, to silence the mind filling "I Want" words that are coming from your animalistic five senses and you certainly do not have to go to a church to do this although this can be VERY useful! For truly it is in this "Mantra" mind controlling way that you can and will become "Self-Aware", which is the first stage in which you will experience that you really are the unified totality of that only child which we call "The Creation", for certainly, this is the target and the purpose of all our world's religions and philosophies'! For it is without doubt, that you will eventually become "Self-Aware" has you experience that you, which is in real truth your inner "Soul", is cared for by the unseen "Mother of the Creation" - whose energy and need did originally create your body! For truly it should also be known that all people are the "Mother of the Creations" only child!

For certainly, you will experience this truth has you, with a silent mind, become "Self-Aware" that you are "Everything"! For truly this sought religious and philosophical experience is due to the mind silencing discipline of your "meditational" praying which is the target that is pursued by all worlds religions and philosophies, these being that which exists all around you! For certainly, via imposed disciplinary religious praying and incanting you will silence the animalistic five senses and so "naturally" sense that you are has one with that world which rests all around, you just has it does in unification within you! Thus meaning that you really experience that you are the totality of all the creation for it is certain that you will really experience that you are has one with Gods world or has one with the "Present" time - for the non-believer!

So yes! The experiencing of this truth, this being that you are the unified totality of "The Creation", is actual the target of ALL our world's religions and philosophises. But sadly, it is also known that this sought unification, with that which we call "The Creation, is often attacked by a person's five animalistic "I want" this creation to be for ME and not for others! It is then that they do endeavour to "animalistic ally" and in a ganging form, claim it for themselves! For certainly again and again it should be said, that this is because a person's five senses are still animalistic in nature and so they are not free from the animal kingdoms "I want for me"! This of course is a constant endeavour to claim for them that reality which we call "The Creation"! This personal claiming "I want for me", could also probably be from a person whose previous life was has a member of the animal kingdom and so they are not yet enabled to experience the true wonder that their new body carries a Soul, this being that which can experience itself to be has one with the creation that exists all around it just has it exists in unification within it! For certainly, this is also that condition in which God, and the "Mother of the Creation", can experience the unified love of their only child – but more about this the purpose of this reality later in "Life's Purpose"!

Therefore and most certainly, it must be true, that with such an "I Want for ME" animalistic way of thinking, you are simply filling your mind with thoughts that are blocking the true you, which is your soul, from seeing and endeavouring to become has one with the "Present", this being that world which can exist only in the "Present Time"!

For certainly, these animalistic "I Want" mind-filling thoughts, these being that animalistic thinking which was inherited from our previous lives within the animal kingdom, is truly a reality which will stop your Soul from seeing through the mind that which we call "The Present"! This reality being, and again it should be said, is because you're past animalistic "I Want" for me thinking did automatically fill your mind with thoughts that were coming from your animalistic five senses!

This being that animalistic reality, which now has a person, will continue to stop the real you, which is your Soul, from becoming has one with that which we call "The Creation"! For certainly, it is a known fact that with an empty mind you will experience your "self", which is the true you, to be has one with the creation that is all around you just has you experience it to be in unification within you. For certainly you will experienced that true reality which is the real you!

Therefore and again it should be said, that has a result of this "I want" animalistic thinking, you will actually experience your body to be separate from that which you see, taste, touch, hear or smell! For that reason, it is good to now understand that it is certainly because of this isolating "I Want for ME" thinking, which is coming from one or from all of your animalistic five senses, that a person can never experience a true "Self-Aware" condition in which they will experience that they are "everything"! This being a "Self-Aware" reality in which a person becomes aware that they are everything that exists in the world that is around them just has it is experienced to be within them! For certainly, they will experience themselves to be has one body with all that exists around them – just has it is experienced to exists within them, therefore the concept of "I Want" cannot exist!

It will also be true that such an animalistic "I Want for ME" person will certainly not be able to experience the second stage of this "Self-Awareness", this second stage being that reality which our wise ancients called "Self-Realisation"! For certainly it is true that "Self-Realisation" is an experience in which our wise ancients state that a person knowingly becomes has one with "Everything", meaning that they experience themselves to be has one with "The Creation and so there is no observer!

This actually being an experience in which the "Soul" becomes has one with its father, whom we knowingly call God, or has one with Nature for the Non-Believer. For without doubt it should now be known that "Self-Realization" is actually a unification of a creation in which there is no observer.

For has our ancient wise say, this "Self-Realization" experience is a realization in which you know that Gods world, or the world of Nature for the Non-Believer, is really "YOU". For certainly, this will be when you experience your "Self" to be the totality of that reality which we call "The Present"! This being a "Present" which can have no relationship with a non existing "I Want" past or a non-existing "I Want" future! For certainly, it should now be known that these "I Want for ME" dreams exist only to be pursued in the minds of people who animalistic ally endeavour to create an imaginary and very unreal *"I Want For Me World"*, which certainly cannot be real world.

So yes! For the believer and the non-believer, the name "Space" is certainly the only place in which this only child that we call "The Creation" could have been born! It is for this reason that "Life's Purpose" scientifically puts forward that the name "Mother" is that which is best used to describe that reality which our believer and our non-believers call "Space". For indeed, is it not a factual truth and also a scientifically stated fact, that a male seed must be planted into a female body, this being why "Life's Purpose" states that "Space" can only be a female and so is

"Scientifically" named in the "Life's Purpose" to be the "Mother of the Creation"? For is it not also true that it is certainly space IE: The "Mother of the Creation", who is recognized to be the one who monitors the growth of this added number three, this being that "child" which we call "The Creation" or that which our Non-believers call "Nature!"

Of course, it is the "Mother of the Creation" who must be the most active and therefore the most important of all that which "Life's Purpose" calls "three in one", for is it not true that it is the mother that looks after the growing child? For certainly, this three in one must be God the father with two being "Nature" who is the mother of the creation and with three being the actual creation, which is the creators only child! For certainly, is it not also true that all our world's natural laws show that it is the Mother who provides the caring energy which nurtures and cares for a growing child, this being from when it is born until it is mature? But what happens when the child becomes mature? Well more about this later in "Life's Purpose"!

But certainly, is it not also true that we see all around us, just has it is within our own lives, this natural law of the Mother being the one who is the carer of the wellbeing of Her growing children? For is it not scientifically confirmed that it is usually the Mother who endeavours to keep Her children fit and healthy? For is it not also usually true that it is the Mother who shows her children how to experience a life that can only be lived in "Present Time"? Also is it not true that it is only within the "Present Time" that there exists Gods ever developing ever mobile and ever pursuing "harmony", this being a harmony that seems to be coming from the attracting future?

Also is it not a naturally known truth that it is within this ever developing ever evolving ever moving and ever still Godly, or for the non-believer a Nature provided "Present" time, that there normally exist an agreeable supporting father? This usually being a constant teaching and caring father who actually brings a cultural self-awareness or even a self-realisation that is based upon the growing Childs ability to understands i.e.: stand under God the fathers harmony seeking laws! These being laws that are constantly unfolding within the "Present" time!

Also is it not true that many people, within all our world's religions, do pursue teaching activities that are based upon their religions controlling and centrally imposed "religious" worshipping laws? For certainly, is it not true that our worlds differently named religions do pursue activities which are usually sought by followers who believe that such charitable pursuits should be supported correctly, frankly, and intelligently? This being that ongoing and ever developing "religious" pursuit in which this ever growing only child, which "Life's Purpose" names to be "The Creation"; can experience the need for a personal and an independent understanding! This being an independent understanding in which there is sought a natural and friendly agreement between the Mother and Her only child – which is the ever-growing ever-developing Creation! For is it not easily confirmed that our natural laws do show that a child is a caring extension of both its parents? So Yes! Is it not true that we see all around us this harmony seeking ongoing truth which is called "Nature" by the non-believer! This being a truth which can only exist in the developing and the growing births and re-births within that which is called "The Present"! For is it not a known truth that this God given "Present" or Nature given "Present" for the non-believer, does actually contain an ever re-birthing life in which it is known that it is only people who are consistently birthed with the "Freedom of Choice"? This being a "Freedom of Choice" in which only people can choose to support or not support the harmony of this ever-growing ever-developing God created "Present" or the Nature created "Present" for the

Even the undecided and individualized "Non-Believers", can recognize nature's constant harmony seeking endeavours that actually target the supporting of life, is this not true? For certainly it is a known truth that even non-believers acknowledge that such "natural" ever-developing harmony can exist and not only within their bodies but also all around their bodies. For is it not true that it is because of our "freedom of choice", that all people can knowingly support or not support God's or Nature for the Non-believer's, harmony seeking endeavours? These being harmony seeking endeavours that can be has purposeful has those that are nature-ally fixed into the rocks of our Earth.

So yes! One of the most important realities that actually cares for this only child that we call "The Creation", is the "Mother of the Creation" or that which is called "Nature" by the non-believer! For certainly it is the "Mother of the Creation" who's caring love can be "scientifically" experienced by any person who has attained the wisdom of a silent mind! This being a silent mind in which all the animalistic "I Want" for me, this being that which is coming from one or all of the animalistic five senses, has been silenced because the Soul has become has one with the creation.

For truly, it is also a fact that only people, because of their God given or Nature given for the non-believer, "Freedom of Choice", are able to create an unthinking mind! This being an unthinking and empty mind condition which allows their Soul to experience a "Self-Aware" condition, a condition in which they become has one with that which exist in the

"Present" time, this being that which is all around them just has it is within them! This certainly being a "Self-Aware" experience which is never misleading, but it also a "Self-Aware" experience which shows the reason why the "Freedom of Choice" has been given only people! For is it not true that it is only people, especially those without a non-animalistic "I Want" nature, that can support the work of the "Mother of the Creation"? This being a much needed support and obviously the reason why God or Nature for the non-believer, gave only to people the "Freedom of Choice"! This being a gift which allows only people to experience the living has one within the "Present" time and so it is only people who can free the harmony that is constantly endeavouring to emerge within the Creations developing "Present"!

For again is it not true that the same act that is being performed under different circumstances, could actually destroy the natural harmony that is endeavouring to emerge within the "Present Time"? For certainly, does not that which we call "Nature", this being that reality which we state controls the growth of all living plants and also the growth of all animals, always reflects a harmonious growing? Even the erupting volcano is compelled by "Nature" to just shrug its shoulders in order to ward off that energy which is emerging within it! For it is certainly it known that energy is also a living reality which also consumes energy? Therefore, is it not true that energy is also consuming reality which actually creates more energy in its never ending target to support the creations growth! For certainly, is it not truly stated by our scientists, that all "Non-Life" can be likened to be just another type of energy that is moving forward into the future – but for what purpose?

Can it not therefore be acclaimed that the harmony seeking "Mother of the Creation" who, when speaking through Jesus the Christian incarnate, did also state this truth by saying, *"My food is to do the will of Him who sent me and to finish His work" John 4.34 -* and also stating *"Whoever eats my flesh and drinks my blood has eternal life, and I will raise him at the last day" John 6.54*! This being explained by "Life's Purpose" to mean that a person who becomes has one with the creation, will become has one with God, meaning that they will not be born again for they have fulfilled the purpose of the creation! For certainly, it was the "Mother of the Creation" or that which is called "Nature" by the non-believer, that was actually speaking through Jesus about Her and Gods only child, this being that only child which we call "The Creation". This truly should be certainly known has an historical fact for it was again spoken by Jesus in the following words that were used to explain the purpose of the creation,

"For my flesh is true food and my blood is true drink" and also the words *"Whoever eats my flesh and drinks my blood remains in me, and I in him."* John 6:54-56. Speaking of course about the unity of that which we call "The Creation", meaning of course that the purpose of life was to become has one with the creation!

So yes! It is good to understand that absorbing this real food, this food being the wisdom which the "Mother of the Creation" is speaking through Jesus about, is actually a food that sustains the soul or sustains the mind for the non-believers, this real food being that which we call the "Present"! This truly being a "Present" that has no connection with time for the knowledge of time cannot exist within this unity that we call "The Creation"! For is it not true that it is only within this mind filling reality, this being that which we call "The Present", that God, who is the creator of this "Present", can actually be acknowledged to exist? For is it not also true that such mind silencing meditation, such has mantra praying and hymn singing, is the primary way to experience an awesome wisdom that will allow such achievers to experience a state of "Self-Awareness"! This experience being the first step towards "Self-Realisation", an experience in which the experiencer becomes has one with the creation that exists all around them and there is no observer!

For certainly, there is only one child, which also means that there is only one Creation which is a understanding that brings forward a good ending for "Life's Purpose"! This understanding being when we remember the following words which actually came from the mouth of Jesus who was certainly has one with the Creation which He truly experienced to be all around him just has it was within him! This being when the Jesus declared that all foods were "clean" but Jesus then added *"what comes out of a man is what makes him unclean, for out of men's hearts come evil thoughts, sexual immorality, theft, murder and adultery". For these evils come from inside and so make a man unclean!* This meaning that animalistic thoughts, these being that which can be heard inside the mind, are truly that which "Life's Purpose" explains to be "I Want" thoughts which are constantly being created by a person's animalistic five senses. For is it not true that you cannot be that which you listen to, or see or smell or taste or touch. For you are the Soul which is the viewer of these animalistic "I Wants", which meditation stops and which praying removes!

For certainly, these mind filling "I Wants", these being that which are being habitually sounded into your mind by one or all of your animalistic five senses, are simply animalistic "I need" pursuits which were originally birthed within the animal kingdom long before the arrival of people! But now in our modern time, it is certainly known that this "I Want" can be silenced by the attending of religious services which contain disciplinary hymn singing and imposed praying plus the mind-silencing listening to the sounding of holy words!

"Life's Purpose" also explains that it is now scientifically and historically known that this constant animalistic mind filling "I Want" can be disciplinary stopped by a private practice such has the repeating in the mind of a single word. This being that which is known to be a mind silencing mantra based meditation which has the purpose of silencing these animalistic "I Want" words which are being sounded into the mind by one or by all of the animalistic five senses! This being a twice daily exercise which is best performed at sunup and at sundown or has close has is possible to these times! For certainly, it is well known that this exercise is a single worded "praying" exercise in which the practitioner will unthinkingly become "Self-Aware" of only the "Present Time"! This being a time in which the observer has no thoughts but a time in which all that is needed to be known is known! This also being a time in which the "Past" and the "Future" do not exist for the "Present" reveals everything that is needed and there is no longer an "I Want" coming from an undisciplined animalistic mind

But YES! It is actually good to understand, that it is the work of the stomach that is the energy provider for all animals, this being that reality which also includes people!   For in the proving of these words, was it not the *"Mother of the Creation"*, who, when speaking through Jesus of the Christian faith, did simply state that *"There is nothing outside of a person which can defile them if it goes into them, but the things which proceed out of a person are what can defile them!";* Also are these words not also supported when Jesus said, *"I am the Bread of Life; whoever comes to me shall not hunger; and whoever believes in me shall never thirst"* Biblical Proverb 23:2.

Therefore and certainly, is it not true that listening to these holistic words coming from Jesus can be likened to a food that brings a feeling of being filled with that which is called "Enlightenment"? This being a "Self-Aware" experience in which a person actually experiences the "Bread of Life" that is spoken of in Proverb 23.2! This being the real world that Jesus speaks about and it is a world that we call "The Present"! This truthful saying means that a believer is no longer an "I Want" observer! This being because a believer will "Self-Realise" that the creation that exists all around them is has one with that world which exists within them! For certainly it is a factual truth that a true believer who exists within all our world's religions and philosophies', will first become "Self-Aware" that they are has one with the world that exists around them. This awareness' meaning that they are without any "I Want" for they actually experience themselves to be attached has one with everything that they observe! For it is certainly true that this "Self-Aware" condition can lead to the above "Self-Realization" that Jesus speaks about - which of coursed is spoken of has being the "Bread of Life"! This being a realization in which they experience themselves to be has one with "Everything" and so there is no observer!

So yes! It should now be again truly and in reminding said that "Self-Awareness" can lead to a condition which our ancients called "Self-Realisation"! This being a religiously targeted realisation in which a believer will silently and religiously experiences that they are "Everything" and that there is no "Observer"! For certainly and again it should be said, that it is then that your silently disciplined mind will refuse to accept the constant "I Want" that can be sounded into your mind by one or several of your animalistic five senses! This being an animalistic "I Want" that was compulsory used in your "four legged" animalistic way of life that your Soul did leave many lives ago! For definitely, it should now be known, has "Life's Purpose" states, that a confirmed believer of our world's religious and philosophical teachings do first experience a "Self-Aware" condition in which a person becomes aware that they are has one with all that exist within the "Present Time"! For certainly it is also "religiously" known that this "Self-Awareness" condition can mature into a "Self-Realization" in which the observer is without any thoughts and so they actually become has one with that which they are observing and there is no observer! This being that reality which can follow the mind silencing "Self-Awareness" in which the mind-filling words of the animalistic five senses are silenced forever and the experiencer becomes has one with the creation and they are no longer an observer for the whole of the creation is "Them"!

For again it should be said; that a silent unthinking mind does factually enable a person to become "Self-Aware" that they are aware of the unity with a creation that exists all around them just has it exists in unification within them. This of course is that unifying experience that will eventually lead the experiencer to become "Self-Realized"! Which actually means that their "Soul", or their consciousness for the non-believer, will actually become has one with the creation and in fact, there is no observer? This actually being the true target and the actual purpose of that only child that we call "The Creation"!

For certainly the creation is that only child which has been birthed so that that reality which we call God, can like all fathers, be enabled to experience a part of "Himself", which is really "Everything": or the entirety of Nature for the Non-Believer. For definitely this is what "Life's Purpose" is endeavouring to explain to those people whose soul is just emerging from the animal kingdom! For certainly, the best known way to achieve this reality is by meditation! This being the disciplined concentration of the mind upon one repeating word which is inwardly sounded in order to stop the "I Want" demands that are coming from one or from all of your animalistic five senses!

9 "THE TARGET AND PURPOSE OF GOD OR OF NATURE FOR THE NON-BELIEVER":

For certainly, it should now be useful to recap the main points made in "Life's Purpose"! We can do this by starting with the fact that the purpose of meditation is to silence the mind and so fully experience the God given "Present" or the Nature given "Present" for the non-believer - this being a "Present" which has no attached "I Want" thought! For certainly it is true that all people are birthed with a Soul that can be likened to be the manager of a private manufacturing company which of course is the body in which the undying Soul exists! This being an animalistic body which can likened to a "Private Enterprise" company that employs five skilled managers who are known has "sight", "taste", "touch", "smell" and "hearing" – is this not true? But now the question is are you a manager who controls these five workers? For is it not also a recognised fact that if you are a manager who does not direct, control and also motivate your five skilled workers, then they would eventually become greed based and very troublesome has they constantly targeted their own "I Want" needs – this being that fact which destroyed the Russian U.S.S.R!

For certainly, this being an "I Want" for me animalistic way of life which brings us to the purpose and also the reason for practicing that prayer which we call "Meditation"! For truly personal "Meditation" is a mind silencing exercise which is practiced in order to disciplinary silence these five animalistic senses that we falsely call "Ourselves" – a reality which ALL our world's religions and philosophies pursue! So now it is important to understand that whatever you believe, the above is the Souls only target, which of course can be explained, has the targeted purpose of the energy that exists within you, which of course is the real YOU!

For certainly it should now be fully understood that the "Target" of your being created is to become has one with the God – or to be has one with the creation for the non-believer: For certainly your constant belief should be: *"I AM NOT THIS BODY IT IS AN INSTRUMENT FOR MY USE"*: This being said so that you are enabled to bring your "Soul", which is the energy that exists within you, back to an unthinking "Self-Aware" reality in which there exists no animalistic "I Want" mind filling thoughts! These again being said are mind-filling words which are coming from one or confusingly from all of your five animalistic senses! This realty being because you are allowing your five animalistic senses to sound their "I Want" within you for truly you cannot be that which you listen too!

So Yes! Is it not good to be "Self-Aware" of the creations stillness which you experience via your unthinking mind! This stillness being that which you became aware of or Realized when you stood at the top of a hill or a mountain and looked at the world below you – and without thought you experienced the love of unity that exists in Gods world or the world of Nature for the Non-Believer. It would also be then that you would fleetingly experience within you that which our ancients call "Enlightenment"!

This certainly being an "Enlightening" experience which is the pursued target of all our world's religions and philosophies! For certainly this is a known happening of unity with the creation which creates a "Self-Aware" experience within all people who have become without thought! Thus it is that such an "un-thinking" observer will become personally aware that they are actually connected in unity to the "Present" - this being that "Present" time which exists not only within you but also that unity which exists all around you!

Thus it is a religious and philosophical fact that you will experience an unthinking "Self-Awareness" of the fullness of this God given creation or this Nature given creation for the non-believer! For certainly it would then be understood just what it is that we call "The Present"! For without doubt, it is true that you will experience that the entire creation, this being that which is within you and also all around you is actually the true "YOU"! For certainly it is with this silent mind experience that you will witness that you are "everything" and there is no "observer"! For without doubt this is a "Self-Awareness" in which you will experience that you are truly has one with everything that exists within that which we call "The Present", this being that world which is within you and also all around you!

For certainly this is also a "Self-Awareness" experience in which our wise ancients say is a wakefulness which comes before that reality which our wise-ancients called "Self-Realization"! This being a "Self-Realization" experience in which the experiencer actually becomes has one with "The Creation" and there is no observer - for you have actually fulfilled the purpose of the creation which is for God to experience "Himself" or for Nature to experience itself for the non-believer!

So the personal question to be answered now is, "Who are you"? Do you now experience that this question was truly answered by the words in the "Christian" bible which state that the answer to this question is "I AM THAT I AM"! This statement meaning that you now understand that you are "Everything" and there is no observer, these being a truth even though you do not yet experience this reality! For certainly this should now be your known truth!

Therefore, and again it should be said, that the actual purpose of all our world's religions and philosophies is by disciplinary imposing group hymn singing and group chanting then unity with the group will and can be experienced! Thus all our worlds' religious meetings do endeavour, in their own cultural way, to silence their attendees' animalistic five senses that constantly claim an "I Want for ME" which can be constantly clouding the mind of a worshipper. This being that truth which can stop your Soul, which exists within you, from becoming has one with that reality which we identify has "The Present"! For indeed are we not now aware or even enabled to realize that this is the targeted purpose of ALL our world's religions and philosophies?

For certainly the targeted purpose of our entire world's religions and philosophies is to stop the animalistic barking of an *"I Want for ME"* or an *"I Want only for my religion"!* This being that isolation thinking which is being created in the mind by one or more of the bodies five animalistic senses! For certainly it is a known truth that you cannot be that which you listen too or see or smell or taste or touch, for you are truly all these realties for you are certainly has one with all that which you listen too or see or smell or taste or touch!

For certainly, this silence within the mind is actually that reality which all our world's religions and philosophies seek! This is because it allows the soul, this being the real you, to see clearly through the mind! It is this fact which enables it to become 100% aware of the unified world that is all around you just has it is within you! This "Self-Awareness" being a religiously sought awareness which can lead to a "Self-Realization" experience in which you "know" who you truly are – which is "everything" that exists within this creation!

For it is certainly a known truth that this personal "religiously" pursued experience does actually bring to the worshipping individual an inner "Self-Awareness" which can lead to a "Self-Realization" that you are actually that which we call "The Creation! This being that realization which all our world religions and philosophies do seek for their worshippers!

For again it should be said, for it is without doubt, that our entire world's religions and philosophies do target and therefore constantly endeavour for their followers to first experience a personal non-thinking "Self-Awareness"! This being a "Self-Aware" experience in which the observer is aware that there is no other for they are has one with the creation that is not only within them but also all around them! This being a "Self-Awareness" which can eventually lead to a "Self-Realization" experience in which you actually become "The Creation", and then you experience that there is no other and you are no longer an observer! For truly God has only one child and the purpose of the creation is so that God can experience "Himself" within this only child! For certainly, God is the father of this only child and "Nature" is the mother of this only child which is physically known has "The Universe"!

Therefore and without doubt, it should now be understood that this personal "Self-Awareness" with the creation is an experience which can only be achieved by religiously silencing the animalistic "I Want" thoughts that are constantly blocking the soul from seeing through the mind! For it is certainly known by our wise that people can be motivated by animalistic mind-filling "I Want" needs rather than spiritual needs in which they experienced that they are actually "everything" and that there is no other!

This ignoring of the truth is because the "thinker" actually believes that their animalistic five senses, these being that who's barking "I wants" are being observed in the mind, are really THEM! But these animalistic five senses cannot be you! For in truth you are everything and so you cannot be separate from that which you hear, see, smell, touch or taste! Therefore and certainly, these "I Want" thoughts, these being that which are blocking your Souls view through the mind, this being that which is the real you, are certainly not coming from the real you but from your animalistic five senses! Therefore, now is the time to become "Self-Aware" that the true you is actually the observer of these animalistic "I Want" thoughts, these being that which you are allowing to fill your mind because you believe that they are you! But now is the time in which the true you should become "Self-Aware"! This meaning that you have become aware that that which is listening to these "I Want" chattering that are coming from your animalistic five senses is your Soul, which is the true YOU! For certainly, this animalistic "I Want" that your five senses are sounding into your mind cannot be you? For you are the observer of these mind filling "I Want" messages that are coming from your animalistic five senses!

So yes! Now we should be aware of whom we really are! For truly we can develop within us a silence in which we eventually realize that we are has one with the creations energy, this being an inner energy that is anciently and historically called "The Soul". For certainly, it is this ancient and historical known experience that we are first Self-Aware" of! This being an awareness which is anciently known to be the first step towards that which is called "Self-Realization", meaning that we actually realise that there is no observer and we are has one with the creation – which is Gods only child or natures only child for the non-believer!!

Therefore the two targets of ALL our world's religions and philosophical teachings are that a person will first become "Self-Aware", meaning that they observe, when without thoughts, that they are has one with that which we call "The Creation" and there is no other! This being an unthinking "Self-Awareness" in which you experience that you are has one with the creation! This being an experience which will lead to that which is called "Self-Realisation"! This being the final experience in which the experiencer actually become "everything" and there is no observer! For certainly they have fulfilled that which is the targeted purpose of all life! This target being the becoming has one with God or with nature for the non-believer and it is then that they are not born again! For again and certainly it should be said, that this is that reality which signifies the purpose of the creation! This being that God can experience "Himself" or Nature can experience itself for the non-believer!

10. HOW TO MEDITATE AND THE PURPOSE OF MEDITATION

For without doubt, it should now be known that the target of meditation, which can also be called "praying", is to achieve a "Self-Aware" experience, this being an experience that occurs when a person's mind becomes without thought. It is then that the non-doer will silently become aware that that which physically exists within them is also has one with that which exists all around them! This being the experience which is sought by all our world's religions and philosophies! For without doubt, it should now be known that a "Self-Aware" experience is the first experience that is targeted by all our world's religions and philosophies.

The reason for this is because it is an experience that occurs when the body is without any mind-filling animalistic "I Want" thoughts! For certainly, it is also a "religiously" known fact that when a "Self-Aware" experience is further continued, it will lead to an even greater experience which is called by our ancient wise "Self-Realization"! This being an experience in which a worshipping person "Self-Realizes" that they are has one with that which we call "The Creation" – for it is an experience in which there is no observer! This being that experience which is certainly targeted by our entire world's religions and philosophies but it is also an experience which is not usually discussed because the "I Want" animalistic five senses show fear at being silenced. For first this is a "Self-Aware" experience in which, and again it should be said, is when a person first becomes aware that they are has one with he creation that is all around them just has it is within them. This certainly this is awareness that can lead to a "Self-Realisation" experience in which the experiencer becomes the creation and there is no observer! This actually being the purpose of the creation, but more about this later in "Life's Purpose"

So again it can be truly said that this **"I am that I am"** experience is first understood to be a "Self-Awareness" experience which is actually the first step towards that which all our worlds religious and or philosophical do target - in their pursuit to achieve "Self-Realisation"! For certainly this is the actual target of ALL our world's religions and philosophises has the worshipper first achieves a mind that does not keep demanding an animalistic "I Want"! For certainly, it is a known truth that a serious worshipper will physically become aware of the ***"Peace That Surpasses All Understanding"***! For truly, is it not factually and religiously known that the first experience of becoming has one with the creation is when a person experiences a "Self-Aware" condition in which they experience the ***"Peace That Surpasses All Understanding"***! For certainly, the first fruits of a personal worshipping is when the worshipper begins to become aware that they are at peace with the unity of the creation that is all around them despite any punishing aspects that are being committed against them – does not our history prove this? Is it not also true that such a worshipper will also eventually "Self-Realise" the fact that they have become lovingly attached to a creation in which they have become "Everything"! This being a realisation which controls their personality and also their actions, for it is a "Realisation" in which they experience that they are has one with the creation that is all around just has it is within them! For without doubt, they experience this to be true for there is no observer for that which they are observing is experienced to be "THEM"!

Also and essentially, this is also a historically known psychological state in which the inner observing self is silently experienced to be a part of "everything" and there is certainly no thoughts coming from any of the five animalistic senses! For certainly worshipping people who are moving towards this realisation know this reality and oft call it *"The peace that surpasses all understanding"!* Is this not true?

For certainly this is a well known "religious" condition which is often experienced by many worshipers to be a unifying condition in which their inner observing self does fleetingly experiences a unified obedience to the world around them! Therefore it should now be known that a continued religious practice will lead the disciplined practiser to be observational aware that they are a living part of that which exists all around them! Also, when such as religious sincerity continues the experiencer will eventually become "Self-Realized"! This being a reality in which there is no observer for the "experiencer" becomes has one with that which we call "The Creation" or the "Present Time" for the non-believer! Within this reality the experiencer will fully understand the meaning of the words *"Forgive them, for they know not what they do!"*

Therefore, and again it should be said, that these two experiences IE: "Self-Awareness" and "Self-Realisation" are the main targets of all our world's religions and philosophies! For without doubt, it is also truly known that disciplinary imposed praying and also disciplinary controlled incantations etc, are the activities that will ensure that the doer, which can be you dear reader, will actually become has one with the creation that exists all around them, just has it exists in unity within them!

For again and definitely it can be said, that it is truly known that such "Self" imposed and disciplinary controlled praying, is actually a self-control that is targeted to silence the "I WANT FOR ME" that is being sounded by one or by all of the animalistic five senses! This certainly being an animalistic "I Want" for me that am being barked into the mind by one or by all of your animalistic five senses! For certainly if you can hear it in the mind it cannot be coming from the real you for you are the listener to this animalistic "I Want"!

For certainly it is then, with a silent mind, that the experienced "prayer" will eventually become aware that the totality of that which is all around them, which is religiously called "The Creation", is truly has one with that which is within them! For truly and again it should be said, that a disciplined incanting prayer will first experience a "Self-Aware" condition in which they know that they are "Everything" and with such repetitive unthinking praying, they will eventually "Self-Realise" that they are the unified totality of creation and so realise that they the only child of GOD! For again and certainly, is it not true and therefore basically understood, that our entire world's religions' and philosophies do constantly and religiously endeavour to remove the *"I Want for Me"* thinking, which knowingly binds people to an animalistic way of life?

Therefore and certainly it should now be accepted has true that a mind filling animalistic "I Want for Me" is an uncontrolled way of thinking that is certainly a verbiage that clouds the purity of the mind! For certainly, and again it should be said, that it is this animalistic mind filling activity that stops the real you, which is your Soul, from seeing the "Present Time" and so you also become animalistic by nature!

For is it not true that this "I Want" way of living creates an inborn animalistic pursuit which can only be coming from one or more of your "animalistic" five senses? This being "I Want" condition which you have inherited from your previous existence has a non-human animal! Also it should be known that the stronger these animalistic "I Want" demands are experienced the more recent it was that you're Soul evolved from such an animalistic existence! For certainly it was also a well know truth that in our ancient times, just has it is in our modern times, that such a disciplined meditation or that which is called praying by many church attendees', is actually and truly pursued in order to silence the mind-clouding "I Want" that actually is coming from the bodies' five "animalistic" senses! This being that "I Want" which actually controls all animals!

But now, in our modern times, it can be understood to be a "religiously" known fact, that it is only people who can disobey this mind filling "I Want" that is repeatedly coming from their "animalistic" five-senses! For certainly it is only people who, by using an imposed discipline, that can silence them! For certainly, is it not a definite truth that it is only people who have been God given or Nature given for the non-believer, a "Freedom of Choice"! This being the "Freedom of Choice" that allows a person to be a believer in God or to not to be a believer in God and even to see or not to see and even to die or not to die!

For certainly, is it not also factual truth that it is also only people that have been birthed with a "Freedom of Choice"? This being a "Freedom of Choice" that is empowered by reason or by rational behaviour and which is based upon a freedom of choice that allows people to be controlled by animalistic instincts or not to be controlled by animalistic instincts and so be motivated by physical appetites rather than spiritual needs! Thus it is that only people are capable of standing back from such desires and choosing which course of action to take.

Therefore it is a known truth that there are no humanitarian rights and also no humanitarian duties normally being pursued within the animal world! For it is a certain truth that every animal lives upon a physical strength in which it is motivated by thoughts of past histories? Does not this fact ensure that within the totality of our animal world there are no common rights and or group duties – except within their own pack!

For again is it not true, that every animal is motivated by its personal needs whereas people have the ability to accept group imposed laws plus their communities and also other communities controlling orders!

This certainly being a group imposed ideology which is founded upon the group's "democratic" ability to use their "Freedom of Choice" in order to refuse internal demands that are based upon another's persons "I Want for ME" animalistic desires! This being a known reality which allows groups of people to control and also silence many a mind filling "I Want" which is being sounded into the mind by one of their five animalistic senses! Therefore and truly, is not this God given or Nature Given gift for the Non-Believer "Freedom of Choice", a gift which actually stops people from blindly pursuing their mind filling animalistic "I Want for ME"!

Also and certainly, is it not also a known truth that people, who have been newly rebirthed from the animal kingdom, just cannot understand this group based controlling democracy? For is it not true that such people believe that their animalistic five senses are truly them and that there is no "unified with everything" observer! This condition being a reality which endeavours to control the lives of those people who have just emerged from the animal kingdom! Therefore is it not a fact that we should now be aware that this animalistic "I Want for ME" demand will actually be a very strong "motivational" pursuit especially for those people who have just been reborn from the animal kingdom! For is it not true that such early animalistic rebirths has people would not know that they possess this mind-filling and controlling "Freedom of Choice"! This "Freedom of Choice" being a reality which enables any person to be or not to be, to choose or not to choose and even to give or not to give, which includes their own death!

So now let us take a further look at these five animalistic controlling systems that rest within us! Theses being that which we call "Touch", "Sight", "Listening", "Taste" and "Smell". The question now being is shall we obey them or should they obey our inner observer, this being that which we call the Soul! Therefore and certainly should it not be known that the voice you listen to in your mind is coming from your five senses and not the real you! For is it not true that you are the observer who is listening to these sounds that are being made in your mind! Now if you have difficulty in accepting these truths, then try this exercise! Just say these words into your mind! *"I am the greatest person in the world today!"* Now say *"I am the worst person in the world today!"* Now ask yourself, who is in charge? This should prove to you conclusively that you are certainly the one who is in charge of your mind and not the five animalistic senses' which you are personally controlling – is this not true? Yet is it not strange that we can believe that our thoughts are coming from that which is really us! For certainly it is VERY true that our thoughts are NOT us! For is it not a fact that we are the listener and observer of these thoughts that enter the mind?

Therefore, is it not true that the purpose of all religions and philosophies is to reveal that you cannot be that which you observe, taste, touch, smell, or listen too! For the truth is that you are really "The Soul! This being that reality which is a unified part of everything that exists not only within you but also everything which exists all around you, for truly there is no other - Amen.

But is it not true that we can be animalistic ally dominated by our five senses? These being **"sight"** and so we spend hours watching sport and many other entertainments such has films and shows etc! Also many people love to paint pictures and create films and also many people take pleasure in long walks in the countryside plus going very often to the theatre? Or are we dominated by the sense of **"taste"** and therefore love the eating of food and our body size actually shows this affection? Or is it **"smell"** that dominates us? Therefore we fill our homes with good smells and also scent our clothes with perfumes in order to make them smell fresh and also scent our body so that it also smells wonderfully? Or is it **touch?** Where we love playing the piano or the violin and also painting pictures plus cuddling our loved ones etc? Or is it **listening?** In which we love the sound of music and if possible listen all day to such favourably chosen sounds etc? But now is the time to remember that the above five senses cannot be the true you, for is it not true that they are just instruments for your use?

So certainly, the question now remaining is "Who are YOU!" and the answer must be that "YOU" are really that energy which we call "The Soul"! Thus it is the Soul that provides the energy that motivates your body for it is the only energy that can be acknowledged to be the real "YOU"! for definitely it is your Soul which is that reality which experiences "Everything"! For is it not a known fact that all the personal energy which rests within you and which automatically empowers you, is actually that unified energising reality which is personally named to be your "Soul"?

Also, is it not a well known fact that "energy" cannot die! For the written law supporting this fact actually states that preservation, protection, upkeep, maintenance, management, maintenance are all words that endeavour to explain the use of an energy that can neither be created nor be destroyed! For certainly, it is this fact which means that an energised ongoing system always has the same amount of energy, unless it's added to by an energy that exists outside of it! For certainly is it not a well known scientific fact that energy cannot die! Also that when it is displaced it just re-creates its existence somewhere else! For is it not a truth that the law regarding the conservation of energy states that the total energy of an isolated system is constant and that energy can neither be created nor can energy be destroyed - but it can be transformed from one form to another.

Therefore it can be said that the energy of life, this being that which exists within all people and which is religiously called "The Soul", cannot be destroyed, but it can be transformed into another form in which it suddenly begins exist has a new life! An example being likened to the driver of car who exchanges an old car for a newer car and simply drives it away! A good confirmation of this truth is that any pregnant mother immediately knows when an energy, which is the Soul, actually enters the child that she is carrying within her. It is certainly an energy that knowingly brings life and it is also an energy that is religiously believed to have originated from God or from Nature for a non-believer! For it is certainly an energy that brings a way of life which is clearly explained in the ten most ancient and most religiously known Christian laws – which are has follows!

1. ***Do not put other gods before me.*** (Live according to the laws of the community within which you live!)
2. ***Honour thy father and thy mother.*** (For being allowed by the creator of all life, they personally gave you your life!)
3. ***Do not murder another person.*** (For all people truly exist because they are sacred!).
4. ***Do not covet thy neighbour's wife and do not commit adultery.*** (Remember that the law of union should not be broken.)
5. ***Do not murder.*** (For all people exist has your true yourself!).
6. ***Do not covet his slaves*** (Paid Workers) ***or his animals, or anything of thy neighbour.*** (For your small finger cannot be your big finger?)
7. ***Remember the Sabbath day.*** (And your being has one with the

creation that is all around you just has it is within you.)
8. ***Do not bear false witness against thy neighbour.*** (For your neighbour is also you).
9. ***Do not take the name of the Lord thy God in vain.*** *(Never blaspheme for it can damage your Soul)*
10. ***Do not make has alive any graven image or idols and neither kneel before them nor worship them!*** (For they have no Soul and so do not exist within the unity of all life!)

Also, is it not a known truth that the energy being used to develop a system can only be developed in relationship to the abilities of the system? An example being the energy that brings to life the light that removes the sleep of an electric light bulb! For certainly, is it not true that the first law of thermodynamics', this being the branch of physics that deals with the conversions from one to another of various forms of energy and how these affect temperature, pressure, volume, mechanical action, and all explanations state that energy is locally conserved. This means that the amount energy contained inside some volume – i.e.: volume meaning the total amount of something and in this discussion this something being the human body, explains that the human body can only change if this energy flows into or out of that which it being energised – which is you body!

So it is a certain truth that energy changes form has it moves around from place to place, but it can never "just appear" nor can it "Just disappear." For energy is un-dying and also very consistent for it creates an ongoing life, meaning that it will continue energising a life until the body dies through age or through damage – which we call death!

But certainly, it is a known truth that the energy that actually fills a body with life is the same energy that is used to bring life again and again into a new body! For is it not a truth that energy cannot die therefore it will certainly be used again when that body, which contains it, "dies"! Thus it is that a new body, which can be likened to being a new electric light bulb, becomes alive with this non-dying energy, which it must obey and so brings to the new recipient that reality which we call "LIFE"! Also is this reality not worldly known to be true? For is it not true that a mother to-be knows exactly when this energy enters the body of the child that is growing inside her! Also is it not a known truth that such "get-up-and-go" energy must be attached in unity to all the creations energy! Which means that your inner "private" Soul is certainly a realty that cannot die? *For truly, is this not also scientifically stated within the first law of thermodynamics which says that energy cannot be created nor can it be destroyed, but it can change the power of its existence by absorbing other energies!* Now does this truth not mean that the energy encased in all life is constantly growing and therefore developing into a unified existence with "The Present"? Thus meaning that we can experience the energy within us to be has one with that energy which is outside of us – meaning our bodies?

Also does this truth not mean all the energy which exists within that reality which we call "The Creation", is acting to unify has one "everything" which exists within it! Meaning that our bodies must contain this growing and needed search for unity, this being a reality which must also becomes stronger life after life after life?

But is it not also a "scientifically" known fact that the body's energy, this being that which brings to the body life, is actually created by that bodies inner Soul! This being that fact which certainly makes it a truth that a person's soul can actually choose to self-destruct, has in wars etc! It is also certainly a "scientifically" known fact that the statement "I am", is the most powerful and personal command statement that can be spoken. This being because it can be used to empower you or disempowering you, so be careful of what you attach to the end of any "I WANT" statement; because it can manifest into a reality.

Also it is certainly a "scientifically" known truth that that animalistic "I Want for ME" feeling is stated to be just a 20-watt cloud of "I Want" energy based verbalisation that is being sounded into your mind by one or by all of your animalistic five senses. For certainly, is it not a truth, has the first law of thermodynamics state, that energy is always locally conserved?

Thus it is scientifically stated that the amount of energy which is contained inside an encasement, which is you, can only change if that energy is permitted, by you, to flow into or out of that encasement! For has Einstein said, *"Energy cannot be created or destroyed, it can only be changed from one form to another".* This being first law of thermodynamics which is also known as *"The Law of Conservation of the Energy, this being that which works in all spheres of life",* so the point is, who allows this changing within a person's mind?

So certainly it is scientifically known fact that such energy can and does move around from place to place, but it never "just appears" or "just disappears"! For according to our world's scientists, energy can never be made and neither can it be destroyed! Therefore it is certainly a well known scientific fact that a person's Soul actually exists has one with not only the energy of the unified creation that actually exists within them, but also the energy that exists all around them!

Therefore, within each living person there is an observing energy which is coming from that which we call "The Soul"! This being that which is known by all religious people and non-religious people to be the provider of life, which we call consciousness! For is it not also a truth that a person's Soul is therefore a non-ageing and also a never dying energy whose wisdom is usually based upon the number of lives that it has lived since leaving the lower animal kingdom! For is it not also a known truth, this being that which is explained within the first law of thermodynamics, that energy is a living entity and also a reality that is used by all life forms to pursue activities that will knowingly support and also develop that life forms aging energy?

For certainly, the first laws of thermodynamics describe how energy, this being that which exists within all systems, can only change in its effort to perform usefully supporting work for the unified "life" which exists all around it – this being that which is supported by the unified energy which exists within it! For it is certainly true, has Einstein said, that energy cannot be created nor can it be destroyed, but it can change from one form to another i.e.; Energy can be strengthened or it can be weakened! This being the first law of thermodynamics which also known to be the "Law of Conservation of Energy" and it is a law that is known to work in all spheres of life! Yet it is also known that it is an energy that can weaken or strengthen or even modify that which it supports! Alas, unfortunately and regrettably it also truly known that some supporting entities, these being that which we call "people", can in efforts to "support" can actually self-destruct, has in wars and suicides etc!

But certainly, it is also known to be true that the inner mind "me" feeling is just a 20-watt cloud of energy that actually exists inside a living person's head. Therefore, and this is a scientifically known truth, that our bodies energy, this being the energy that is coming from what we call "The Soul", cannot cease to exist upon the death of the body in which it previously existed! This being because it is a scientifically known fact that energy, which provides the life that exists within a living body, is like all energy, meaning that it cannot cease to exist! Or more simply put, "The Soul", this being the energy that brings life to a person - cannot die!

So yes! It is now useful to first become knowingly "Self-Aware" and so develop an awareness in order to eventually "Self-Realise" and so experience the reality of just what is the simple meaning of the creations energy! For certainly what is now known and also now being scientifically stated, is that the first law of thermodynamics states that the total energy of an "isolated" system, which is experienced to be on its own, is an unchanging constant. It is also known that any isolated energy, such has the energy supporting a human body, can neither be created nor can it be destroyed! For it is certainly a known fact that this inner energy is enabled to transform itself from one form to another form. This meaning that energy cannot die, but the newly inhabited forms shape and its structure, which can be likened to a person's body, will give this inner energy a distinctive personality which is considered to be separate from its power, which of course emits is its colour, plus its texture and its composition.

So yes! This is the natural law regarding energy and it is certainly a natural law in which only people are enabled to become "Self-Aware" that they are has one with the "unified" energy that empowers the world upon which they live! For truly, this is an historical known condition in which it is "religiously" known that a person can experience that their body is has one and so being without thought they "experience" that they are the totality of the creation that exists all around them, just has it experienced to exist within them. For certainly, does not this truth give full meaning to the words of Jesus, who when being nailed to a cross said, *"Father, forgive them, for they do not know what they are doing."* Then upon His death, the people that killed him stole his clothes for themselves!

Thus it is now certainly known that Jesus was certainly an unthinking unified part of a creation which existed all around and within the people who painfully nailed Him to a cross – for Jesus was certainly was has one body with those that destroyed him! This meaning that Jesus was has one life with all that was all around him just has had been the life that had been within him. For certainly Jesus knew and so experienced that He was the totality of the creation, which also means that He experienced himself to be, has one with all people, even those who were destroying him! This certainly being known has a "Self-Realisation" condition in which the experiencer realises that they are "Everything", which of course they are; for they have knowingly "Self-Realized" that they are everything and that there is no observer!

For certainly the purpose of life is so God or Nature for the Non-Believer, can realize their "self"! For certainly is it not also scientifically stated that there is a management of life in which a system i.e. say your body, can change from its initial unknowing state to a final all knowing state, this being based upon a thermodynamic agreement. In broad scientific terms, thermodynamic agreements deal with the transfer of energy from one place to another and also from one form into another. The key concept is that the Soul, this being that which energizes a person's body, is a form of thermodynamic energy which does also achieve a definite amount of "unthinking" mechanical work.

For analytical purposes, in regarding thermodynamic energy, it is helpful to divide your personal activity has to be either a quasi-state or a non-quasi-state, with quasi meaning to mindfully reflect something or somebody in ways that are not exactly the same! Therefore, your Soul has an isolated "singularity", cannot exchange matter or energy with its surroundings, but has an enclosed system it can experience an incoming force which can then be reflected into an outgoing force! This reality being achieved by combining this "inner" pressure, which is emanating from your Soul, with Natures energy, meaning the physical world including all natural phenomena and living things, or by the combining and so joining up this energy with somebody else's Soul or their inner personality for the non-believer. This certainly being an all combined energy release, which is achieved in order to accomplish a jointly pursued effort such has that which can be read in all our worlds various religions and philosophies.

But it is certainly believed that the inner soul cannot inwardly change or even exchange matter, for it is only an open system, this being that which is observationally alive only in the "Present Time", can interact with its surroundings! This fact simply means that only energy can increase or exchange itself. For certainly, it is also known, has stated in the first law of thermodynamics, that energy can neither be created nor can it be destroyed for it can only be altered in its own form – which explains the limits of the human body!

For within any "living" system, this energy is always being transferred from one life to another life, for it is an energy which also creates thoughts that arise in an observing mind, for certainly, this is an energy which can actually "Choose" a third energy to be associated with! This third energy usually being that which is sought to remove the existing boundary in which the "Present Times" isolated energy is encased within a person's body! This being a silent exercise which is normally achieved by repeating a chosen mantra into the mind and it is also meditation that can only be achieved in the "Present Time"!

Therefore and certainly meditation, i.e.: the repeating of one word into the mind in order to keep silent the mind filling animalistic five senses, does certainly aid the actual crossing of that boundary which rests between an animalistic "I Want for ME" mind filling dream world and into an unthinking world in which the beholder becomes "Self-Aware" or even "Self-Realises" that they are "Everything" that exists in the "Present" time and that there is certainly no observer! Thus truly, they will physically experience the meaning of the words "I AM THAT I AM", for they will experience that they are "Everything"!

For certainly, disciplined single word mantra praying, which is the disciplined repeating into the mind of only one word, a person will experience that they are has one with the creation! This being the creation which exists not only within them but also all around them for the sounding of only one word into the mind disciplinary silences the chattering "I want" of the animalistic five senses which is a verbiage that always takes consciousness' away from that which we wisely call "The Present"!

For truly, is it not also well known fact that all our world's religions and all our worlds philosophies, do disciplinary introduce these mind controlling activities via imposed hymn singing and praying etc, this being that disciplined culture which abounds in all our worlds religious gatherings! For certainly it is well known that single worded mantra praying, which is called "Meditation", certainly silences the "I Want" mind-filling verbiage which is coming from the animalistic five senses

For certainly and again it should be said, that it is certainly true that the five animalistic senses, whose mind filling "I Want for me", is certainly that reality which stops the Soul from seeing through such a cloudily filled "I Want" mind! This being a mind-filling reality which makes it difficult if not impossible for the Soul to see through such an active mind and so experience the world that we call "The Present"!

For certainly, is it not a well known religious and also a philosophical understanding, that the first law regarding the managing of our everyday life, is the need to support the law of energy and also its conservation, which is called a thermodynamic process. This being the branch of physics that deals with the conversions of energy to energy, such as that which happens when a person dies but is reborn again! For certainly, all energy has various forms which actually affect temperature, pressure, volume, mechanical action, and of course work output.

For is it not true that the law regarding the creations energy, this being that energy which exists all around us and also within us, states that energy cannot be created nor can it be destroyed, but it can be converted from one form of energy into to another form of energy. Thus it is known and also accepted, that an ongoing repetitive working system always has the same amount of energy within it, unless it is added to or subtracted from by another source of energy which must exists outside of it! So scientifically and therefore factually, it is a known scientific truth that our living source of energy, must come from that which we call "The Soul", so certainly the body dies when the Soul leaves it!

Also, is it not a known truth, that this undying energy, this being an energy which is coming to us from that which call the Soul, can certainly leave the body to which it is attached, which brings death to the body it is empowering! For certainly, is it not a known truth that a person's Soul, when leaving the body it is occupying, will bring death to that body which it had previously energised. This being exactly the same has when the light of an aging light-bulb ceases to function, but the electricity which is empowering the light-bulb, does not die but will be enabled to empower another replacing light-bulb – is this not truly called "The Energy of Life"?

For certainly, is it not also a well known truth that this inner-energy, this being that which supports of all "Life", is also known to be a group motivator, for it actually groups together differing life forms! Is this because it enlightens the mind in order for it to support friendship or is it the need of support has in a pack culture! For certainly, a pack of animals is an exceedingly complex social unit with an extended family consisting of parents, offspring, siblings, aunts, uncles, and sometimes friends from other groups! But they all endeavour to fully experience that which we call "The Present"! This being a "Present" which actually gives all life forms a need and a reason to live! For does not their inner energy empowers them to do something to support the creation which feeds them and which exists within and around them plus around all life and all non-life! Therefore and truly, this inner "animalistic" energy actually enables all life to become freely committed to doing something that will support their life, which of course is the reason why some activities are also animalistic ally preoccupied with physical rather than spiritual need!

For certainly all people have been given the "Freedom of Choice"! But again is it not true that energy, such as that which activates your rooms lighting, is also an energy which can also work in another room when requested to do so? Therefore and again, should it should be said, that all energy is has one entity and so it cannot die! Therefore you're Soul, which is the energy that brings life to your body, will live a life after life after life, which of course it does – until it achieves its target! For that reason the question should now be "Who are YOU and also what is your target"?

For certainly it is known that within the Christian Bible, Jesus stated, has in the Gospel of John, that *"you are the bread of life!"* This being a saying which can be modernly understood to mean that you are a unified part of that energy which feeds that which we call "The Creation", which is the totality of everything that exists! For certainly it is true that we are a part of that unified energy which is known to rest within that which we call "The Creation" – which again should be known has "Everything"! For certainly and again it should be known, that this is an energy which brings to life that part of the creation which you call your body! Or even more scientifically put you can say, "I am that I am"! This being a phrase which is generally understood to mean that you are self-existent and also eternal and that you need no explanation for your being alive! This meaning that you really know that you are that undying energy which you call "The Soul", which is actually the energy which exists not only within you, but also within everything that is around you!

Therefore and again we can say that the real you are really your undying "Soul", which is actually the energy that brings life to the body within which it exists! For is it not a definite truth, that it is really your "Soul" that actually experiences all life and also all that which has no life?

Should it not also be known to be true that the target of your Soul, which is also the target of ALL life, is to actually become has one with all that exists within that which we call the "Present", which is commonly known has "The Creation"?

Therefore should it not be said again and again that that which ALL our world's religions and all our worlds philosophies' actually target, is for the worshipper to become has one with Gods "Present" or with Nature given "Present" for the non-believer! This being a "Present" which undoubtedly makes a person un-compromisingly and ungrudgingly "Self-Aware" that they are has one with the energy coming from the world that exists all around them becomes has one with the energy that exists within them! This being the knowledge gained when the inner Soul or the source of your bodies energy for the non-believer, is experienced to be has one with not only the energy that exists in unification within your body, but also has one with the unified world which exists all around you!

So yes! Now it should be known that the real you cannot be the animalistic body which carries the "Soul", this being that which creates your body's energy? For you are certainly "The Soul", this being the source of that energy which your current body is using in order for you to experience sight, taste, smell, touch and which experiences the creation that exists around your current body! This being because the real you, is a "Soul" that cannot die and for certain you are the "Soul" and this is where your body's energy for life does come from!

For truly and certainly, it should be now known and so said again, that our body's energy truly comes from that which you really are, which the "The Soul" is truly! This also being a personal "Soul" which, via your God given or Nature given for the non-believer "Freedom of Choice", does constantly bear witness to the mind filling "I Want" verbiage world that is being created in your mind by your five "animalistic" senses! For is it not true that this is an "I Want" that is born from your animalistic five senses? These being that which you are personally allowing to control you because you have been Godly allowed or Nature allowed for the non-believer, with a "Freedom of Choice"! Thus you are allowed to decide what do or what not to do and what to be or what not to be? But now it should be known that that consciousness, which exists within you, is also the same consciousness that exists within all animals!

For certainly is it not a definite truth that it was from the animal kingdom that people did truly originate? But now it must be said, that after many thousands of years of your body being controlled by the animalistic "I Want" that is coming from your five senses, you now know that this "I Want" cannot be coming from you! For you now know that you are truly the controller of these "I Want" words! Therefore you now know that you cannot be that, which you listen too, or taste, or smell, or touch and neither can you be that which you see! For you are truly the experiencer of these messages that are coming from your five animalistic senses – is this not true? For certainly you should now be aware or actually realise, that the real truth is in the knowing that your Soul, which is the real you, is the witness to that world which is being sounded into your mind! For is it not true that such mind filling "I Want" verbiage can only come from your five animalistic senses which the real you, which is your silent Soul, does observe and also evaluate!

So yes! Now is the time for you to create a silent non-active mind within which you will "silently" experience a "Self-Aware" reality in which all these "I Want for ME" words, these being words that are being sounded into your mind by your five animalistic senses, will be stopped, for they are NOT YOU – for you cannot experience an "I Want" when you are "Everything"! For certainly, our worlds religiously sought and or philosophically sought truth, is actually experienced when you either become "Self-Aware" that you are the world that you experience to be within you and all around you, or you may "Self-Realise" that you are has one with everything that exists in the "Present" and that in truth, there is no observer! These being worlds that can only be fully experienced when the observing Soul is enabled to see through a clear and empty mind in which there is no mind-blocking "I Want" thoughts that are coming from one or more of your animalistic five senses.

It is then that you will experience that you are has one with that which we call "The Creation" or that which is called the "Present" by the non-believer! For certainly this is a truth that all our world's religions and philosophies' do target and it is also a truth that any person can personally experience when their Soul, or that which is called consciousness by the non-believer, does actually observe the reality of the "Present" time", but only through a clear and silent mind! For certainly and again it should be said, that within this silent empty mind condition you will first become "Self-Aware" that you, or your Soul for the believer, are really a unified part of "Everything"! This being an awareness which can lead to that which our wise ancients called "Self-Realization"!

This being reality in which the experiencer, which can be YOU, does actually "Self-Realize" that they are a unified "everything" with that which exists within that which is called "The Creation", also known by non-believers has "The Present Time"! For factually it is certainly a known religious truth, that everything that can be experienced to exist within the "Present" time, is actually experienced to be "Them"! For is it not a known truth that Jesus of the Christian faith, when being savagely nailed upon a cross, did say to his persecutors *"Forgive them for they know not what they do!"*

For certainly again and again it should be religiously said, that you can, via a "Self" discipline, actually experience the truth of that which is the true YOU! For certainly and factually, the true you is your observing Soul, this being that realty which rests within you and which is a reality that is has one with "everything" that exists in the "Present Time"! Therefore, is it not a truth that your bodies inner "Soul", this being that which provides the energy for your body, is a silent witness to these animalistic "I Want for ME"?

These being thoughts that are being constantly sounded into your mind by one or by all of your five animalistic senses, these being taste, sight, smell, listening and touch! Therefore is it not true that they cannot be the real you! For is it not true that the real you is the silent observer that experiences this creation which exists in unity all around you and also in unity within you – but why is the true you, which is your "Soul" just a silent and oft not participating witness to these developing events that are constantly being created in the "Present Time"! Therefore again and again it should be said, this being until it is habitually and acceptably understood, that the true you is that which is your inner Soul, this being that which is an integral part of everything, or that which is known to be your consciousness for the non-believer!

For certainly it is factually true, that your inner Soul is the silent analyser and also the acceptor of all that which your current life experiences! This being because your Soul is an integral energy that is unified with everything that exists and it is this energy which is called consciousness by non-religious people!

Thus it should now be accepted that a "Self-Aware" experience, means that you have experienced that you are has one with the entirety of the creation, which is that experience which is religiously pursued by all our worlds' religions and philosophies'! For certainly the experiencer will religiously and also factually, become "Self-Aware" that their life's energy comes from that which is called "The Soul"!

This also being that energy which actually experienced to exist has one with everything that exists within them just has it also exists has one with the creation that is developing all around them. For is it not a certain truth that the "Enlightened" Jesus of the Christian faith, did constantly say to his listeners - *"No one can serve two masters. Either you will hate the one and love the other, or you will be devoted to the one and despise the other. You cannot serve both God and money.* Meaning that you must truly serve only your "self", which, has stated above, is "Everything" or that which is called "THE CREATION" by many people! For truly there is no separation within that which we call "The Creation", which is the known name of this only child!

For is it not true that Jesus of the Christian faith did say to His listeners *"I am the light of the world. He who follows Me shall not walk in darkness, but have the light of life"!* Also in John 8:58 Jesus stated, *"I tell you the truth, before Abraham was even born, I Am!"* Which "Life's Purpose" translates to mean that we are everything that exists within that which we call "The Creation" and that your energy cannot die and so your will certainly be born again? Also in another quotation, this being in Exodus 3:14, *"God said to Moses, "I AM WHO I AM";* meaning that He was everything and then it was also stated that God added *"Thus you shall say to the sons of Israel, 'I AM has sent me to you",* with "I AM" meaning "Everything"! For certainly, Jesus knowingly speaks the word of God, because He knows that He is a part of a God which give him the freedom to say "I AM that I AM", which is everything! For certainly there is only one life and it is called "The Creation" and is it not true that this experience is targeted by ALL our world's various religions and philosophies?

So yes! This "I am the I am" is that experience which is certainly pursued by all our world's religions and philosophical for all know it to be true that a silent mind, this being that which is not filled by any animalistic "I Want" thoughts, will enable your inner Soul to experience itself to be has one with that which we call the creation! For certainly this is an inner experience in which you become "Self-Aware" that your life's energy, which is coming from your "Soul", is actually experienced to be has one with the creation that exists all around it just has it knowingly exists has one within the bodies energy, this being that is within YOU! For certainly it should now be known that this "Self-Aware" experience is the an experience in which you will become "Self-Aware" that you are has one with that energy from which all life is coming from and that there is no observer for you are experiencing that you are actually that which we call "The Creation"!

So yes! Now it must be accepted that an empty non-thinking mind will factually bring forth an enlightened "Self-Aware" experience in which your inner Soul will know that it is has one with the totality of the creation! This being an inner awareness which can only be experienced when the mind is empty and without the "I Want" thinking, which can only be coming from one or more of your animalistic five senses! It is then, with an empty mind, that you will "unthinkingly" experience that you are has one with the world which is all around just has it rests within you! This being that which we call "The Creation" and it is this "Self-Aware" reality which our entire world's religions and philosophies do pursue for their followers to experience!

This without doubt is a spiritual experience which is knowingly achieved by religiously imposed praying and it is also an experience which can be achieved by the unified singing of hymns, all of which are religiously targeted to silence the mind! These being religious exercises such has the disciplined imposition of group "praying" and group "listening", which is pursued in order to disciplinary silence a person's "I Want" animalistic five senses, this being that "I Want" animalism which rest within all life forms!

For positively, it is known by all our world's religions and philosophies', that this mind silencing pursuit is a much needed activity! The reason being that it endeavours to silence a person mind filling animalistic five senses which enables their religious followers to become "Self-Aware" of an unthinking world that exists only in the "Present" time! This certainly being a "Self-Aware" experience in which their religious followers do, when not thinking, experience that they are has one with Gods world, this being the world that we call the "Present"!

For definitely, this is a personal "Self-Aware" experience in which the observer becomes aware that they are has one with that which exists all around them just has it is experienced to be has one entity within them! It is also known to be a "Self-Awareness" which can lead to that which is known has a "Self-Realisation" experience, this being that which is the target of all our worlds' religions and philosophies! This being because it is a "Self-Realisation" in which the experiencer realises that they are has one with the "Present Time" and there is no observer! This realisation actually being the main target of all our world's religions and philosophies' for it achieves a singularity with Gods world or the world of Nature for the non-believer! For positively this experience is a religious and philosophically known experience in which the observer ceases to exist! This reality being because they become has one with the creation and there is no observer!

Therefore and again for certain, is it not a historically known fact that this "Self-Realization" of being has one with the creation, is preached by all our ancient wise? This being a realisation that you dear reader, are has one with the "Creation" or has one with that which we is called "The Present" by the non-believer and so you become has one within God's love or within Natures love for the non-believer! For truly, is it not a positive fact, that all our worlds' religions and philosophies do endeavour to bring to their followers an experience in which they become personally "Self-Aware" of this unifying love? This being an individual awareness which can eventually lead to the realisation that the "experiencer" is truly has one with Gods world or the world of Nature for the Non-Believer, and that there is no observer! For unquestionably certainly, this religious and/or philosophical target, this being that there is no observer, is the target which is being pursued by all our world's religions and philosophies'! Therefore, again and again it should be said, that the target of all our world's religions and philosophies, is for their followers to become has one with that which we call "The Creation"! This "Oneness" being a personal experience in which a person first becomes aware that all they observe and so experience, is truly them! It is also from this "Self-Aware" experience that a person, if so desired, can become "Self-Realized"! This being a realization in which a person experiences that they are no longer an observer of the world around them, this being because they fully experience that they are "Everything" and there is no observer! It is then that their energy, upon a bodily death, becomes has one with God or with "Nature" for the non-believer", which of course is the targeted purpose of all the life that exist in that which we call "The Creation"!

For certainly, and if you wish to achieve this experience, this being that which is targeted by all our worlds' religions and philosophies' - then read on! For all readers should now be aware or even be enabled to realise, that it is the silencing of these animalistic "I Want" mind-filling thoughts, these being that which are being sounded into the mind by one or more of your body's animalistic five senses, that actually brings the experiencing of a oneness with that which we call "The Creation"! For truly, this is that experience which is being sought by all our world's religions and philosophies' – is this not true? For without doubt, it is also known that being without any mind filling thoughts does actually enable your Soul to see through your mind and so enable it to silently experience, without thought, its oneness with that which we call "The Creation"!

For definitely the experiencing of your Souls oneness with the world around it, is certainly that "singularity" experience which is pursued by all our world's religions and philosophies'! For our entire world's religions and philosophies do ceremoniously target the emptying of the mind from all "I Want" thoughts, these being thoughts which are now known to be coming from one or from all of your animalistic five senses.

So yes! It is well known that a disciplined exercise is needed in order to support this "religious" search for a mental and/or spiritual development! For it is well known that a non-thinking empty-minded experience of being "Self-Aware", means that you actually experience that you are aware that you are has one with that which exists in the "Present! Time! This certainly being an awareness which can lead to the experiencing of that which is called "Self-Realisation"! This being that reality in which you realise that you are "Everything" and there is no observer! Therefore it is certainly a known truth, that all our worlds regions and philosophies are aware and so do realise, that the practise of chanting prayers and other such disciplined praying methods does actually stop the mind, via this discipline, from being constantly filled by the "I Want" thoughts that are coming from one or from more of your animalistic five senses!

This again being stated for it is a religious or a philosophical truth for the non-believer, that it is this imposed "Self-Discipline" that truly stops the animalistic five senses from sounding their mind-filling "I Want" verbiage into the mind of the thinker! For it is certainly a known truth, that it is this "Self" imposed religious or philosophical mind-silencing discipline that does allow a person's Soul to witness the correct happening that are occurring in that which we call the "Present"!

For unquestionably, when you experience the silencing of these mind filling animalistic "I Wants", these being that which are being sounded into your mind by one or more of your animalistic five senses, this experience will certainly arouse within you a desire to pursue this "personal" and very spiritual development! This being a spiritual development in which the observing Soul, which is the undying energy that rests within you, experiences its oneness with that which we call "The

Creation", this being that which is more commonly known has "The Present"!

For truly it should now be known that such disciplined praying activity, which also includes the harmonious and unified singing of hymns, is that mind silencing activity which is being pursued by ALL our world's religions and philosophies - and this being for thousands of years! For certainly, it should also be known that this mind-silencing activity is achieved only by a personal mind-silencing pursuit such has private praying and also group hymn singing, this being that which is knowingly targeted by all our world's religions and philosophies. For certainly, this imposed activity will ensure that no "I WANT" can be sounded into the mind by any of the animalistic five senses!

Thus it is that such a silent and unthinking mind reveals a "Self-Awareness" or a "Self-Realization" experience which our entire world's religious and philosophical followers are being targeted to physically experience, this experience being that they are has one with the creation! Therefore and certainly, this is the main and only target of all our world's religions and philosophies via prayer and the singing of hymns so that the doer will experience that they really are has one with the creation!

Therefore and certainly, all our world religions and philosophies' do target various ways that will silence the animalistic "I Want" that is being sounded into the mind by one or by all of the bodies animalistic five senses. For certainly, is it not a known fact that praying and hymn singing, this being that which takes place in the "Present Time", is certainly that mind silencing discipline which is pursued by all our world's religions and philosophies! This being because such a mind-silencing pursuit actually stops the five animalistic senses from barking into the mind and therefore will, via this imposed discipline, stop the mind filling "I WANT", which is coming from one or from several of your animalistic five senses. For certainly, it is then, via this silent mind, that your Soul, which is the undying real you, will be enabled to experience a unity with that which we call "The Present", meaning that you actually experience that you truly are that which is "Everything" for there is no observer!

For it is then that the real you, which is your soul or your consciousness for the non-believer, will actually experience that the energy, this being that which rests within your body, is truly has one with that energy which we call "The Creation"!

Therefore and truly, it is then that you will have achieved the target which is pursued by ALL our world's religions and philosophies! This being the experience that you are not an observer of the present time but that you are has one with that which we call the "Present" and it is truly then that you will actually experience that which is religiously called "Enlightenment"! This being the enlightenment in which the main experience is the undying joyfulness of being has one with this "Present" and all that exists within that which you now know to be the only child of God or of Nature for the non-believer!

For certainly this means that you truly experience that you are "Everything" and that there is no observer! For it is then, within this "Enlightenment", you will experience yourself to be the totality of that which we call the creation or that which is called Nature by the non-believer. Therefore and truly, when the mind becomes silent and is without any animalistic "I WANT" thoughts, these being that which are coming from one or all of your "animalistic" five senses, you will knowingly become has one with God or has one with Nature for the non-believer - and therefore you will never be born again! This reality being because you have fulfilled the purpose of all life, which is so God, can experience "Him-Self" or Nature can experience itself for the Non-Believer. ... The end:

A FINAL NOTE ON AN ENDING OF THE BOOK CALLED "LIFES PURPOSE-
The truth being that everything that exists is "You"!

This book, which is called "Life's Purpose", is written in order to reveal that you are has one with God or with Nature for the Non-Believer and so be enabled to experience that there is no observer for everything that exists within this creation is the unified YOU! Thus it is that the awareness or the realization of this truth is the target of all our world's religions and philosophies. For certainly it is known that by disciplined praying and group hymn singing that the disciplined worshipper will achieve a "Self-Aware" reality in which they unthinkingly become "observationally" aware that they are an integral part of "everything"!

For certainly this "Self-Aware" experience is a personal experience in which a person becomes conscious that they are truly the observer and experiencer of everything that exists around them and also that which exists within them. This being an experience which is religiously known to be the first step towards fulfilling the target all our world's religions or natures target for the non-believer, which is to experience that which is religiously called "Self-Realization"! This being an experience in which, when without thought, a person truly realizes that they are "Everything" and that there is no observer!

So yes! Now it should be realized that this is the "Self-Realization" experience which all our worlds' religions and philosophies do pursue and that they do so in a way which is based upon a person's cultural understanding! Therefore and without any doubts, it should now be known that this un-dying energy, this being that which is emanating from that which is named to be "The Soul", is also an energy that has silently shown us how to create all our world's religions and philosophies'! For is it not true that all religions and philosophies' do target their worshipper to become enabled to "Self-Realize" that they are has one with God, who is the Father of the creation or to become has one with Nature for the Non-Believer, who is truly the "Mother of the Creation".

For definitely it is true that this personal "Self-Realization" is a religiously known experience in which it is automatically experienced that, when without any thoughts, the worshipper will experience themselves to be has one with the creation and that there is truly no observer! Consequently, and has an experienced result, a person will be enabled to say "I AM THAT I AM", which the Jesus stated in the Christian Bible.

This being an experience in which the prayer will actually realize that they are has one with everything, which truly means that they are without thoughts and so are free from any "I Want" perceptions or any "I Want" associations! Thus they are without thoughts and therefore have no thoughts of any future mind-filly "I Want" – these being mind entering "I Want" thoughts that are coming from one or from all of a person five animalistic senses which are listening, seeing, smelling, tasting and of course touch.

For certainly is it not also a known truth that you cannot be that which you listen too, or see, or smell, or taste and of course touch – with the touching of your body being the most difficult to accept has not being you! But is it not true that your arms and legs plus most of you body parts can be removed including your heart when a machine replaces it. Also can the silent observer of your thoughts and the experiencer of your body parts change? This being that which is called "The Soul", who is the silent observer of that life which exists all around you just has it does within you – is this not true?

Also is it not true that you're Soul, which is that energy which lives only within people – cannot die! For the known truth, which is stated in the first law of thermodynamics, is that energy cannot be destroyed! Thus meaning that the energy which exists only within people has always existed and will always do so! Therefore and certainly this constant re-birthing of the Soul actually means that it is only people who have the knowledge and wisdom of that which has been experienced in their past lives – this being the wisdom and the knowledge which is in accordance to the number of lives that they have had when living has people!

For again is it not true to say that energy cannot be changed nor can it be destroyed and has nature shows, it is a scientifically known fact that all living people do contain pure energy! This being an energy which is needed in order to bring life to their body and which is also an energy that was truly provided by God or provided by Nature for the Non-Believer – who is really the Mother of a creation! Also is it not known to be a factual truth that this energy, which is truthfully called "The Soul", is actually seen to leave the body them when the body dies–is this not true?

Back Cover

This book is a religious and philosophical approach to life, where the reader is taken through a journey to enlightenment. This is suitable for both believers and non-believers. Before you approach this book, the author suggests an act to help you on your journey. Place 'Life's Purpose' between your hands, has if in prayer, then with closed eyes open to a random page and place your finger upon the page. Silently read where your finger is placed and reflect on these words, and their meaning to you. You can then read the whole page for further understanding. This is a personal message, only for you, to reach a peace that surpasses all understanding.

This book can then be read to progress to the state of "Enlightenment" and so live without fear and to advance your life and all your endeavours, which can only be achieved in the "Present Time".

Where do you come from? What is the point of our existence? Who are we? Who or what is God? What is the Nature of the Soul or Consciousness for the Non-Believer? Most People have asked themselves these fundamental questions – "The Book" targets the answer to these questions – for the Believer and the Non-Believer

Spine

Life's Purpose

The Purpose of All Religions and Phylosophies
For the Believer and the Non-Believer

William Finley
25-12-1938

Front Cover

DISCOVER-

'The Peace that surpasses all Understanding',
'A Realm beyond the Ability of Words to Properly Convey'
"The Natural Way of the Universe"
The World of Nature and Natural Law"
Achieve the "Present" That Rests in Time

Life's Purpose

The Purpose of All Religions and Phylosophies
For the Believer and the Non-Believer
William Finley

NIRVANA TAOISM
BODHI LIBERATION HOLY GHOST
ISLAM zoroastrianism
THE WAY CHRISTIAN MOKSHA
PEACE USHTA
HOLY SPIRIT
CONFUCIANISM KENSHO BHAGAVAD GITA
BUDDISM SRI RAMAKRISNA
SWAMI VIVEKANDA HINDU
Elightenment BORN AGAIN

Printed in Great Britain
by Amazon